# The Complete Keto Diet Cookbook 2021

Easy and Affordable Keto Recipes Book 800 | Low Carb High Fat
Recipes for Keto Lifestyle Lovers to Burn Fat Quickly

**By Alice G. Bolyard**

# Table of Content

**Chapter 9 Beef and Lamb**

# Chapter 1 Sauces and Dressings

## Spicy Enchilada Sauce

**Prep time: 10 minutes | Cook time: 7 to 8 hours | Makes 4 cups**

¼ cup extra-virgin olive oil, divided
2 cups puréed tomatoes
1 cup water
1 sweet onion, chopped
2 jalapeño peppers, chopped
2 teaspoons minced garlic
2 tablespoons chili powder
1 teaspoon ground coriander

1. Lightly grease the insert of the slow cooker with 1 tablespoon of the olive oil.
2. Place the remaining 3 tablespoons of the olive oil, tomatoes, water, onion, jalapeño peppers, garlic, chili powder, and coriander in the insert.
3. Cover and cook on low 7 to 8 hours.
4. Serve over poultry or meat. After cooling, store the sauce in a sealed container in the refrigerator for up to 1 week.

**Per Serving (½ cup)**
calories: 92 | fat: 8g | protein: 2g
carbs: 4g | net carbs: 2g | fiber: 2g

## Remoulade

**Prep time: 5 minutes | Cook time: 0 minutes | Makes ½ cup**

⅓ cup sugar-free mayonnaise
1 tablespoon dill pickle relish
1 teaspoon Cajun Seasoning
1 teaspoon capers, drained
1 teaspoon Dijon mustard
1 teaspoon lemon juice
1 teaspoon prepared horseradish
½ teaspoon minced garlic

1. Place all of the ingredients in a small bowl and mix well. Serve immediately or store in an airtight container in the refrigerator for up to 5 days.

**Per Serving**
calories: 161 | fat: 18.8g | protein: 0g
carbs: 1.1g | net carbs: 1.1g | fiber: 0g

## Lemony Caper Dressing

**Prep time: 5 minutes | Cook time: 0 minutes | Makes ¾ cup**

½ cup sugar-free mayonnaise
2 tablespoons extra-virgin olive oil
1 tablespoon capers, drained
1 tablespoon lemon juice
1 tablespoon white vinegar
1 teaspoon grated lemon zest
½ teaspoon dried dill weed

1. Place all of the ingredients in a small blender and blend for 30 seconds, until creamy and nearly entirely smooth. Store in an airtight container in the refrigerator for up to 1 week.

**Per Serving**
calories: 106 | fat: 13.0g | protein: 0g
carbs: 0g | net carbs: 0g | fiber: 0g

## Basil Kale Pesto

**Prep time: 15 minutes | Cook time: 0 minutes | Makes 1½ cup**

1 cup chopped kale
1 cup fresh basil leaves
3 garlic cloves
2 teaspoons nutritional yeast
¼ cup extra-virgin olive oil

1. Place the kale, basil, garlic, and yeast in a food processor and pulse until the mixture is finely chopped, about 3 minutes.
2. With the food processor running, drizzle the olive oil into the pesto until a thick paste forms, scraping down the sides of the bowl at least once.
3. Add a little water if the pesto is too thick.
4. Store the pesto in an airtight container in the refrigerator for up to 1 week

**Per Serving (2 tablespoons)**
calories: 44 | fat: 4g | protein: 1g
carbs: 1g | net carbs: 1g | fiber: 0g

## Dill Feta Dressing

**Prep time: 5 minutes | Cook time: 0 minutes | Makes 1 cup**

¼ cup sugar-free mayonnaise
1/3 cup crumbled Feta cheese
2 tablespoons full-fat sour cream
2 tablespoons heavy whipping cream

1 tablespoon chopped fresh dill
1 tablespoon white vinegar
⅛ teaspoon ground black pepper
⅛ teaspoon onion powder

1. Place all of the ingredients in a small blender and blend for 30 seconds, until creamy and nearly entirely smooth. Store in an airtight container in the refrigerator for up to 1 week.

**Per Serving**

calories: 75 | fat: 8.1g | protein: 1.2g
carbs: 0.3g | net carbs: 0.3g | fiber: 0g

## Marinara Sauce

**Prep time: 10 minutes | Cook time: 7 to 8 hours | Serves 12**

3 tablespoons extra-virgin olive oil, divided
2 (28-ounce / 794-g) cans crushed tomatoes
½ sweet onion, finely chopped

2 teaspoons minced garlic
½ teaspoon salt
1 tablespoon chopped fresh basil
1 tablespoon chopped fresh oregano

1. Lightly grease the insert of the slow cooker with 1 tablespoon of the olive oil.
2. Add the remaining 2 tablespoons of the olive oil, tomatoes, onion, garlic, and salt to the insert, stirring to combine.
3. Cover and cook on low for 7 to 8 hours.
4. Remove the cover and stir in the basil and oregano.
5. Store the cooled sauce in a sealed container in the refrigerator for up to 1 week.

**Per Serving (½ cup)**

calories: 66 | fat: 5g | protein: 1g
carbs: 7g | net carbs: 5g | fiber: 2g

## Bolognese Sauce

**Prep time: 15 minutes | Cook time: 7 to 8 hours | Serves 10**

3 tablespoons extra-virgin olive oil, divided
1 pound (454 g) ground pork
½ pound (227 g) ground beef
½ pound (227 g) bacon, chopped
1 sweet onion, chopped

1 tablespoon minced garlic
2 celery stalks, chopped
2 (28-ounce / 794-g) cans diced tomatoes
½ cup coconut milk
¼ cup apple cider vinegar

1. Lightly grease the insert of the slow cooker with 1 tablespoon of the olive oil.
2. In a large skillet over medium-high heat, heat the remaining 2 tablespoons of the olive oil. Add the pork, beef, and bacon, and sauté until cooked through, about 7 minutes.
3. Stir in the onion and garlic and sauté for an additional 2 minutes.
4. Transfer the meat mixture to the insert and add the celery, tomatoes, coconut milk, and apple cider vinegar.
5. Cover and cook on low for 7 to 8 hours.
6. Serve, or cool completely, and store in the refrigerator in a sealed container for up to 4 days or in the freezer for 1 month.

**Per Serving (½ cup)**

calories: 333 | fat: 23g | protein: 25g
carbs: 5g | net carbs: 2g | fiber: 3g

## Creamy Duo-Cheese Dipping Sauce

**Prep time: 10 minutes | Cook time: 0 minutes | Serves 10**

4 ounces (113 g) Feta cheese
1 cup Asiago cheese,

shredded
1 cup double cream
1 tablespoon paprika

1. Melt the cheese and cream in a saucepan over medium-low heat.
2. Transfer to a serving bowl and top with paprika.
3. Serve with fresh celery sticks if desired. Enjoy!

**Per Serving**

calories: 127 | fat: 10.8g | protein: 5.5g
carbs: 1.3g | net carbs: 1.3g | fiber: 0g

## Tahini Dressing

**Prep time: 5 minutes | Cook time: 0 minutes | Makes ⅓ cup**

| | |
|---|---|
| 3 tablespoons filtered water | 1 teaspoon minced garlic |
| 2 tablespoons tahini | ½ teaspoon kosher salt |
| 1 tablespoon lemon juice | |

1. Place all of the ingredients in a small blender and blend until smooth. Store in an airtight container in the refrigerator for up to 1 week.

**Per Serving**

calories: 62 | fat: 5.0g | protein: 2.0g
carbs: 3.0g | net carbs: 1.0g | fiber: 2.0g

## Cheesy Spinach Basil Pesto

**Prep time: 10 minutes | Cook time: 0 minutes | Serves 2 cups**

| | |
|---|---|
| 2 cups fresh spinach | Parmesan cheese |
| 1 cup fresh basil leaves | ½ cup good-quality olive oil |
| 3 garlic cloves, smashed | Sea salt, for seasoning |
| ¼ cup pecans | Freshly ground black pepper, for seasoning |
| ¼ cup grated | |

1. Blend the base. Put the spinach, basil, garlic, pecans, and Parmesan in a blender and pulse until the mixture is finely chopped, scraping down the sides of the blender once.
2. Finish the pesto. While the blender is running, pour in the olive oil in a thin stream and blend until the pesto is smooth. Season it with salt and pepper.
3. Store. Store in a sealed container in the refrigerator for up to one week.
4. Swap: Pesto comes in many variations because this delectable creation is versatile. Try kale, basil, or cilantro in place of the spinach in the same amount.

**Per Serving (2 tablespoons)**

calories: 60 | fat: 6g | protein: 1g
carbs: 1g | net carbs: 1g | fiber: 0g

## Spanish Queso Sauce

**Prep time: 10 minutes | Cook time: 3 to 4 hours | Makes 4 cups**

| | |
|---|---|
| 1 tablespoon extra-virgin olive oil | 1 cup sour cream |
| 12 ounces (340-g) cream cheese | 2 cups salsa verde |
| | 1 cup monterey jack cheese, shredded |

1. Lightly grease the insert of the slow cooker with the olive oil.
2. In a large bowl, stir together the cream cheese, sour cream, salsa verde, and Monterey Jack cheese, until blended.
3. Transfer the mixture to the insert.
4. Cover and cook on low for 3 to 4 hours.
5. Serve warm.

**Per Serving (½ cup)**

calories: 278 | fat: 25g | protein: 9g
carbs: 4g | net carbs: 4g | fiber: 0g

## Basil Pesto

**Prep time: 5 minutes | Cook time: 0 minutes | Makes ¾ cup**

| | |
|---|---|
| 1 cup fresh basil leaves | 1 tablespoon chopped garlic |
| ¼ cup extra-virgin olive oil | ¼ teaspoon kosher salt |
| ¼ cup grated Parmesan cheese | ⅛ teaspoon ground black pepper |
| ¼ cup pine nuts | |

1. Put all of the ingredients in a small blender or mini food processor. Pulse until fully combined but not quite smooth. Store in an airtight container in the refrigerator for up to 1 week or in the freezer for up to 3 months.

**Per Serving**

calories: 140 | fat: 14.0g | protein: 2.9g
carbs: 1.4g | net carbs: 1.0g | fiber: 0.4g

## Raita

**Prep time: 8 minutes | Cook time: 0 minutes | Makes 1 cup**

⅓ cup full-fat Greek yogurt
⅓ cup full-fat sour cream
¼ cup finely chopped cucumbers
1 tablespoon chopped fresh cilantro
1 tablespoon chopped fresh mint
1 teaspoon granulated erythritol
1 teaspoon minced red onions
¼ teaspoon ground cumin

1. Place all of the ingredients in a small bowl and mix well. Serve immediately or store in an airtight container in the refrigerator for up to 3 days.

**Per Serving**

calories: 30 | fat: 2.1g | protein: 0.9g
carbs: 1.0g | net carbs: 1.0g | fiber: 0g

## Homemade Dijon Vinaigrette

**Prep time: 5 minutes | Cook time: 0 minutes | Serves 4**

2 tablespoons Dijon mustard
Juice of ½ lemon
1 garlic clove, finely minced
1½ tablespoons red
wine vinegar
Pink Himalayan salt
Freshly ground black pepper, to taste
3 tablespoons olive oil

1. In a small bowl, whisk the mustard, lemon juice, garlic, and red wine vinegar until well combined. Season with pink Himalayan salt and pepper, and whisk again.
2. Slowly add the olive oil, a little bit at a time, whisking constantly.
3. Keep in a sealed glass container in the refrigerator for up to 1 week

**Per Serving**

calories: 99 | fat: 11g | protein: 1g
carbs: 1g | net carbs: 1g | fiber:0g

## Oregano Balsamic Vinegar

**Prep time: 4 minutes | Cook time: 0 minutes | Makes 1 cup**

1 cup extra-virgin olive oil
¼ cup balsamic vinegar
2 tablespoons chopped fresh oregano
1 teaspoon chopped
fresh basil
1 teaspoon minced garlic
Sea salt, to taste
Freshly ground black pepper, to taste

1. Whisk the olive oil and vinegar in a small bowl until emulsified, about 3 minutes.
2. Whisk in the oregano, basil, and garlic until well combined, about 1 minute.
3. Season the dressing with salt and pepper.
4. Transfer the dressing to an airtight container, and store it in the refrigerator for up to 1 week. Give the dressing a vigorous shake before using it.

**Per Serving (1 tablespoon)**

calories: 83 | fat: 9g | protein: 0g
carbs: 0g | net carbs: 0g | fiber: 0g

## Alfredo Sauce

**Prep time: 5 minutes | Cook time: 1 minute | Makes 1½ cups**

½ cup mascarpone cheese (4 ounces / 113 g)
¼ cup grated Parmesan cheese
¼ cup (½ stick) butter
½ cup heavy whipping cream
½ teaspoon kosher salt
¼ teaspoon ground black pepper

1. Place the mascarpone, Parmesan, and butter in a medium-sized microwave-safe bowl. Microwave on high for 30 seconds, then stir.
2. Microwave on high for 30 seconds more. Add the cream, salt, and pepper to the bowl. Whisk together until smooth. Serve immediately.

**Per Serving**

calories: 240 | fat: 23.9g | protein: 3.1g
carbs: 1.2g | net carbs: 1.2g | fiber: 0g

## Hollandaise Sauce

**Prep time: 20 minutes | Cook time: 10 minutes | Makes 2 cups**

1½ cups unsalted butter
4 large egg yolks
2 teaspoons cold water

Juice of 1 small lemon, about 4 teaspoons
Pinch sea salt

1. Place a medium heavy-bottomed saucepan over very low heat and melt the butter.
2. Remove the saucepan from the heat and let the melted butter stand for 5 minutes.
3. Carefully skim the foam from the top of the melted butter.
4. Very slowly pour the clarified part of the butter (it should be a clear yellow color) into a container, leaving the milky solids in the bottom of the saucepan.
5. Discard the milky solids and let the clarified butter cool in the container until it is just warm, about 15 minutes.
6. Put a medium saucepan with about 3 inches of water in it over medium heat until the water simmers gently.
7. In a large stainless steel bowl, add the egg yolks and 2 teaspoons of cold water and whisk them until they are foamy and light, about 3 minutes.
8. Add 3 or 4 drops of the lemon juice to the yolks and whisk for about 1 minute.
9. Place the bowl onto the mouth of the saucepan, making sure the bottom of the bowl does not touch the simmering water.
10. Whisk the yolks until they thicken a little, about 1 to 2 minutes, then remove the bowl from the simmering water.
11. In a very thin stream, add the clarified butter to the yolk mixture, whisking continuously, until you have used up all the butter and your sauce is thick and smooth. If you add the butter too quickly, the sauce will break.
12. Whisk in the remaining lemon juice and the salt.
13. This sauce should be used right away or held for only about 1 hour. Throw away any unused sauce.

**Per Serving (1 tablespoon)**
calories: 173 | fat: 17g | protein: 5g | carbs: 1g | net carbs: 1g | fiber: 0g

# Chapter 2 Breakfast

## Colby Broccoli Frittata

**Prep time: 8 minutes | Cook time: 12 minutes | Serves 4**

| | |
|---|---|
| 2 tablespoons olive oil | pepper, minced |
| ½ cup onions, chopped | Salt and red pepper, to taste |
| 1 cup broccoli, chopped | ¾ cup colby cheese, grated |
| 8 eggs, beaten | ¼ cup fresh cilantro, to serve |
| ½ teaspoon jalapeño | |

1. Set an ovenproof frying pan over medium heat and warm the oil. Add onions and sauté until caramelized. Place in the broccoli and cook until tender. Add in jalapeño pepper and eggs; season with red pepper and salt. Cook until the eggs are set.
2. Scatter colby cheese over the frittata. Set oven to 370ºF (188ºC) and cook for approximately 12 minutes, until frittata is set in the middle. Slice into wedges and decorate with fresh cilantro before serving.

**Per Serving**

calories: 249 | fat: 17.2g | protein: 17.5g carbs: 6.7g | net carbs: 6.1g | fiber: 0.6g

## Eggs Stuffed Avocados

**Prep time: 5 minutes | Cook time: 10 minutes | Serves 4**

| | |
|---|---|
| 2 large avocados, halved and pitted | to season |
| 4 small eggs | Chopped parsley to garnish |
| Salt and black pepper | |

1. Preheat the oven to 400ºF (205ºC).
2. Crack each egg into each avocado half and place them on a greased baking sheet. Bake the filled avocados in the oven for 8 or 10 minutes or until eggs are cooked. Season with salt and pepper, and garnish with parsley.

**Per Serving**

calories: 235 | fat: 19.2g | protein: 8.1g carbs: 8.7g | net carbs: 2.0g | fiber: 6.7g

## Spinach Fontina Chorizo Waffles

**Prep time: 10 minutes | Cook time: 5 minutes | Serves 6**

| | |
|---|---|
| 6 eggs | pepper, to taste |
| 6 tablespoons almond milk | 3 chorizo sausages, cooked, chopped |
| 1 teaspoon Spanish spice mix or allspice | 1 cup Fontina cheese, shredded |
| Sea salt and black | |

1. Using a mixing bowl, beat the eggs, Spanish spice mix, black pepper, salt, and almond milk. Add in shredded cheese and chopped sausage. Use a nonstick cooking spray to spray a waffle iron.
2. Cook the egg mixture for 5 minutes. Serve alongside homemade sugar-free tomato ketchup.

**Per Serving**

calories: 315 | fat: 24.9g | protein: 20.1g carbs: 1.4g | net carbs: 1.4g | fiber: 0g

## Rosemary Turkey Sausage Egg Muffins

**Prep time: 5 minutes | Cook time: 15 minutes | Serves 3**

| | |
|---|---|
| 1 teaspoon butter | rosemary |
| 6 eggs | 1 cup pecorino romano cheese, grated |
| Salt and black pepper, to taste | 3 turkey sausages, chopped |
| ½ teaspoon dried | |

1. Preheat oven to 400ºF (205ºC) and grease muffin cups with cooking spray.
2. In a skillet over medium heat add the butter and cook the turkey sausages for 4-5 minutes.
3. Beat 3 eggs with a fork. Add in sausages, cheese, and seasonings. Divide between the muffin cups and bake for 4 minutes. Crack in an egg to each of the cups. Bake for an additional 4 minutes. Allow cooling before serving.

**Per Serving**

calories: 422 | fat: 34.2g | protein: 26.4g carbs: 2.1g | net carbs: 2.1g | fiber: 0g

## Mozzarella and Chorizo Omelet

**Prep time: 8 minutes | Cook time: 7 minutes | Serves 1**

2 eggs
6 basil leaves
2 ounces (57 g) Mozzarella cheese
1 tablespoon butter
1 tablespoon water
4 thin slices chorizo
1 tomato, sliced
Salt and black pepper, to taste

1. Whisk the eggs along with the water and some salt and pepper. Melt the butter in a skillet and cook the eggs for 30 seconds. Spread the chorizo slices over. Arrange the tomato and Mozzarella over the chorizo. Cook for about 3 minutes. Cover the skillet and cook for 3 minutes until omelet is set.
2. When ready, remove the pan from heat; run a spatula around the edges of the omelet and flip it onto a warm plate, folded side down. Serve garnished with basil leaves and green salad.

**Per Serving**

calories: 452 | fat: 36.4g | protein: 30.1g
carbs: 5.4g | net carbs: 2.9g | fiber: 2.5g

## Avocado-Coconut Protein Shake

**Prep time: 5 minutes | Cook time: 0 minutes | Serves 4**

3 cups flax milk, chilled
3 teaspoons unsweetened cocoa powder
1 medium avocado, pitted, peeled, sliced
1 cup coconut milk, chilled
3 mint leaves plus extra to garnish
3 tablespoons erythritol
1 tablespoon low carb Protein powder
Whipping cream for topping

1. Combine the flax milk, cocoa powder, avocado, coconut milk, 3 mint leaves, erythritol, and protein powder into the smoothie maker, and blend for 1 minute to smooth.
2. Pour the drink into serving glasses, lightly add some whipping cream on top, and garnish with 1 or 2 mint leaves. Serve immediately.

**Per Serving**

calories: 266 | fat: 15.6g | protein: 11.9g
carbs: 7.8g | net carbs: 4.0g | fiber: 3.8g

## Aioli Eggs with Tuna and Veggies

**Prep time: 15 minutes | Cook time: 0 minutes | Serves 8**

8 eggs, hard-boiled, chopped
28 ounces (794 g) tuna in brine, drained
½ cup lettuces, torn into pieces
**Aioli:**
1 cup mayonnaise
2 cloves garlic, minced
1 tablespoon lemon
½ cup green onions, finely chopped
½ cup Feta cheese, crumbled
¹⁄₃ cup sour cream
½ tablespoon mustard

juice
Salt and black pepper, to taste

1. Set the eggs in a serving bowl. Place in tuna, onion, mustard, cheese, lettuce, and sour cream.
2. To prepare aioli, mix in a bowl mayonnaise, lemon juice, and garlic. Add in black pepper and salt. Stir in the prepared aioli to the bowl to incorporate everything. Serve with pickles.

**Per Serving**

calories: 356 | fat: 22.6g | protein: 29.6g
carbs: 2.2g | net carbs: 1.7g | fiber: 0.5g

## Double Cheese Omelet

**Prep time: 10 minutes | Cook time: 0 minutes | Serves 2**

3 tablespoons olive oil
4 eggs, beaten
Salt and black pepper, to taste
¼ teaspoon paprika
¼ teaspoon cayenne pepper
½ cup Asiago cheese, shredded
½ cup Cheddar cheese, shredded
2 tablespoons fresh basil, roughly chopped

1. Set a pan over medium heat and warm the oil. Season eggs with cayenne pepper, salt, paprika, and black pepper. Transfer to the pan and ensure they are evenly spread. Top with the Asiago and Cheddar cheeses. Slice the omelet into two halves. Decorate with fresh basil, to serve.

**Per Serving**

calories: 491 | fat: 44.5g | protein: 22.8g
carbs: 4.8g | net carbs: 4.6g | fiber: 0.2g

## Bacon and Zucchini Hash

**Prep time: 10 minutes | Cook time: 15 minutes | Serves 1**

1 medium zucchini, diced
2 bacon slices
1 egg
1 tablespoon coconut oil
½ small onion, chopped
1 tablespoon chopped parsley
¼ teaspoon salt

1. Place the bacon in a skillet and cook for a few minutes, until crispy. Remove and set aside.
2. Warm the coconut oil and cook the onion until soft, for about 3-4 minutes, occasionally stirring. Add the zucchini, and cook for 10 more minutes until zucchini is brown and tender, but not mushy. Transfer to a plate and season with salt.
3. Crack the egg into the same skillet and fry over medium heat. Top the zucchini mixture with the bacon slices and a fried egg. Serve hot, sprinkled with parsley.

**Per Serving**

calories: 341 | fat: 26.7g | protein: 17.3g
carbs: 7.3g | net carbs: 6.5g | fiber: 0.8g

## Almond Shake

**Prep time: 5 minutes | Cook time: 0 minutes | Serves 1**

1½ cups almond milk
2 tablespoons almond butter ½ teaspoon almond extract
½ teaspoon cinnamon
2 tablespoons flax
meal
1 tablespoon collagen peptides
A pinch of salt
15 drops of stevia
A handful of ice cubes

1. Add almond milk, almond butter, flax meal, almond extract, collagen peptides, a pinch of salt, and stevia to the bowl of a blender. Blitz until uniform and smooth, for about 30 seconds. Add a bit more almond milk if it's very thick.
2. Then taste, and adjust flavor as needed, adding more stevia for sweetness or almond butter to the creaminess. Pour in a smoothie glass, add the ice cubes and sprinkle with cinnamon.

**Per Serving**

calories: 325 | fat: 26.9g | protein: 19.1g
carbs: 8.1g | net carbs: 6.0g | fiber: 2.1g

## Roquefort Kielbasa Waffles

**Prep time: 15 minutes | Cook time: 5 minutes | Serves 2**

2 tablespoons butter, melted
Salt and black pepper, to taste
½ teaspoon parsley flakes
½ teaspoon chili pepper flakes
4 eggs
½ cup Roquefort cheese, crumbled
4 slices kielbasa, chopped
2 tablespoons fresh chives, chopped

1. In a mixing bowl, combine all ingredients except fresh chives. Preheat waffle iron and spray with a cooking spray. Pour in the batter and close the lid.
2. Cook for 5 minutes or until golden-brown, do the same with the rest of the batter. Decorate with fresh chives and serve while warm.

**Per Serving**

calories: 471 | fat: 40.2g | protein: 24.5g
carbs: 3.0g | net carbs: 2.8g | fiber: 0.2g

## Chia Walnut Coconut Pudding

**Prep time: 5 minutes | Cook time: 5 minutes | Serves 1**

½ teaspoon vanilla extract
½ cup water
1 tablespoon chia seeds
2 tablespoons hemp seeds
1 tablespoon flax seed meal
2 tablespoons almond meal
2 tablespoons shredded coconut
¼ teaspoon granulated stevia
1 tablespoon walnuts, chopped

1. Put chia seeds, hemp seeds, flaxseed meal, almond meal, granulated stevia, and shredded coconut in a nonstick saucepan and pour over the water. Simmer over medium heat, occasionally stirring, until creamed and thickened, for about 3-4 minutes. Stir in vanilla. When the pudding is ready, spoon into a serving bowl, sprinkle with walnuts and serve warm.

**Per Serving**

calories: 335 | fat: 29.1g | protein: 15.1g
carbs: 14.5g | net carbs: 1.4g | fiber: 13.1g

## Cream Cheese Salmon Omelet Roll

**Prep time: 10 minutes | Cook time: 5 minutes | Serves 1**

½ avocado, sliced
2 tablespoons chopped chives
½ package smoked salmon, cut into strips
1 spring onions, sliced
3 eggs
2 tablespoons cream cheese
1 tablespoon butter
Salt and black pepper, to taste

1. In a small bowl, combine the chives and cream cheese; set aside. Beat the eggs in a large bowl and season with salt and black pepper.
2. Melt the butter in a pan over medium heat. Add the eggs to the pan and cook for about 3 minutes. Flip the omelet over and continue cooking for another 2 minutes until golden.
3. Remove the omelet to a plate and spread the chive mixture over. Arrange the salmon, avocado, and onion slices. Wrap the omelet and serve immediately.

**Per Serving**

calories: 512 | fat: 47.8g | protein: 36.8g
carbs: 13.0g | net carbs: 5.7g | fiber: 7.3g

## Pepperoni Ciabatta

**Prep time: 10 minutes | Cook time: 5 minutes | Serves 6**

10 ounces (283 g) cream cheese, melted
2½ cups Mozzarella cheese, shredded
4 large eggs, beaten
3 tablespoons Romano cheese, grated
½ cup pork rinds, crushed
2½ teaspoon baking powder
½ cup tomato purée
12 large slices pepperoni

1. Combine eggs, Mozzarella cheese and cream cheese. Place in baking powder, pork rinds, and Romano cheese. Form into 6 chiabatta shapes. Set a nonstick pan over medium heat. Cook each ciabatta for 2 minutes per side. Sprinkle tomato purée over each one and top with pepperoni slices to serve.

**Per Serving**

calories: 465 | fat: 33.5g | protein: 31.2g
carbs: 10.5g | net carbs: 9.2g | fiber: 1.3g

## Feta Spinach Frittata

**Prep time: 15 minutes | Cook time: 25 minutes | Serves 4**

5 ounces (142 g) spinach
8 ounces (227 g) crumbled Feta cheese
1 pint halved cherry tomatoes
10 eggs
3 tablespoons olive oil
4 scallions, diced
Salt and black pepper, to taste

1. Preheat your oven to 350ºF (180ºC).
2. Drizzle the oil in a casserole and place in the oven until heated. In a bowl, whisk the eggs along with the black pepper and salt, until thoroughly combined. Stir in the spinach, Feta cheese, and scallions.
3. Pour the mixture into the casserole, top with the cherry tomatoes and place back in the oven. Bake for 25 minutes until your frittata is set in the middle.
4. When done, remove the casserole from the oven and run a spatula around the edges of the frittata; slide it onto a warm platter. Cut the frittata into wedges and serve with salad.

**Per Serving**

calories: 462 | fat: 35.1g | protein: 25.9g
carbs: 8.2g | net carbs: 6.1g | fiber: 2.1g

## Strawberry Kefir Smoothie

**Prep time: 5 minutes | Cook time: 0 minutes | Serves 1**

¾ cup unsweetened vanilla-flavored almond milk
¼ cup full-fat unsweetened kefir, store-bought or homemade
1 tablespoon granulated erythritol,
or more to taste
¼ teaspoon pure vanilla extract
4 medium-sized fresh strawberries, hulled, plus 1 fresh strawberry for garnish (optional)
3 ice cubes

1. Place all of the ingredients in a blender and blend until smooth and creamy. Taste and add more sweetener if desired. Pour into a 12-ounce (340-g) glass and serve immediately. If desired, rest a strawberry on the rim for garnish.

**Per Serving**

calories: 74 | fat: 3.9g | protein: 2.9g
carbs: 4.8g | net carbs: 4.0g | fiber: 0.8g

## Double Cheese Stuffed Bell Peppers

**Prep time: 10 minutes | Cook time: 17 minutes | Serves 4**

4 summer bell peppers, divined and halved
1 clove garlic, minced
4 ounces (113 g) cream cheese

2 ounces (57 g) Mozzarella cheese, crumbled
2 tablespoons Greek-style yogurt

1. Cook the peppers in boiling water in a Dutch oven until just tender or approximately 7 minutes.
2. Mix the garlic, cream cheese, mozzarella, and yogurt until well combined. Then, stuff the peppers with the cheese mixture.
3. Arrange the stuffed peppers on a tinfoil-lined baking pan.
4. Bake in the preheated oven at 360ºF (182ºC) for 10 to 12 minutes. Serve at room temperature. Bon appétit!

**Per Serving**

calories: 140 | fat: 10g | protein: 8g
carbs: 6g | net carbs: 5g | fiber: 1g

## Crabmeat Egg Bake

**Prep time: 5 minutes | Cook time: 10 minutes | Serves 3**

1 tablespoon olive oil
6 eggs, whisked
1 (6-ounce / 170-g) can crabmeat, flaked
Salt and black pepper to taste For the Salsa:
¾ cup crème fraiche
½ cup scallions,

chopped
½ teaspoon garlic powder
Salt and black pepper to taste
½ teaspoon fresh dill, chopped

1. Set a sauté pan over medium heat and warm olive oil. Crack in eggs and scramble them. Stir in crabmeat and season with salt and black pepper; cook until cooked thoroughly.
2. In a mixing dish, combine all salsa ingredients. Equally, split the egg/crabmeat mixture among serving plates; serve alongside the scallions and salsa to the side.

**Per Serving**

calories: 335 | fat: 26.1g | protein: 21.0g
carbs: 4.8g | net carbs: 4.2g | fiber: 0.6g

## Pumpkin Coffee Latte

**Prep time: 5 minutes | Cook time: 0 minutes | Serves 1**

6 ounces (170 g) brewed hot coffee
1 tablespoon coconut oil
1 tablespoon granulated erythritol

1 tablespoon solid-pack pumpkin purée
1 tablespoon unsalted butter
¼ teaspoon pumpkin pie spice

1. Place all of the ingredients in a small blender and blend until smooth. Pour into a 10-ounce (283-g) mug and serve immediately.

**Per Serving**

calories: 225 | fat: 35.1g | protein: 0g
carbs: 3.0g | net carbs: 2.0g | fiber: 1.0g

## Cacao Nib Nut Granola

**Prep time: 5 minutes | Cook time: 30 minutes | Serves 6**

½ cup chopped raw pecans
½ cup flax seeds
½ cup superfine blanched almond flour
½ cup unsweetened dried coconut
¼ cup chopped cacao nibs
¼ cup chopped raw walnuts
¼ cup sesame seeds

¼ cup sugar-free vanilla-flavored protein powder
3 tablespoons granulated erythritol
1 teaspoon ground cinnamon
⅛ teaspoon kosher salt
⅓ cup coconut oil
1 large egg white, beaten

1. Preheat the oven to 300ºF (150ºC). Line a 15 by 10-inch sheet pan with parchment paper.
2. Place all of the ingredients in a large bowl. Stir well until the mixture is crumbly and holds together in small clumps. Spread out on the parchment-lined pan. Bake for 30 minutes, or until golden brown and fragrant.
3. Let the granola cool completely in the pan before removing. Store in an airtight container in the refrigerator for up to 2 weeks.

**Per Serving**

calories: 442 | fat: 40.0g | protein: 15.0g
carbs: 14.0g | net carbs: 4.0g | fiber: 10.0g

## Avocado Smoothie with Mixed Berries

**Prep time: 5 minutes | Cook time: 0 minutes | Serves 4**

1 avocado, pitted and sliced
3 cups mixed blueberries and strawberries
2 cups unsweetened almond milk
6 tablespoons heavy cream
2 teaspoons erythritol
1 cup ice cubes
1/3 cup nuts and seeds mix

1. Combine the avocado slices, blueberries, strawberries, almond milk, heavy cream, erythritol, ice cubes, nuts and seeds in a smoothie maker; blend in high-speed until smooth and uniform.
2. Pour the smoothie into drinking glasses, and serve immediately.

**Per Serving**

calories: 336 | fat: 25g | protein: 8g
carbs: 18g | net carbs: 12g | fiber: 6g


## Carrot and Ham Egg Frittata

**Prep time: 15 minutes | Cook time: 26 minutes | Serves 4**

2 tablespoons butter, at room temperature
1/2 cup green onions, chopped
2 garlic cloves, minced
1 jalapeño pepper, chopped
1 carrot, chopped
8 ham slices
8 eggs, whisked
Salt and black pepper, to taste
1/2 teaspoon dried thyme

1. Set a pan over medium heat and warm the butter. Stir in green onions and sauté for 4 minutes.
2. Place in garlic and cook for 1 minute. Stir in carrot and jalapeño pepper, and cook for 4 more minutes. Remove the mixture to a lightly greased baking pan, with cooking spray, and top with ham slices.
3. Place in the eggs over vegetables and ham; add thyme, black pepper, and salt for seasoning. Bake in the oven for about 18 minutes at 360ºF (182ºC). Serve warm alongside a dollop of full-fat natural yogurt.

**Per Serving**

calories: 311 | fat: 26.3g | protein: 15.3g
carbs: 4.5g | net carbs: 3.8g | fiber: 0.7g


## Double Cheese and Egg Stuffed Avocados

**Prep time: 5 minutes | Cook time: 15 minutes | Serves 4**

3 avocados, halved and pitted, skin on
1/2 cup Feta cheese, crumbled
1/2 cup Cheddar cheese, grated
2 eggs, beaten
Salt and black pepper, to taste
1 tablespoon fresh basil, chopped

1. Set oven to 360ºF (182ºC) and lay the avocado halves in an ovenproof dish. In a mixing dish, mix both types of cheeses, black pepper, eggs, and salt. Split the mixture equally into the avocado halves. Bake thoroughly for 15 to 17 minutes. Decorate with fresh basil before serving.

**Per Serving**

calories: 343 | fat: 30.5g | protein: 11.2g
carbs: 17.5g | net carbs: 7.4g | fiber: 10.1g


## Spinach and Cucumber Smoothie

**Prep time: 5 minutes | Cook time: 0 minutes | Serves 1**

1 small very ripe avocado, peeled and pitted
1 cup almond milk or water, plus more as needed
1 cup tender baby spinach leaves, stems removed
1/2 medium cucumber,
peeled and seeded
1 tablespoon extra-virgin olive oil or avocado oil
8 to 10 fresh mint leaves, stems removed
Juice of 1 lime (about 1 to 2 tablespoons)

1. In a blender or a large wide-mouth jar, if using an immersion blender, combine the avocado, almond milk, spinach, cucumber, olive oil, mint, and lime juice and blend until smooth and creamy, adding more almond milk or water to achieve your desired consistency.

**Per Serving**

calories: 330 | fat: 30g | protein: 4g
carbs: 19g | net carbs:10 g | fiber: 9g

## Cinnamon Cream Cheese Pancakes

**Prep time: 5 minutes | Cook time: 12 minutes | Makes 4 pancakes**

2 ounces (57 g) cream cheese (¼ cup), softened
2 large eggs
1 teaspoon granulated erythritol
½ teaspoon ground cinnamon
1 tablespoon butter, for the pan

1. Place the cream cheese, eggs, sweetener, and cinnamon in a small blender and blend for 30 seconds, or until smooth. Let the batter rest for 2 minutes.
2. Heat the butter in a 10-inch nonstick skillet over medium heat until bubbling. Pour ¼ cup of the batter into the pan and tilt the pan in a circular motion to create a thin pancake about 6 inches in diameter. Cook for 2 minutes, or until the center is no longer glossy. Flip and cook for 1 minute on the other side. Remove and repeat with the rest of the batter, making a total of 4 pancakes.

**Per Serving**

calories: 396 | fat: 35.0g | protein: 17.0g
carbs: 3.0g | net carbs: 3.0g | fiber: 0g

## Triple Cheese and Bacon Zucchini Balls

**Prep time: 20 minutes | Cook time: 10 minutes | Serves 6**

4 cups zucchini, spiralized
½ pound (227 g) bacon, chopped
6 ounces (170 g) cottage cheese, curds
6 ounces (170 g) cream cheese
1 cup Fontina cheese
½ cup dill pickles, chopped, squeezed
2 cloves garlic, crushed
1 cup grated Parmesan cheese
½ teaspoon caraway seeds
¼ teaspoon dried dill weed
½ teaspoon onion powder
Salt and black pepper, to taste
1 cup crushed pork rinds
Cooking oil

1. Thoroughly mix zoodles, cottage cheese, dill pickles, ½ cup of Parmesan cheese, garlic, cream cheese, bacon, and Fontina cheese until well combined. Shape the mixture into balls. Refrigerate for 3 hours.
2. In a mixing bowl, mix the remaining ½ cup of Parmesan cheese, crushed pork rinds, dill, black pepper, onion powder, caraway seeds, and salt. Roll cheese ball in Parmesan mixture to coat.
3. Set a skillet over medium heat and warm 1-inch of oil. Fry cheeseballs until browned on all sides. Set on a paper towel to soak up any excess oil.

**Per Serving**

calories: 406 | fat: 26.7g | protein: 33.3g
carbs: 8.6g | net carbs: 5.7g | fiber: 2.9g

## Mediterranean Shakshuka

**Prep time: 10 minutes | Cook time: 0 minutes | Serves 3**

1 tablespoon avocado oil
½ cup diced onion
2 cloves garlic, minced
1 (10-ounce / 283-g) can no-salt-added diced tomatoes with green chilies
½ cup tomato purée
1 teaspoon paprika
1 teaspoon ground cumin
½ teaspoon sea salt, plus more for taste
6 large eggs
2 tablespoons chopped fresh parsley

1. In a 12-inch sauté pan, heat the oil over medium-low heat. Add the diced onion and cook for about 10 minutes, until browned. Add the minced garlic and sauté for about 1 minute, until fragrant.
2. Add the diced tomatoes (with juices), tomato purée, paprika, and cumin and mix. Add the sea salt. Cover and simmer 12 to 15 minutes, until the tomato mixture has thickened and most of the liquid is gone. If needed, cook for a couple of minutes uncovered to reduce.
3. Crack the eggs into the pan so that each egg is surrounded by tomato mixture. If desired, you can create a little well for each egg first. Sprinkle the eggs lightly with more sea salt.
4. Cover and cook for 4 to 6 minutes, until the egg whites are opaque, but the yolks are still runny. If you prefer them more done, continue cooking the eggs to your liking.
5. Sprinkle with parsley to serve.

**Per Serving**

calories: 248 | fat: 15g | protein: 16g
carbs: 10g | net carbs: 8g | fiber: 2g

## Chorizo and Spanish Tortilla

**Prep time: 10 minutes | Cook time: 18 minutes | Serves 4**

8 ounces (227 g) Mexican-style fresh (raw) chorizo
2 tablespoons avocado oil or other light-tasting oil
1 cup peeled and thinly sliced celery root
½ cup thinly sliced yellow onions
1 teaspoon kosher salt
½ teaspoon ground black pepper
8 large eggs, beaten
½ cup shredded Manchego cheese
2 tablespoons chopped fresh cilantro, for garnish (optional)

1. Remove the chorizo from the casing (if applicable) and place in a 10-inch skillet. Cook over medium heat, stirring to break into crumbles, for 5 minutes, or until cooked through. Remove the chorizo from the skillet and set aside.
2. Add the oil, celery root, and onions to the same skillet and cook over medium heat until lightly browned and softened, about 7 minutes. Season with the salt and pepper.
3. Return the cooked chorizo to the skillet and stir to combine. Reduce the heat to low. Add the beaten eggs and stir. Sprinkle with the cheese. Cook on low for 2 minutes, or until the cheese is melting.
4. Stir and bring all of the cooked egg from the sides of the skillet into the center. Stir again, then smooth the mixture back out to the edges with a rubber spatula and cook for 2 minutes, uncovered, until it's beginning to set. Cover the skillet with a lid and cook for another 2 minutes, or until the center is firm.
5. Loosen the edges with a rubber spatula and gently flip over onto a serving dish. Cut into 4 wedges and serve hot. Garnish with chopped cilantro, if desired.
6. Leftovers can be stored in an airtight container in the refrigerator for up to 5 days or in the freezer for up to 3 months. To reheat, thaw if frozen, then place in a baking dish and heat in the oven at 325°F (163°C) for 8 minutes. Alternatively, you can microwave on high for 30 seconds.

**Per Serving**

calories: 380 | fat: 32.0g | protein: 22.0g
carbs: 5.0g | net carbs: 4.0g | fiber: 1.0g

## Cream Cheese Snickerdoodle Crepes

**Prep time: 8 minutes | Cook time: 24 minutes | Makes 8 crepes**

**Crepes:**

6 large eggs
5 ounces (142 g) cream cheese (½ cup plus 1 tablespoon), softened
1 tablespoon granulated erythritol
1 teaspoon ground cinnamon
2 tablespoons butter, for the pan

**Filling/Topping:**

⅓ cup granulated erythritol
1 tablespoon ground cinnamon
½ cup (1 stick) butter, softened

1. Make the crepes: Place the eggs, cream cheese, sweetener, and cinnamon in a blender and blend for 30 seconds, or until smooth. Let the batter rest for 5 minutes.
2. Heat a small pat of the butter in a 10-inch nonstick skillet over medium heat until bubbling. Pour about ¼ cup of the batter into the pan and tilt in a circular motion to create a round crepe about 6 inches in diameter. Cook for 2 minutes, or until no longer glossy in the middle. Flip and cook for 1 more minute. Remove the crepe and place on a plate or serving platter. Repeat with the remaining butter and batter to make a total of 8 crepes.
3. Meanwhile, make the filling: Mix the sweetener and cinnamon in a small bowl until combined. Place half of the cinnamon mixture and the softened butter in another small bowl. (Set the other half of the cinnamon mixture aside for the topping.) Stir with a fork until the butter is smooth and the cinnamon mixture is fully incorporated.
4. To serve, spread 1 tablespoon of the filling in the center of each crepe. Roll up each crepe and sprinkle each with 1 teaspoon of the reserved filling.

**Per Serving**

calories: 435 | fat: 42.1g | protein: 12.0g
carbs: 4.5g | net carbs: 3.5g | fiber: 1.0g

## Sausage Stuffed Mushrooms

**Prep time: 8 minutes | Cook time: 27 minutes | Serves 4**

4 large portobello mushroom caps
Kosher salt and ground black pepper
1 pound (454 g) raw country sausage (aka breakfast sausage)
4 medium eggs
1 tablespoon chopped fresh parsley, for garnish

1. Preheat the oven to 375ºF (190ºC). Remove the stems from the mushroom caps and scrape out the ribs with a spoon. Season the caps with salt and pepper.
2. Divide the sausage into 4 equal portions. Press a portion of the sausage along the bottom and up the sides of each mushroom cap to form a cup for the egg. Place the sausage-stuffed mushrooms on a sheet pan and bake for 15 minutes.
3. Remove the mushroom caps from the oven and blot any liquid from the centers. Crack an egg into each mushroom cap. Return to the oven and bake for 12 more minutes for firm whites and slightly runny yolks. If you prefer hard yolks, increase the cooking time to 15 minutes, or until the eggs are cooked to your liking.
4. Serve hot or at room temperature, garnished with fresh parsley.
5. Store in an airtight container in the refrigerator for up to 3 days. To reheat, microwave on high for 30 seconds.

**Per Serving**

calories: 466 | fat: 34.1g | protein: 25.9g
carbs: 3.6g | net carbs: 2.5g | fiber: 1.1g

## Cheesy Omelet and Vegetables

**Prep time: 15 minutes | Cook time: 5 minutes | Serves 2**

2 teaspoons olive oil
2 scallion stalks, chopped
2 garlic cloves, minced
bell peppers, chopped
½ cup cauliflower florets
eggs
½ teaspoon cayenne pepper
Kosher salt and
ground black pepper, to season
½ teaspoon dried Mexican oregano
½ teaspoon chili pepper flakes
½ teaspoon dried parsley flakes
2 ounces (57 g) Cotija cheese, crumbled

1. Heat the olive oil in a medium-sized pan over moderate heat. Sauté the scallions and garlic until just tender and fragrant.
2. Now, stir in the peppers and cauliflower and continue sautéing an additional 2 to 3 minutes.
3. Meanwhile, mix the eggs with the cayenne pepper, salt, black pepper, oregano, chili pepper flakes, and parsley.
4. Pour the egg mixture over the sautéed vegetables. Let it cook, tilting your pan so the raw parts can cook.
5. Add the Cotija cheese, fold over and leave for 1 minute before slicing and serving. Enjoy!

**Per Serving**

calories: 287 | fat: 20g | protein: 17g
carbs: 7g | net carbs: 4g | fiber: 3g

## Spicy Brown Mushroom Omelet

**Prep time: 10 minutes | Cook time: 5 minutes | Serves 2**

1 tablespoon olive oil
½ brown onion, thinly sliced
1 garlic clove, thinly sliced
1 green chili, minced
½ pound (227 g) brown mushrooms, sliced
4 eggs, whisked
1 tablespoon fresh coriander, chopped
Sea salt and ground black pepper, to taste
½ teaspoon Kashmiri chili powder
½ teaspoon garam masala

1. In a nonstick skillet, heat the olive oil until sizzling. Then, sauté the onion until translucent. Now, stir in the garlic, chili pepper, and mushrooms and continue sautéing until just tender and fragrant or about 2 minutes. Reserve.
2. Add in the whisked eggs, fresh coriander, salt, black pepper, Kashmiri chili powder, and garam masala. Give it a quick swirl to distribute the eggs evenly across the skillet. Cook for 2 to 3 minutes.
3. Flip your omelet over and cook an additional minute or so. Fill with the mushroom mixture, fold and serve immediately. Bon appétit!

**Per Serving**

calories: 217 | fat: 16g | protein: 14g
carbs: 5g | net carbs: 4g | fiber: 1g

## Egg, Scallion, Jalapeño Pepper Salad

**Prep time: 10 minutes | Cook time: 10 minutes | Serves 2**

3 eggs
¼ cup scallions, chopped
1 jalapeño pepper, deseeded and minced
¼ cup mayonnaise

1 teaspoon Dijon mustard
Kosher salt and ground black pepper, to taste
1 tablespoon fresh parsley, roughly chopped
½ teaspoon sweet paprika

1. Arrange the eggs in a small saucepan. Pour in water (1-inch above the eggs) and bring to a boil.
2. Heat off and let it sit, covered, for 9 to 10 minutes.
3. When the eggs are cool enough to handle, peel away the shells, and rinse the eggs under running water. Chop the eggs and transfer them to a serving bowl.
4. Add in the scallions, jalapeno pepper, mayonnaise, mustard, salt, and black pepper.
5. Sprinkle fresh parsley and paprika over the salad and serve well chilled.

**Per Serving**

calories: 398 | fat: 35g | protein: 15g | carbs: 5g | net carbs: 4g | fiber: 1g

## Streusel Walnut Muffins

**Prep time: 5 minutes | Cook time: 22 minutes | Makes 12 muffins**

**Muffins:**

1 cup unsweetened vanilla-flavored almond milk
½ cup (1 stick) butter, softened
3 large eggs
1 teaspoon pure vanilla extract
1½ cups superfine blanched almond flour

¾ cup granulated erythritol
½ cup coconut flour
2 teaspoons baking powder
1 teaspoon ground cinnamon
¼ teaspoon xanthan gum
Pinch of kosher salt

**Streusel Topping:**

3 tablespoons butter, melted
¾ cup superfine blanched almond flour
¼ cup chopped raw walnuts

¼ cup granulated erythritol
1 teaspoon ground cinnamon
Pinch of kosher salt

1. Preheat the oven to 375ºF (190ºC). Line a standard-size 12-cup muffin tin with paper or foil liners.
2. Place all of the muffin ingredients in a blender and blend until smooth. Spoon the batter (it will be thick) into the lined muffin cups, filling them about two-thirds full.
3. Place all of the streusel topping ingredients in a small bowl and stir with a fork until a crumbly dough forms. Using your fingers, crumble the streusel into pea-sized pieces over the muffin batter. Bake the muffins for 22 minutes, or until a toothpick inserted in the center of a muffin comes out clean.
4. Remove the muffins from the pan and let cool for at least 10 minutes before serving. Store in an airtight container in the refrigerator for up to 1 week or in the freezer for up to 3 months.

**Per Serving**

calories: 273 | fat: 25.1g | protein: 7.2g | carbs: 7.9g | net carbs: 3.9g | fiber: 4.0g

# Chapter 3 Soups

## Creamy Beef Soup

**Prep time: 10 minutes | Cook time: 4 hours | Serves 6**

1 pound (454 g) lean ground beef
1 cup beef broth
1 cup heavy cream
½ cup shredded Mozzarella cheese
½ cup diced tomatoes
1 yellow onion, chopped
2 cloves garlic, chopped
1 tablespoon Italian seasoning
Salt and pepper, to taste

1. Add all the ingredients to a slow cooker minus the heavy cream and Mozzarella cheese. Cook on high for 4 hours.
2. Warm the heavy cream, and then add the warmed cream and cheese to the soup. Stir well and serve.

**Per Serving**

calories: 242 | fat: 14.0g | protein: 24.8g
carbs: 4.0g | net carbs: 3.0g | fiber: 1.0g

## Italian Mozzarella Chicken Soup

**Prep time: 10 minutes | Cook time: 4 hours | Serves 6**

6 cups chicken broth
3 boneless, skinless chicken breasts
1 cup canned diced tomatoes
1 yellow onion, chopped
2 cloves garlic, chopped
1 cup shredded Mozzarella cheese
1 jalapeño pepper, seeded and sliced
1 teaspoon dried thyme
1 teaspoon dried oregano
Salt and black pepper, to taste

1. Add all the ingredients minus the salt and black pepper to the base of a slow cooker minus the cheese and cook on high for 4 hours.
2. Stir in the cheese and season with salt and black pepper.
3. Shred the chicken and serve.

**Per Serving**

calories: 126 | fat: 4.0g | protein: 16.9g
carbs: 4.9g | net carbs: 3.8g | fiber: 1.1g

## Chicken and Jalapeño Soup

**Prep time: 10 minutes | Cook time: 4 hours | Serves 6**

6 cups chicken broth
3 boneless, skinless chicken breasts
Juice from 1 lime
1 yellow onion, chopped
2 cloves garlic, chopped
1 jalapeño pepper, seeded and sliced
1 handful fresh cilantro
Salt and black pepper, to taste

1. Add all the ingredients minus the cilantro, salt and black pepper to the base of a slow cooker and cook on high for 4 hours.
2. Add the cilantro and season with salt and black pepper.
3. Shred the chicken and serve.

**Per Serving**

calories: 110 | fat: 3.0g | protein: 16.0g
carbs: 4.0g | net carbs: 3.0g | fiber: 1.0g

## Chicken Lemon Soup

**Prep time: 10 minutes | Cook time: 4 hours | Serves 6**

6 cups chicken broth
3 boneless, skinless chicken breasts
Juice from 1 lemon
1 yellow onion, chopped
2 cloves garlic, chopped
1 teaspoon cayenne pepper
1 teaspoon dried thyme
1 handful of fresh parsley, minced
Salt and black pepper, to taste

1. Add all the ingredients minus the salt, black pepper and parsley to the base of a slow cooker minus the parsley and cook on high for 4 hours.
2. Add the parsley and season with salt and black pepper.
3. Shred the chicken and serve.

**Per Serving**

calories: 110 | fat: 3.0g | protein: 15.9g
carbs: 4.1g | net carbs: 2.9g | fiber: 1.2g

## Beef and Bacon Soup

**Prep time: 15 minutes | Cook time: 40 minutes | Serves 6**

| | |
|---|---|
| 1 pound (454 g) of lean ground beef | powder |
| 6 slices uncured bacon | ½ teaspoon onion powder |
| 6 cups beef broth | ½ teaspoon cumin |
| 1 cup heavy cream | ½ teaspoon paprika |
| 1 cup shredded Cheddar cheese | ½ cup sour cream, for serving |
| 1 yellow onion, chopped | 1 tablespoon coconut oil, for cooking |
| 1 teaspoon garlic | |

1. Add the coconut oil to a skillet and cook the bacon until crispy. Allow the bacon to cool and chop into small pieces. Set aside.
2. Once cooked, add the lean ground beef to the same skillet with the bacon fat and cook until browned.
3. Add the onions and cook for another 2 to 3 minutes.
4. Add all the ingredients minus the bacon, heavy cream, sour cream and cheese to a stockpot and stir. Cook for 25 minutes.
5. Warm the heavy cream, and then add the warmed cream and cheese and serve with the bacon and a dollop of sour cream.

**Per Serving**

calories: 500 | fat: 34.0g | protein: 41.0g
carbs: 5.0g | net carbs: 4.0g | fiber: 1.0g

## Guacamole and Tomato Soup

**Prep time: 10 minutes | Cook time: 0 minutes | Serves 4**

| | |
|---|---|
| 3 cups chicken broth | cilantro |
| ½ cup heavy cream | 1 tomato, chopped |
| 2 ripe avocados pitted | Salt and black pepper, to taste |
| ½ cup freshly chopped | |

1. Add all the ingredients to a high-speed blender and blend until creamy.
2. Chill in the refrigerator for 1 hour before serving.

**Per Serving**

calories: 290 | fat: 25.9g | protein: 6.1g
carbs: 10.1g | net carbs: 3.0g | fiber: 7.1g

## Chicken Soup

**Prep time: 10 minutes | Cook time: 2 minutes | Serves 4**

| | |
|---|---|
| 2 cups cooked and shredded chicken | cilantro |
| 1 tablespoon butter, melted | ⅓ cup buffalo sauce |
| | ½ cup cream cheese |
| 4 cups chicken broth | Salt and black pepper, to taste |
| 1 tablespoon chopped | |

1. Blend the butter, buffalo sauce, and cream cheese, in a food processor, until smooth. Transfer to a pot, add chicken broth and heat until hot but do not bring to a boil. Stir in chicken, salt, black pepper and cook until heated through.
2. When ready, remove to soup bowls and serve garnished with cilantro.

**Per Serving**

calories: 406 | fat: 29g | protein: 27g
carbs: 5g | net carbs: 5g | fiber: 0g

## Chicken Garlic Soup

**Prep time: 10 minutes | Cook time: 15 minutes | Serves 6**

| | |
|---|---|
| 2 boneless, skinless chicken breasts | chopped |
| | 1 teaspoon thyme |
| 4 cups chicken broth | 1 teaspoon salt |
| ½ cup whipped cream cheese | ¼ teaspoon black pepper |
| 3 cloves garlic, | 1 tablespoon butter |

1. Preheat a stockpot over medium heat with the butter.
2. Add the chicken and brown until completely cooked through. Remove from heat.
3. Shred the chicken and add it back to the stockpot along with the remaining ingredients minus the cream cheese.
4. Bring to a simmer.
5. Add in the cream cheese and whisk until there are no more clumps.
6. Simmer for 10 minutes and serve.

**Per Serving**

calories: 130 | fat: 6.1g | protein: 15.9g
carbs: 2.1g | net carbs: 2.1g | fiber: 0g

## Avocado and Cucumber Soup 20

**Prep time: 10 minutes | Cook time: 0 minutes | Serves 4**

1 ripe avocado
½ cucumber, sliced
1 cup full-fat unsweetened coconut milk
1 tablespoon freshly chopped mint leaves
1 tablespoon freshly squeezed lemon juice
Pinch of salt

1. Add all the ingredients to a high-speed blender and blend until creamy.
2. Chill in the refrigerator for 1 hour before serving.

**Per Serving**

calories: 250 | fat: 24.1g | protein: 2.9g
carbs: 8.9g | net carbs: 4.1g | fiber: 4.8g

## Coconut Cheesy Cauliflower Soup

**Prep time: 10 minutes | Cook time: 15 minutes | Serves 4**

½ head cauliflower, chopped
1 tablespoon coconut oil
½ cup leeks, chopped
1 celery stalk, chopped
1 serrano pepper, finely chopped
1 teaspoon garlic puree
1½ tablespoon flax seed meal
2 cups water
1½ cups coconut milk
6 ounces (170 g) Monterey Jack cheese, shredded
Salt and black pepper, to taste
Fresh parsley, chopped

1. In a deep pan over medium heat, melt the coconut oil and sauté the serrano pepper, celery and leeks until soft, for about 5 minutes. Add in coconut milk, garlic puree, cauliflower, water and flax seed.
2. While covered partially, allow simmering for 10 minutes or until cooked through. Whizz with a immersion blender until smooth. Fold in the shredded cheese, and stir to ensure the cheese is completely melted and you have a homogenous mixture. Season with pepper and salt to taste.
3. Divide among serving bowls, decorate with parsley and serve while warm.

**Per Serving**

calories: 312 | fat: 16g | protein: 13g
carbs: 9g | net carbs: 7g | fiber: 2g

## Tangy Cucumber and Avocado Soup

**Prep time: 10 minutes | Cook time: 0 minutes | Serves 4**

4 large cucumbers, seeded, chopped
1 large avocado, peeled and pitted
Salt and black pepper to taste
2 cups water
1 tablespoon cilantro, chopped
1 tablespoon olive oil
2 limes, juiced
1 teaspoon minced garlic
2 tomatoes, chopped
1 chopped avocado for garnish

1. Pour the cucumbers, avocado halves, salt, black pepper, olive oil, lime juice, cilantro, water, and garlic in the food processor. Puree the ingredients for 2 minutes or until smooth. Pour the mixture in a bowl and top with avocado and tomatoes. Serve chilled with zero-carb bread.

**Per Serving**

calories: 170 | fat: 7g | protein: 4g
carbs: 10g | net carbs: 4g | fiber: 6g

## Spicy Chicken Soup

**Prep time: 10 minutes | Cook time: 20 minutes | Serves 4**

1 tablespoon coconut oil
1 pound (454 g) chicken thighs
¾ cup red enchilada sauce
¼ cup water
¼ cup onion, chopped
3 ounces (85 g)
canned diced green chilis
1 avocado, sliced
1 cup cheddar cheese, shredded
¼ cup pickled jalapeños, chopped
½ cup sour cream
1 tomato, diced

1. Put a large pan over medium heat. Add coconut oil and warm. Place in the chicken and cook until browned on the outside. Stir in onion, chilies, water, and enchilada sauce, then close with a lid.
2. Allow simmering for 20 minutes until the chicken is cooked through. Spoon the soup on a serving bowl and top with the sauce, cheese, sour cream, tomato, and avocado.

**Per Serving**

calories: 643 | fat: 44g | protein: 46g
carbs: 12g | net carbs: 10g | fiber: 2g

## Cream Cheese Chicken Soup

**Prep time: 20 minutes | Cook time: 40 minutes | Serves 6**

2 boneless, skinless chicken breasts
2 cups chicken broth
2 cups water
1 cup whipped cream cheese
½ cup shredded Cheddar cheese
1 yellow onion, chopped

2 cloves garlic, chopped
1 teaspoon chili powder
½ teaspoon cumin
½ teaspoon salt
¼ teaspoon black pepper
1 tablespoon coconut oil, for cooking

1. Heat a large skillet over medium heat with a ½ tablespoon of the coconut oil.
2. Brown the chicken breasts until cooked through. Set aside.
3. Add the garlic and onion to a large stockpot with the remaining 1 tablespoon of the coconut oil and sauté until translucent over low to medium heat. This should take about 3 to 5 minutes.
4. Add this chicken broth and water.
5. Whisk in the cream cheese and keep whisking over low to medium heat until combined.
6. Add in the spices and bring to a boil.
7. While the water is boiling, cut the chicken into bite-sized pieces and add to the stockpot.
8. Reduce to a simmer and cook for 30 to 35 minutes.
9. Stir in the Cheddar cheese and serve.

**Per Serving**

calories: 158 | fat: 6.9g | protein: 17.2g
carbs: 5.1g | net carbs: 3.9g | fiber: 1.2g

## Shrimp Jalapeño Soup

**Prep time: 10 minutes | Cook time: 35 minutes | Serves 6**

4 cups chicken broth
Juice from 1 lime
1 pound (454 g) peeled, deveined shrimp
1 yellow onion, chopped
1 shallot, chopped

3 cloves garlic, chopped
1 jalapeño pepper, seeded and sliced
Salt and black pepper, to taste
1 tablespoon coconut oil for cooking

1. Add the coconut oil to a large stockpot over medium heat.
2. Add the shrimp, onion, shallot and garlic and cook until the shrimp are cooked through and pink.
3. Add the remaining ingredients minus the salt and black pepper, and bring to a boil.
4. Reduce the heat to a simmer and cook for 30 minutes.
5. Season with salt and black pepper and serve.

**Per Serving**

calories: 154 | fat: 4.9g | protein: 21.2g
carbs: 5.9g | net carbs: 4.8g | fiber: 1.1g

## Red Curry Shrimp and Bean Soup

**Prep time: 10 minutes | Cook time: 11 minutes | Serves 4**

1 onion, chopped
1 tablespoon red curry paste
1 tablespoon butter
1 pound jumbo shrimp, deveined
1 teaspoon ginger-garlic puree

1 cup coconut milk
Salt and chili pepper, to taste
1 bunch green beans, halved
1 tablespoon cilantro, chopped

1. Add the shrimp to melted butter in a saucepan over medium heat, season with salt and pepper, and cook until they are opaque, 2 to 3 minutes. Remove to a plate. Add in the ginger-garlic puree, onion, and red curry paste and sauté for 2 minutes until fragrant.
2. Stir in the coconut milk; add the shrimp, salt, chili pepper, and green beans. Cook for 4 minutes. Reduce the heat to a simmer and cook an additional 3 minutes, occasionally stirring. Adjust taste with salt, fetch soup into serving bowls, and serve sprinkled with cilantro.

**Per Serving**

calories: 351 | fat: 32g | protein: 8g
carbs: 4g | net carbs: 3g | fiber: 1g

## Broccoli Cheddar Soup

**Prep time: 10 minutes | Cook time: 20 minutes | Serves 6**

4 cloves garlic, minced
3½ cups chicken broth
1 cup heavy cream

4 cups broccoli florets
3 cups shredded Cheddar cheese

1. In a large pot, cook the garlic over medium heat for 1 minute, until fragrant.
2. Add the chicken broth, cream, and broccoli. Increase the heat to bring to a boil, then reduce the heat and simmer for 10 to 20 minutes, until the broccoli is tender.
3. Use a slotted spoon to remove about one-third of the broccoli pieces and set aside.
4. Use an immersion blender to purée the mixture, or transfer to a regular blender in batches if you don't have an immersion blender.
5. Reduce the heat to low. Add the Cheddar ½ cup at a time, stirring constantly, and continue to stir until melted. Puree again until smooth.
6. Remove from the heat. Return the reserved broccoli florets to the soup.

**Per Serving**

calories: 395 | fat: 33.1g | protein: 16.9g
carbs: 7.2g | net carbs: 5.9g | fiber: 1.3g

## Italian Pork Sausage and Zoodle Soup

**Prep time: 15 minutes | Cook time: 25 minutes | Serves 8**

1 tablespoon olive oil
4 cloves garlic, minced
1 pound (454 g) pork sausage (no sugar added)
½ tablespoon Italian seasoning

3 cups regular beef broth
3 cups beef bone broth
2 medium zucchini (6 ounces / 170 g each), spiralized

1. In a large soup pot, heat the oil over medium heat. Add the garlic and cook for about 1 minute, until fragrant.
2. Add the sausage, increase the heat to medium-high, and cook for about 10 minutes, stirring occasionally and breaking apart into small pieces, until browned.
3. Add the seasoning, regular broth, and bone broth, and simmer for 10 minutes.

4. Add the zucchini. Bring to a simmer again, then simmer for about 2 minutes, until the zucchini is soft. (Don't overcook or the zoodles will be mushy.)

**Per Serving**

calories: 215 | fat: 16.8g | protein: 12.2g
carbs: 2.1g | net carbs: 2.1g | fiber: 0g

## Bacon and Cauliflower Soup

**Prep time: 15 minutes | Cook time: 4 or 8 hours | Serves 5**

10 slices bacon
2 large or 3 small heads cauliflower
4 cups chicken broth
½ large yellow onion, chopped (about 1⅓ cups)
3 cloves garlic, pressed

¼ cup (½ stick) salted butter
2 cups shredded Cheddar cheese, plus extra for garnish
1 cup heavy whipping cream
Salt and pepper

1. Snipped fresh chives or sliced green onions, for garnish (optional) 1 Fry the bacon in a large skillet over medium heat. Transfer to a paper towel–lined plate, allow to cool, and then chop. Set aside in the refrigerator.
2. Core the heads of cauliflower and cut the cauliflower into florets. Place the florets in a food processor and chop into small to medium-sized pieces. (Don't rice it.)
3. In a large slow cooker (I use a 5½-quart slow cooker), combine the chicken broth, onion, garlic, butter, and cauliflower. Stir, cover, and cook on high for 4 hours or on low for 8 hours.
4. Once the cauliflower is tender, switch the slow cooker to the keep warm setting and use a whisk to stir and mash the cauliflower to a smooth consistency.
5. Add about three-quarters of the chopped bacon, the cheese, and the cream. Season with salt and pepper to taste. Stir well until the cheese is melted.
6. Serve garnished with additional cheese, the remaining bacon, and chives or green onions, if desired.

**Per Serving**

calories: 283 | fat: 22.1g | protein: 11.9g
carbs: 8.1g | net carbs: 6.2g | fiber: 1.9g

## Chicken, Carrot and Cauliflower Soup

**Prep time: 15 minutes | Cook time: 7 to 8 hours | Serves 6**

1 tablespoon extra-virgin olive oil
4 cups chicken broth
2 cups coconut milk
2 cups diced chicken breast
½ sweet onion, chopped
2 celery stalks, chopped
1 carrot, diced
½ cup chopped cauliflower
2 teaspoons minced garlic
1 teaspoon chopped thyme
1 teaspoon chopped oregano
¼ teaspoon freshly ground black pepper

1. Lightly grease the insert of the slow cooker with the olive oil.
2. Add the broth, coconut milk, chicken, onion, celery, carrot, cauliflower, garlic, thyme, oregano, and pepper.
3. Cover and cook on low for 7 to 8 hours.
4. Serve warm.

**Per Serving**

calories: 300 | fat: 25.1g | protein: 13.9g
carbs: 8.1g | net carbs: 4.9g | fiber: 3.2g

## Easy Egg Drop Soup

**Prep time: 5 minutes | Cook time: 5 minutes | Serves 4**

4 cups chicken broth
2 tablespoons unsalted butter
3 large eggs
Salt and pepper
1 green onion, sliced, for garnish

1. In a medium-sized pot over high heat, bring the chicken broth and butter to a boil.
2. Crack the eggs into a bowl, beat with a fork, and set aside.
3. Once the broth is boiling, slowly stir in the beaten eggs, then remove the pot from the heat. Season with salt and pepper to taste.
4. Serve garnished with the sliced green onion.

**Per Serving**

calories: 156 | fat: 9.4g | protein: 9.6g
carbs: 1.1g | net carbs: 1.1g | fiber: 0g

## Cheesy Coconut Carrot Soup

**Prep time: 15 minutes | Cook time: 6 hours | Serves 6**

1 tablespoon butter
5 cups chicken broth
1 cup coconut milk
2 celery stalks, chopped
1 carrot, chopped
½ sweet onion, chopped
Pinch cayenne pepper
8 ounces (227 g)
cream cheese, cubed
2 cups shredded Cheddar cheese
Salt, for seasoning
Freshly ground black pepper, for seasoning
1 tablespoon chopped fresh thyme, for garnish

1. Lightly grease the insert of the slow cooker with the butter.
2. Place the broth, coconut milk, celery, carrot, onion, and cayenne pepper in the insert.
3. Cover and cook on low for 6 hours.
4. Stir in the cream cheese and Cheddar, then season with salt and pepper.
5. Serve topped with the thyme.

**Per Serving**

calories: 405 | fat: 36.0g | protein: 14.9g
carbs: 6.9g | net carbs: 5.9g | fiber: 1.0g

## Cauliflower and Leek Soup

**Prep time: 10 minutes | Cook time: 35 minutes | Serves 4**

4 cups vegetable broth
2 heads cauliflower, cut into florets
1 celery stalk, chopped
1 onion, chopped
1 cup leeks, chopped
1 tablespoon butter
1 tablespoon olive oil
1 cup heavy cream
½ teaspoon red pepper flakes

1. Warm butter and olive oil in a pot set over medium heat and sauté onion, leeks, and celery for 5 minutes.
2. Stir in vegetable broth and cauliflower and bring to a boil; simmer for 30 minutes.
3. Transfer the mixture to an immersion blender and puree; add in the heavy cream and stir. Decorate with red pepper flakes to serve.

**Per Serving**

calories: 231 | fat: 18g | protein: 4g
carbs: 9g | net carbs: 5g | fiber: 4g

## Cauliflower and Double-Cheese Soup

**Prep time: 15 minutes | Cook time: 6 hours | Serves 6**

1 tablespoon extra-virgin olive oil
4 cups chicken broth
2 cups coconut milk
2 cups chopped cooked chicken
1 cup chopped cooked bacon
2 cups chopped cauliflower
1 sweet onion, chopped
3 teaspoons minced garlic
½ cup cream cheese, cubed
2 cups shredded Cheddar cheese

1. Lightly grease the insert of the slow cooker with the olive oil.
2. Place the broth, coconut milk, chicken, bacon, cauliflower, onion, and garlic in the insert.
3. Cover and cook on low for 6 hours.
4. Stir in the cream cheese and Cheddar and serve.

**Per Serving**

calories: 541 | fat: 44.1g | protein: 35.1g
carbs: 6.9g | net carbs: 5.9g | fiber: 1.0g

## Buffalo Cheese Chicken Soup

**Prep time: 10 minutes | Cook time: 7 minutes | Serves 4**

1 onion, chopped
2 cups cooked, shredded chicken
1 tablespoon butter
4 cups chicken broth
1 tablespoon cilantro, chopped
⅓ cup buffalo sauce
½ cup cream cheese
Salt and black pepper, to taste

1. In a skillet over medium heat, warm butter and sauté the onion until tender, about 5 minutes.
2. Add to a food processor and blend with buffalo sauce and cream cheese, until smooth.
3. Transfer to a pot, add chicken broth and heat until hot but do not bring to a boil. Stir in chicken, salt, pepper and cook until heated through. When ready, remove to soup bowls and serve garnished with cilantro.

**Per Serving**

calories: 487 | fat: 41g | protein: 16g
carbs: 5g | net carbs: 3g | fiber: 2g

## Sauerkraut and Organic Sausage Soup

**Prep time: 15 minutes | Cook time: 6 hours | Serves 6**

1 tablespoon extra-virgin olive oil
6 cups beef broth
1 pound (454 g) organic sausage, cooked and sliced
2 cups sauerkraut
2 celery stalks, chopped
1 sweet onion, chopped
2 teaspoons minced garlic
2 tablespoons butter
1 tablespoon hot mustard
½ teaspoon caraway seeds
½ cup sour cream
2 tablespoons chopped fresh parsley, for garnish

1. Lightly grease the insert of the slow cooker with the olive oil.
2. Place the broth, sausage, sauerkraut, celery, onion, garlic, butter, mustard, and caraway seeds in the insert.
3. Cover and cook on low for 6 hours.
4. Stir in the sour cream.
5. Serve topped with the parsley.

**Per Serving**

calories: 333 | fat: 27.9g | protein: 15.2g
carbs: 5.9g | net carbs: 2.0g | fiber: 3.9g

## Cucumber Cream Soup

**Prep time: 10 minutes | Cook time: 0 minutes | Serves 6**

2 cups heavy cream
1 cup sour cream
1 cucumber, diced
1 tablespoon spicy brown mustard
1 tablespoon horseradish
2 tablespoons freshly chopped parsley
2 tablespoons freshly chopped dill
2 tablespoons freshly chopped mint
Salt and black pepper, to taste

1. Add all the ingredients to a large mixing bowl minus the cucumber. Use an immersion blender and blend until smooth.
2. Stir in the cucumber, and chill in the refrigerator for at least 1 hour before serving.

**Per Serving**

calories: 234 | fat: 22.9g | protein: 3.1g
carbs: 5.9g | net carbs: 4.7g | fiber: 1.2g

## Almond Soup with Sour Cream and Cilantro

**Prep time: 10 minutes | Cook time: 21 minutes | Serves 4**

1 tablespoon olive oil
1 cup onion, chopped
1 celery, chopped
2 cloves garlic, minced
2 turnips, peeled and chopped
4 cups vegetable broth

Salt and white pepper, to taste
¼ cup ground almonds
1 cup almond milk
1 tablespoon fresh cilantro, chopped
1 teaspoon sour cream

1. Warm oil in a pot over medium heat and sauté celery, garlic, and onion for 6 minutes. Stir in white pepper, broth, salt, and ground almonds.
2. Bring to the boil and simmer for 15 minutes.
3. Transfer soup to an immersion blender and puree. Serve garnished with sour cream and cilantro.

**Per Serving**

calories: 125 | fat: 7g | protein: 5g
carbs: 12g | net carbs: 8g | fiber: 4g

## Lush Vegetable Soup

**Prep time: 15 minutes | Cook time: 25 minutes | Serves 4**

1 teaspoon olive oil
1 onion, chopped
1 garlic clove, minced
½ celery stalk, chopped
1 cup mushrooms, sliced
½ head broccoli, chopped

1 cup spinach, torn into pieces
Salt and black pepper, to taste
2 thyme sprigs, chopped
3 cups vegetable stock
1 tomato, chopped
½ cup almond milk

1. Heat olive oil in a saucepan. Add onion, celery and garlic; sauté until translucent, stirring occasionally, about 5 minutes.
2. Place in spinach, mushrooms, salt, rosemary, tomatoes, bay leaves, black pepper, thyme, and vegetable stock. Simmer the mixture for 15 minutes while the lid is slightly open. Stir in almond milk and cook for 5 more minutes.

**Per Serving**

calories: 140 | fat: 6g | protein: 3g
carbs: 4g | net carbs: 1g | fiber: 3g

## Turnip and Soup with Pork Sausage

**Prep time: 10 minutes | Cook time: 32 minutes | Serves 4**

3 turnips, chopped
2 celery sticks, chopped
1 tablespoon butter
1 tablespoon olive oil
1 pork sausage, sliced
2 cups vegetable broth

½ cup sour cream
3 green onions, chopped
2 cups water
Salt and black pepper, to taste

1. Sauté green onions in melted butter over medium heat until soft and golden, about 3 minutes. Add celery and turnip, and cook for another 5 minutes. Pour over the vegetable broth and water over.
2. Bring to a boil, simmer covered, and cook for about 20 minutes until the vegetables are tender. Remove from heat. Puree the soup with a hand blender until smooth. Add sour cream and adjust the seasoning. Warm the olive oil in a skillet. Add the pork sausage and cook for 5 minutes. Serve the soup in deep bowls topped with pork sausage.

**Per Serving**

calories: 275 | fat: 23g | protein:7 g
carbs: 10g | net carbs: 6g | fiber: 4g

## Creamy Tomato Soup

**Prep time: 10 minutes | Cook time: 40 minutes | Serves 6**

3 cups canned whole, peeled tomatoes
4 cups chicken broth
1 cup heavy cream
3 cloves garlic, chopped

2 tablespoons butter
1 teaspoon freshly chopped thyme
Salt and black pepper, to taste

1. Add the butter to the bottom of a stockpot.
2. Add in all the remaining ingredients minus the heavy cream. Bring to a boil, and then simmer for 40 minutes.
3. Warm the heavy cream, and then stir into the soup.

**Per Serving**

calories: 144 | fat: 12g | protein: 4g
carbs: 4g | net carbs: 3g | fiber: 1g

## White Mushroom Cream Soup with Herbs

**Prep time: 10 minutes | Cook time: 23 minutes | Serves 4**

1 onion, chopped  
½ cup crème fraiche  
¼ cup butter  
12 ounces (340 g) white mushrooms, chopped  
1 teaspoon thyme  
leaves, chopped  
1 teaspoon parsley leaves, chopped  
2 garlic cloves, minced  
4 cups vegetable broth  
Salt and black pepper, to taste

1. Add butter, onion and garlic to a pot over high heat and cook for 3 minutes. Add in mushrooms, salt and pepper, and cook for 10 minutes. Pour in broth and bring to a boil.
2. Reduce heat and simmer for 10 minutes. Puree soup with a hand blender. Stir in crème fraiche. Garnish with herbs before serving.

**Per Serving**

calories: 190 | fat: 15g | protein: 3g  
carbs: 6g | net carbs: 4g | fiber: 2g

## Spinach Mozzarella Soup

**Prep time: 10 minutes | Cook time: 15 minutes | Serves 4**

2 cups chicken broth  
1 cup heavy cream  
1 cup shredded mozzarella cheese  
1 cup fresh spinach, chopped  
3 cloves garlic,  
chopped  
1 teaspoon onion powder  
1 teaspoon dried thyme  
Salt and black pepper, to taste

1. Add all the ingredients minus the heavy cream and mozzarella to the base of a stockpot.
2. Bring to a boil, and then simmer for 10 minutes.
3. Warm the heavy cream, and then add to the soup along with mozzarella. Stir until the cheese has melted.

**Per Serving**

calories: 151 | fat: 13g | protein: 6g  
carbs: 3g | net carbs: 3g | fiber: 0g

## Heavy Cream-Cheese Broccoli Soup

**Prep time: 10 minutes | Cook time: 13 minutes | Serves 4**

1 tablespoon olive oil  
1 tablespoon peanut butter  
¾ cup heavy cream  
1 onion, diced  
1 garlic, minced  
4 cups chopped broccoli  
4 cups veggie broth  
2¾ cups cheddar cheese, grated  
¼ cup cheddar cheese to garnish  
Salt and black pepper, to taste  
½ bunch fresh mint, chopped

1. Warm olive oil and peanut butter in a pot over medium heat. Sauté onion and garlic for 3 minutes, stirring occasionally. Season with salt and pepper. Add the broth and broccoli and bring to a boil.
2. Reduce the heat and simmer for 10 minutes. Puree the soup with a hand blender until smooth. Add in the cheese and cook about 1 minute. Stir in the heavy cream.
3. Serve in bowls with the reserved grated cheddar cheese and sprinkled with fresh mint.

**Per Serving**

calories: 508 | fat: 28g | protein: 26g  
carbs: 11g | net carbs: 7g | fiber: 4g

## Turkey and Celery Soup

**Prep time: 15 minutes | Cook time: 4 hours | Serves 7**

1 pound (454 g) turkey breast, cubed  
5 cups chicken broth  
1 cup cream cheese  
1 stalk celery, chopped  
3 cloves garlic,  
chopped  
1 teaspoon freshly chopped rosemary  
Salt and black pepper, to taste

1. Add all the ingredients minus the cream cheese to the base of a slow cooker.
2. Cook on high for 4 hours.
3. Stir in the cream cheese until well combined.

**Per Serving**

calories: 216 | fat: 14g | protein: 17g  
carbs: 3g | net carbs: 2g | fiber: 1g

## Turkey and Veggies Soup

**Prep time: 10 minutes | Cook time: 25 minutes | Serves 4**

1 onion, chopped
1 garlic clove, minced
3 celery stalks, chopped
2 leeks, chopped
1 tablespoon butter
4 cups chicken stock
Salt and black pepper,
to taste
¼ cup fresh parsley, chopped
1 large zucchini, spiralized
2 cups turkey meat, cooked and chopped

1. In a pot over medium heat, add in leeks, celery, onion, and garlic and cook for 5 minutes.
2. Place in the turkey meat, black pepper, salt, and stock, and cook for 20 minutes. Stir in the zucchini, and cook turkey soup for 5 minutes. Serve in bowls sprinkled with parsley.

**Per Serving**

calories: 312 | fat: 13g | protein: 16g
carbs: 9g | net carbs: 4g | fiber: 5g

## Tomato Soup with Basil

**Prep time: 10 minutes | Cook time: 14 minutes | Serves 4**

1 tablespoon olive oil
1 onion, diced
1 garlic clove, minced
¼ cup raw cashew nuts, diced
14 ounces canned
tomatoes
1 teaspoon fresh basil leaves
Salt and black pepper, to taste
1 cup crème fraîche

1. Warm olive oil in a pot over medium heat and sauté the onion and garlic for 4 minutes until softened. Stir in the tomatoes, basil, 1 cup water, cashew nuts, and season with salt and black pepper.
2. Cover and bring to simmer for 10 minutes until thoroughly cooked. Puree the ingredients with an immersion blender. Adjust to taste and stir in the crème fraîche. Serve sprinkled with basil.

**Per Serving**

calories: 189 | fat: 14g | protein: 5g
carbs: 4g | net carbs: 2g | fiber: 2g

## Broccoli and Spinach Soup

**Prep time: 10 minutes | Cook time: 16 minutes | Serves 4**

1 tablespoon butter
1 onion, chopped
1 garlic clove, minced
2 heads broccoli, cut in florets
2 stalks celery, chopped
4 cups vegetable broth
1 cup baby spinach
Salt and black pepper, to taste
1 tablespoon basil, chopped
Parmesan cheese, shaved to serve

1. Melt the butter in a saucepan over medium heat. Sauté the garlic and onion for 3 minutes until softened. Mix in the broccoli and celery, and cook for 4 minutes until slightly tender.
2. Pour in the broth, bring to a boil, then reduce the heat to medium-low and simmer covered for about 5 minutes.
3. Drop in the spinach to wilt, adjust the seasonings, and cook for 4 minutes. Ladle soup into serving bowls. Serve with a sprinkle of grated Parmesan cheese and chopped basil.

**Per Serving**

calories: 123 | fat: 11g | protein: 1g
carbs: 4g | net carbs: 3g | fiber: 1g

## Butternut Squash Soup

**Prep time: 15 minutes | Cook time: 4 to 6 hours | Serves 8**

1½ cups butternut squash, cubed
1 cup heavy cream
5 cups chicken broth
3 cloves garlic, chopped
2 teaspoons ground
cinnamon
½ teaspoon ground nutmeg
½ teaspoon ground cloves
Salt and black pepper, to taste

1. Add all the ingredients minus the heavy cream to the base of a slow cooker.
2. Cook on high for 4 to 6 hours.
3. Warm the heavy cream, and then add to the soup.
4. Use an immersion blender and blend until smooth.

**Per Serving**

calories: 95 | fat: 7g | protein: 4g
carbs: 3g | net carbs: 2g | fiber: 1g

## Asparagus Parmesan Soup

**Prep time: 10 minutes | Cook time: 15 minutes | Serves 4**

2 cups chicken broth
1 cup heavy cream
1 cup shredded Parmesan cheese
1 cup asparagus finely chopped
1 yellow onion, chopped
3 cloves garlic, chopped
1 teaspoon dried thyme
Salt and black pepper, to taste

1. Add all the ingredients minus the heavy cream and Parmesan cheese to the base of a stockpot.
2. Bring to a boil, and then simmer for 10 minutes.
3. Warm the heavy cream, and then add to the soup along with the Parmesan cheese. Stir until the cheese has melted and serve.

**Per Serving**

calories: 228 | fat: 17g | protein: 12g
carbs: 7g | net carbs: 5g | fiber: 2g

## Broccoli and Bacon Soup

**Prep time: 10 minutes | Cook time: 10 minutes | Serves 6**

2 cups chicken broth
1 cup broccoli florets finely chopped
1 cup heavy cream
1 cup shredded cheddar cheese
½ white onion, chopped
2 cloves garlic, chopped
3 slices cooked bacon, crumbled for serving
½ teaspoon salt
¼ teaspoon black pepper

1. Add all the ingredients minus the heavy cream, cheddar cheese and bacon to a stockpot over medium heat.
2. Bring to a simmer and cook for 5 minutes.
3. Warm the cream, and then add the warm cream and cheddar cheese. Whisk until smooth.
4. Serve with crumbled bacon.

**Per Serving**

calories: 220 | fat: 18g | protein: 11g
carbs: 4g | net carbs: 3g | fiber: 1g

## Spiced Pumpkin Soup

**Prep time: 15 minutes | Cook time: 4 to 6 hours | Serves 8**

1½ cups pumpkin, cubed
1 cup heavy cream
5 cups chicken broth
3 cloves garlic, chopped
2 teaspoons ground cinnamon
½ teaspoon ground nutmeg
½ teaspoon ground cloves
Salt and black pepper, to taste

1. Add all the ingredients minus the heavy cream to the base of a slow cooker.
2. Cook on high for 4 to 6 hours.
3. Warm the heavy cream, and then add to the soup.
4. Use an immersion blender and blend until smooth.

**Per Serving**

calories: 96 | fat: 7g | protein: 4g
carbs: 6g | net carbs: 4g | fiber: 2g

## Tomato and Onion Soup

**Prep time: 15 minutes | Cook time: 30 minutes | Serves 6**

4 cups vegetable broth
1 cup heavy cream
1 cup canned diced tomatoes
1 yellow onion, chopped
2 cloves garlic, chopped
1 cup shredded mozzarella cheese
Freshly chopped basil, for serving

1. Add all of the ingredients minus the heavy cream, cheese and fresh basil to a stockpot over medium heat. Bring to a boil, and then reduce to a simmer.
2. Simmer for 30 minutes.
3. While the soup is cooking, warm the heavy cream over low heat and add to the soup once cooked.
4. Use an immersion blender and blend until smooth.
5. Stir in the mozzarella cheese and top with fresh basil.

**Per Serving**

calories: 122 | fat: 9g | protein: 6g
carbs: 5g | net carbs: 4g | fiber: 1g

# Chapter 4 Salads

## Mexican Egg and Avocado Salad

**Prep time: 15 minutes | Cook time: 10 minutes | Serves 2**

4 large eggs
½ cup shredded cheese, divided
1 jalapeño
1 avocado, halved
Pink Himalayan salt
Freshly ground black pepper
2 tablespoons chopped fresh cilantro

1. Preheat the oven to 350ºF (180ºC).
2. Line a baking sheet with parchment paper or a silicone baking mat.
3. In a medium saucepan, cover the eggs with water. Place over high heat, and bring the water to a boil. Once it is boiling, turn off the heat, cover, and leave on the burner for 10 to 12 minutes.
4. Use a slotted spoon to remove the eggs from the pan and run them under cold water for 1 minute or submerge in an ice bath.
5. Gently tap the shells and peel. (I like to run cold water over my hands as I peel the shells off.)
6. While the eggs are cooking, put 2 (¼-cup) mounds of shredded cheese on the prepared pan and bake for about 7 minutes, or until the edges are brown and the middle has fully melted.
7. Remove the cheese chips from the oven and allow to cool for 5 minutes; they will be floppy when they first come out but will crisp as they cool.
8. In a medium bowl, chop the hardboiled eggs.
9. Stem, rib, seed, and dice the jalapeño, and add it to the eggs.
10. Mash the avocado with a fork. Season with pink Himalayan salt and pepper. Add the avocado and cilantro to the eggs, and stir to combine.
11. Place the cheese chips on two plates, top with the egg salad, and serve.

**Per Serving**

calories: 360 | fat: 28.9g | protein: 20.9g
carbs: 8.0g | net carbs: 2.9g | fiber: 5.1g

## Dijon Broccoli Slaw Salad

**Prep time: 10 minutes | Cook time: 0 minutes | Serves 6**

1 tablespoon granulated Swerve
1 tablespoon Dijon mustard
1 tablespoon olive oil
4 cups broccoli slaw
⅓ cup mayonnaise,
sugar-free
1 teaspoon celery seeds
1½ tablespoon apple cider vinegar
Salt and black pepper, to taste

1. Whisk together all ingredients except the broccoli slaw. Place broccoli slaw in a large salad bowl. Pour the dressing over. Mix with your hands to combine well.

**Per Serving**

calories: 110 | fat: 10g | protein: 3g
carbs: 5g | net carbs: 2g | fiber: 3g

## Baby Arugula and Walnuts Salad

**Prep time: 10 minutes | Cook time: 0 minutes | Serves 4**

4 tablespoons extra-virgin olive oil
Zest and juice of 2 lemon (2 to 3 tablespoons)
1 tablespoon red wine vinegar
½ teaspoon salt
¼ teaspoon freshly
ground black pepper
8 cups baby arugula
1 cup coarsely chopped walnuts
1 cup crumbled goat cheese
½ cup pomegranate seeds

1. In a small bowl, whisk together the olive oil, zest and juice, vinegar, salt, and pepper and set aside.
2. To assemble the salad for serving, in a large bowl, combine the arugula, walnuts, goat cheese, and pomegranate seeds. Drizzle with the dressing and toss to coat.

**Per Serving**

calories: 444 | fat: 40g | protein: 10g
carbs: 11g | net carbs: 8g | fiber: 3g

## Charred Broccoli and Sardine Salad

**Prep time: 5 minutes | Cook time: 5 minutes | Serves 4**

| | |
|---|---|
| 1 pound (454 g) broccoli florets | drained |
| ½ white onion, thinly sliced | 2 tablespoons fresh lime juice |
| 2 (4-ounce / 113-g) cans sardines in oil, | 1 teaspoon stone-ground mustard |

1. Heat a lightly greased cast-iron skillet over medium-high heat. Cook the broccoli florets for 5 to 6 minutes until charred; work in batches.
2. In salad bowls, place the charred broccoli with onion and sardines. Toss with the lime juice and mustard. Serve at room temperature. Bon appétit!

**Per Serving**

calories: 160 | fat: 7.2g | protein: 17.6g
carbs: 5.6g | net carbs: 2.6g | fiber: 3.0g

## Spicy Leek and Green Cabbage Salad

**Prep time: 15 minutes | Cook time: 40 minutes | Serves 4**

| | |
|---|---|
| 3 tablespoons extra-virgin olive oil | Sea salt, to taste |
| 1 medium-sized leek, chopped | 4-5 black peppercorns |
| ½ pound (227 g) green cabbage, shredded | 1 garlic clove, minced |
| | 1 teaspoon yellow mustard |
| ½ teaspoon caraway seeds | 1 tablespoon balsamic vinegar |
| | ½ teaspoon Sriracha sauce |

1. Drizzle 2 tablespoons of the olive oil over the leek and cabbage; sprinkle with caraway seeds, salt, black peppercorns.
2. Roast in the preheated oven at 420ºF (216ºC) for 37 to 40 minutes. Place the roasted mixture in a salad bowl.
3. Toss with the remaining tablespoon of olive oil garlic, mustard, vinegar, and Sriracha sauce. Serve immediately and enjoy!

**Per Serving**

calories: 116 | fat: 10.1g | protein: 1.0g
carbs: 6.5g | net carbs: 4.7g | fiber: 1.8g

## Zucchini and Bell Pepper Slaw

**Prep time: 15 minutes | Cook time: 0 minutes | Serves 3**

| | |
|---|---|
| 1 zucchini, shredded | vinegar |
| 1 yellow bell pepper, sliced | 1 teaspoon Dijon mustard |
| 1 red onion, thinly sliced | ¼ teaspoon cumin seeds |
| 2 tablespoons extra-virgin olive oil | ¼ teaspoon ground black pepper |
| 1 tablespoon balsamic | Sea salt, to taste |

1. Thoroughly combine all ingredients in a salad bowl.
2. Refrigerate for 1 hour before serving or serve right away. Enjoy!

**Per Serving**

calories: 97 | fat: 9.5g | protein: 0.8g
carbs: 2.7g | net carbs: 2.4g | fiber: 0.3g

## Chicken and Sunflower Seed Salad

**Prep time: 15 minutes | Cook time: 15 minutes | Serves 3**

| | |
|---|---|
| 1 chicken breast, skinless | ¼ cup sunflower seeds, hulled and roasted |
| ¼ mayonnaise | |
| ¼ cup sour cream | ½ avocado, peeled and cubed |
| 2 tablespoons Cottage cheese, room temperature | ½ teaspoon fresh garlic, minced |
| Salt and black pepper, to taste | 2 tablespoons scallions, chopped |

1. Bring a pot of well-salted water to a rolling boil.
2. Add the chicken to the boiling water; now, turn off the heat, cover, and let the chicken stand in the hot water for 15 minutes.
3. Then, drain the water; chop the chicken into bite-sized pieces. Add the remaining ingredients and mix well.
4. Place in the refrigerator for at least one hour. Serve well chilled. Enjoy!

**Per Serving**

calories: 401 | fat: 35.2g | protein: 16.2g
carbs: 5.7g | net carbs: 2.9g | fiber: 2.8g

## Asparagus and Mozzarella Caprese Salad

**Prep time: 15 minutes | Cook time: 0 minutes | Serves 2**

| | |
|---|---|
| 1 teaspoon fresh lime juice | 1 cup grape tomatoes, halved |
| 1 tablespoon hot Hungarian paprika infused oil | 2 tablespoon red wine vinegar |
| ½ teaspoon kosher salt | 1 garlic clove, pressed |
| ¼ teaspoon red pepper flakes | 1-2 drops liquid stevia |
| ½ pound (227 g) asparagus spears, trimmed | 1 tablespoon fresh basil |
| | 1 tablespoon fresh chives |
| | ½ cup Mozzarella, grated |

1. Heat your grill to the hottest setting. Toss your asparagus with the lime juice, hot Hungarian paprika infused oil, salt, and red pepper flakes.
2. Place the asparagus spears on the hot grill. Grill until one side chars; then, grill your asparagus on the other side.
3. Cut the asparagus spears into bite-sized pieces and transfer to a salad bowl. Add the grape tomatoes, red wine, garlic, stevia, basil, and chives; toss to combine well.
4. Top with freshly grated Mozzarella cheese and serve immediately.

**Per Serving**

calories: 190 | fat: 13.2g | protein: 9.6g
carbs: 7.5g | net carbs: 4.2g | fiber: 3.3g

## Mediterranean Tomato and Zucchini Salad

**Prep time: 15 minutes | Cook time: 10 minutes | Serves 4**

| | |
|---|---|
| ½ pound (227 g) Roma tomatoes, sliced | black pepper |
| ½ pound (227 g) zucchini, sliced | Sea salt, to season |
| 1 Lebanese cucumber, sliced | 4 tablespoons extra-virgin olive oil |
| 1 cup arugula | 2 tablespoons fresh lemon juice |
| ½ teaspoon oregano | ½ cup Kalamata olives, pitted and sliced |
| ½ teaspoon basil | 4 ounces (113 g) Feta cheese, cubed |
| ½ teaspoon rosemary | |
| ½ teaspoon ground | |

1. Arrange the Roma tomatoes and zucchini slices on a roasting pan; spritz cooking oil over your vegetables.
2. Bake in the preheated oven at 350ºF (180ºC) for 6 to 7 minutes. Let them cool slightly, then, transfer to a salad bowl.
3. Add in the cucumber, arugula, herbs, and spices. Drizzle olive oil and lemon juice over your veggies; toss to combine well.
4. Top with Kalamata olives and Feta cheese. Serve at room temperature and enjoy!

**Per Serving**

calories: 242 | fat: 22.1g | protein: 6.4g
carbs: 6.9g | net carbs: 5.1g | fiber: 1.8g

## Israeli Veggies, Nut, and Seed Salad

**Prep time: 15 minutes | Cook time: 0 minutes | Serves 4**

| | |
|---|---|
| ¼ cup pine nuts | ½ small red onion, finely chopped |
| ¼ cup shelled pistachios | ½ cup finely chopped fresh flat-leaf Italian parsley |
| ¼ cup coarsely chopped walnuts | ¼ cup extra-virgin olive oil |
| ¼ cup shelled pumpkin seeds | 2 to 3 tablespoons freshly squeezed lemon juice (from 1 lemon) |
| ¼ cup shelled sunflower seeds | 1 teaspoon salt |
| 2 large English cucumbers, unpeeled and finely chopped | ¼ teaspoon freshly ground black pepper |
| 1 pint cherry tomatoes, finely chopped | 4 cups baby arugula |

1. In a large dry skillet, toast the pine nuts, pistachios, walnuts, pumpkin seeds, and sunflower seeds over medium-low heat until golden and fragrant, 5 to 6 minutes, being careful not to burn them. Remove from the heat and set aside.
2. In a large bowl, combine the cucumber, tomatoes, red onion, and parsley.
3. In a small bowl, whisk together olive oil, lemon juice, salt, and pepper. Pour over the chopped vegetables and toss to coat.
4. Add the toasted nuts and seeds and arugula and toss with the salad to blend well. Serve at room temperature or chilled.

**Per Serving**

calories: 414 | fat: 34g | protein: 10g
carbs: 17g | net carbs: 11g | fiber: 6g

## Roasted Asparagus Salad

**Prep time: 15 minutes | Cook time: 15 minutes | Serves 5**

14 ounces (397 g) asparagus spears, trimmed
2 tablespoons olive oil
½ teaspoon oregano
½ teaspoon rosemary
Sea salt and freshly ground black pepper, to taste
5 tablespoons

mayonnaise
3 tablespoons sour cream
1 tablespoon wine vinegar
1 teaspoon fresh garlic, minced
1 cup cherry tomatoes, halved

1. In a lightly greased roasting pan, toss the asparagus with the olive oil, oregano, rosemary, salt, and black pepper.
2. Roast in the preheated oven at 425ºF (220ºC) for 13 to 15 minutes until just tender.
3. Meanwhile, in a mixing bowl, thoroughly combine the mayonnaise, sour cream, vinegar, and garlic; dress the salad and top with the cherry tomato halves.
4. Serve at room temperature. Bon appétit!

**Per Serving**

calories: 180 | fat: 17.6g | protein: 2.6g
carbs: 4.5g | net carbs: 2.5g | fiber: 2.0g

## Grilled Chicken and Cucumber Salad

**Prep time: 10 minutes | Cook time: 15 minutes | Serves 2**

2 chicken breasts
2 tablespoons extra-virgin olive oil
4 tablespoons apple cider vinegar

1 cup grape tomatoes, halved
1 Lebanese cucumber, thinly sliced

1. Preheat your grill to medium-high temperature. Now, grill the chicken breasts for 5 to 7 minutes on each side.
2. Slice the chicken into strips and transfer them to a nice salad bowl. Toss with the olive oil, vinegar, grape tomatoes, and cucumber.
3. Garnish with fresh snipped chives if desired. Bon appétit!

**Per Serving**

calories: 402 | fat: 18.1g | protein: 51.5g
carbs: 5.2g | net carbs: 3.7g | fiber: 1.5g

## Bell Pepper, Cabbage, and Arugula Coleslaw

**Prep time: 15 minutes | Cook time: 0 minutes | Serves 4**

2 teaspoons balsamic vinegar
1 teaspoon fresh garlic, minced
2 tablespoons tahini (sesame paste)
1 tablespoon yellow mustard
Sea salt and ground black pepper, to taste
¼ teaspoon paprika
1 red bell pepper,

deveined and sliced
1green bell pepper, deveined and sliced
½ pound (227 g) Napa cabbage, shredded
2 cups arugula, torn into pieces
1 Spanish onion, thinly sliced into rings
4 tablespoons sesame seeds, lightly toasted

1. Make a dressing by whisking the balsamic vinegar, garlic, tahini, mustard, salt, black pepper, and paprika.
2. In a salad bowl, combine the bell peppers, cabbage, arugula, and Spanish onion. Dress the salad and toss until everything is well incorporated.
3. Garnish with sesame seeds just before serving. Serve well chilled and enjoy!

**Per Serving**

calories: 123 | fat: 9.2g | protein: 4.6g
carbs: 5.8g | net carbs: 2.8g | fiber: 3.0g

## Homemade Albacore Tuna Salad

**Prep time: 5 minutes | Cook time: 0 minutes | Serves 4**

2 (5-ounce / 142-g) cans albacore tuna packed in water, drained
¼ cup avocado oil mayonnaise

2 teaspoons Dijon mustard
3 teaspoons dried dill
2 teaspoons lime juice
½ cup diced bell pepper

1. In a small bowl, combine the tuna, mayonnaise, mustard, dill, lime juice, and bell pepper.
2. Serve on a bed of mixed greens.

**Per Serving**

calories: 294 | fat: 21g | protein: 13g
carbs: 19g | net carbs: 12g | fiber: 7g

## Roasted Asparagus and Cherry Tomato Salad

**Prep time: 15 minutes | Cook time: 20 minutes | Serves 3**

1 pound (454 g) asparagus, trimmed
¼ teaspoon ground black pepper
Flaky salt, to season
3 tablespoons sesame seeds
1 tablespoon Dijon mustard
½ lime, freshly squeezed
3 tablespoons extra-virgin olive oil
2 garlic cloves, minced
1 tablespoon fresh tarragon, snipped
1 cup cherry tomatoes, sliced

1. Start by preheating your oven to 400ºF (205ºC). Spritz a roasting pan with nonstick cooking spray.
2. Roast the asparagus for about 13 minutes, turning the spears over once or twice. Sprinkle with salt, pepper, and sesame seeds; roast an additional 3 to 4 minutes.
3. To make the dressing, whisk the Dijon mustard, lime juice, olive oil, and minced garlic.
4. Chop the asparagus spears into bite-sized pieces and place them in a nice salad bowl. Add the tarragon and tomatoes to the bowl; gently toss to combine.
5. Dress your salad and serve at room temperature. Enjoy!

**Per Serving**

calories: 160 | fat: 12.4g | protein: 5.7g
carbs: 6.2g | net carbs: 2.2g | fiber: 4.0g

## Herbed Chicken Salad

**Prep time: 15 minutes | Cook time: 15 minutes | Serves 4**

**Poached Chicken:**

2 chicken breasts, skinless and boneless
½ teaspoon salt
**Salad:**
4 scallions, trimmed and thinly sliced
1 tablespoon fresh coriander, chopped
1 teaspoon Dijon
2 bay laurels
1 thyme sprig
1 rosemary sprig

mustard
2 teaspoons freshly squeezed lemon juice
1 cup mayonnaise, preferably homemade

1. Place all ingredients for the poached chicken in a stockpot; cover with water and bring to a rolling boil.

2. Turn the heat to medium-low and let it simmer for about 15 minutes or until a meat thermometer reads 165ºF (74ºC). Let the poached chicken cool to room temperature.
3. Cut into strips and transfer to a nice salad bowl.
4. Toss the poached chicken with the salad ingredients; serve well chilled and enjoy!

**Per Serving**

calories: 540 | fat: 48.9g | protein: 18.9g
carbs: 3.2g | net carbs: 2.8g | fiber: 0.4g

## Spring Vegetable Salad with Cheese Balls

**Prep time: 15 minutes | Cook time: 10 minutes | Serves 6**

**Cheese balls:**

3 eggs
1 cup feta cheese, crumbled
½ cup pecorino cheese, shredded
1 cup almond flour
**Salad:**
1 head iceberg lettuce, leaves separated
½ cup cucumber, thinly sliced
2 tomatoes, seeded and chopped
½ cup red onion, thinly sliced
1 tablespoon flax meal
1 teaspoon baking powder
Salt and black pepper, to taste

½ cup radishes, thinly sliced
⅓ cup mayonnaise
1 teaspoon mustard
1 teaspoon paprika
1 teaspoon oregano
Salt, to taste

1. Set oven to 390ºF (199ºC). Line a piece of parchment paper to a baking sheet.
2. In a mixing dish, mix all ingredients for the cheese balls; form balls out of the mixture. Set the balls on the prepared baking sheet. Bake for 10 minutes until crisp. Arrange lettuce leaves on a large salad platter; add in radishes, tomatoes, cucumbers, and red onion. In a small mixing bowl, mix the mayonnaise, paprika, salt, oregano, and mustard. Sprinkle this mixture over the vegetables. Add cheese balls on top and serve.

**Per Serving**

calories: 234 | fat: 17g | protein: 12g
carbs: 11g | net carbs: 8g | fiber: 3g

## Strawberry and Spinach Salad

**Prep time: 5 minutes | Cook time: 10 minutes | Serves 2**

4 cups spinach
4 strawberries, sliced
½ cup flaked almonds
1½ cup grated hard goat cheese

1 tablespoon raspberry vinaigrette
Salt and black pepper, to taste

1. Preheat your oven to 400ºF (205ºC). Arrange the grated goat cheese in two circles on two pieces of parchment paper. Place in the oven and bake for 10 minutes.
2. Find two same bowls, place them upside down, and carefully put the parchment paper on top to give the cheese a bowl-like shape. Let cool that way for 15 minutes. Divide spinach among the bowls stir in salt, pepper and drizzle with vinaigrette. Top with almonds and strawberries.

**Per Serving**

calories: 445 | fat: 34g | protein: 33g
carbs: 7g | net carbs: 5g | fiber: 2g

## Blue Cheese Green Salad with Bacon

**Prep time: 5 minutes | Cook time: 6 minutes | Serves 4**

2 (8-ounce / 227-g) pack mixed salad greens
8 strips bacon
1½ cups crumbled blue cheese

1 tablespoon white wine vinegar
1 tablespoon extra virgin olive oil
Salt and black pepper to taste

1. Pour the salad greens in a salad bowl; set aside. Fry bacon strips in a skillet over medium heat for 6 minutes, until browned and crispy. Chop the bacon and scatter over the salad. Add in half of the cheese, toss and set aside.
2. In a small bowl, whisk the white wine vinegar, olive oil, salt, and black pepper until dressing is well combined. Drizzle half of the dressing over the salad, toss, and top with remaining cheese. Divide salad into four plates and serve with crusted chicken fries along with the remaining dressing.

**Per Serving**

calories: 205 | fat: 20g | protein: 4g
carbs: 5g | net carbs: 2g | fiber: 3g

## Mozzarella Bacon and Tomato Salad

**Prep time: 5 minutes | Cook time: 5 minutes | Serves 2**

1 large tomato, sliced
4 basil leaves
8 mozzarella cheese slices
1 teaspoon olive oil

4 bacon slices, chopped
1 teaspoon balsamic vinegar
Salt, to taste

1. Place the bacon in a skillet over medium heat and cook until crispy, about 5 minutes. Divide the tomato slices between two serving plates. Arrange the mozzarella slices over and top with the basil leaves. Add the crispy bacon on top, drizzle with olive oil and vinegar. Sprinkle with salt and serve.

**Per Serving**

calories: 279 | fat: 26g | protein: 21g
carbs: 3g | net carbs: 2g | fiber: 1g

## Tuscan Kale Salad with Lemony Anchovies

**Prep time: 15 minutes | Cook time: 0 minutes | Serves 4**

1 large bunch lacinato or dinosaur kale
¼ cup toasted pine nuts
1 cup shaved or coarsely shredded fresh Parmesan cheese
¼ cup extra-virgin olive oil

8 anchovy fillets, roughly chopped
2 to 3 tablespoons freshly squeezed lemon juice (from 1 large lemon)
2 teaspoons red pepper flakes (optional)

1. Remove the rough center stems from the kale leaves and roughly tear each leaf into about 4-by-1-inch strips. Place the torn kale in a large bowl and add the pine nuts and cheese.
2. In a small bowl, whisk together the olive oil, anchovies, lemon juice, and red pepper flakes (if using). Drizzle over the salad and toss to coat well. Let sit at room temperature 30 minutes before serving, tossing again just prior to serving.

**Per Serving**

calories: 337 | fat: 25g | protein: 16g
carbs: 12g | net carbs: 10g | fiber: 2g

## Mustard Eggs Salad

**Prep time: 10 minutes | Cook time: 10 minutes | Serves 8**

10 eggs
¾ cup mayonnaise
1 teaspoon sriracha sauce
1 tablespoon mustard
½ cup scallions
½ stalk celery, minced
½ teaspoon fresh

lemon juice
½ teaspoon sea salt
½ teaspoon black pepper
1 head romaine lettuce, torn into pieces

1. Add the eggs in a pan and cover with enough water and boil. Get them from the heat and allow to set for 10 minutes while covered. Chop the eggs and add to a salad bowl. Stir in the remaining ingredients until everything is well combined. Refrigerate until ready to serve.

**Per Serving**

calories: 174 | fat: 13g | protein: 7g
carbs: 10g | net carbs: 8g | fiber: 2g

## Caesar Salad with Chicken and Cheese

**Prep time: 10 minutes | Cook time: 11 minutes | Serves 4**

4 boneless, skinless chicken thighs
¼ cup lemon juice
2 garlic cloves, minced
1 tablespoon olive oil
½ cup Caesar salad

dressing, sugar-free
12 bok choy leaves
3 Parmesan crisps
Parmesan cheese, grated for garnishing

1. Mix chicken, lemon juice, 1 tablespoon olive oil and garlic in a ziploc bag. Seal the bag, shake well, and refrigerate for 1 hour.
2. Preheat the grill to medium and grill the chicken for 4 minutes per side. Cut bok choy lengthwise, and brush with the remaining oil. Grill the bok choy for about 3 minutes.
3. Place on a bowl. Top with chicken and Parmesan; drizzle the dressing over. Top with Parmesan crisps to serve.

**Per Serving**

calories: 529 | fat: 39g | protein: 33g
carbs: 6g | net carbs: 5g | fiber: 1g

## Shrimp, Cauliflower and Avocado Salad

**Prep time: 10 minutes | Cook time: 13 minutes | Serves 6**

1 cauliflower head, florets only
1 pound (454 g) medium shrimp
¼ cup plus 1 tablespoon olive oil
1 avocado, chopped

1 tablespoon chopped dill
¼ cup lemon juice
1 tablespoon lemon zest
Salt and black pepper to taste

1. Heat 1 tablespoon olive oil in a skillet and cook shrimp for 8 minutes. Microwave cauliflower for 5 minutes.
2. Place shrimp, cauliflower, and avocado in a bowl. Whisk the remaining olive oil, lemon zest, juice, dill, and salt, and pepper, in another bowl. Pour the dressing over, toss to combine and serve immediately.

**Per Serving**

calories: 214 | fat: 17g | protein: 15g
carbs: 9g | net carbs: 5g | fiber: 4g

## Skirt Steak and Pickled Peppers Salad

**Prep time: 10 minutes | Cook time: 10 minutes | Serves 4**

1 pound (454 g) skirt steak, sliced
Salt and black pepper to season
1 teaspoon olive oil
1½ cups mixed salad greens

3 chopped pickled peppers
1 tablespoon red wine vinaigrette
½ cup crumbled queso fresco

1. Brush the steak slices with olive oil and season with salt and black pepper on both sides. Heat pan over high heat and cook the steaks on each side for about 5-6 minutes. Remove to a bow.
2. Mix the salad greens, pickled peppers, and vinaigrette in a salad bowl. Add the beef and sprinkle with queso fresco.

**Per Serving**

calories: 315 | fat: 26g | protein: 18g
carbs: 3g | net carbs: 2g | fiber: 1g

## Lush Greek Salad

**Prep time: 10 minutes | Cook time: 0 minutes | Serves 4**

2 large English cucumbers
4 Roma tomatoes, quartered
1 green bell pepper, cut into 1- to 1½-inch chunks
¼ small red onion, thinly sliced
4 ounces pitted Kalamata olives
¼ cup extra-virgin olive oil

2 tablespoons freshly squeezed lemon juice
1 tablespoon red wine vinegar
1 tablespoon chopped fresh oregano or 1 teaspoon dried oregano
¼ teaspoon freshly ground black pepper
4 ounces (113 g) crumbled traditional feta cheese

1. Cut the cucumbers in half lengthwise and then into ½-inch-thick half-moons. Place in a large bowl.
2. Add the quartered tomatoes, bell pepper, red onion, and olives.
3. In a small bowl, whisk together the olive oil, lemon juice, vinegar, oregano, and pepper. Drizzle over the vegetables and toss to coat.
4. Divide between salad plates and top each with 1 ounce of feta.

**Per Serving**

calories: 278 | fat: 22g | protein: 8g
carbs: 12g | net carbs: 8g | fiber: 4g

## Tangy Shrimp Ceviche Salad

**Prep time: 15 minutes | Cook time: 0 minutes | Serves 4**

1 pound fresh shrimp, peeled and deveined
1 small red or yellow bell pepper, cut into ½-inch chunks
½ English cucumber, peeled and cut into ½-inch chunks
½ small red onion, cut into thin slivers
¼ cup chopped fresh cilantro or flat-leaf Italian parsley
⅓ cup freshly

squeezed lime juice
2 tablespoons freshly squeezed lemon juice
2 tablespoons freshly squeezed lemon juice
½ cup extra-virgin olive oil
1 teaspoon salt
½ teaspoon freshly ground black pepper
2 ripe avocados, peeled, pitted, and cut into ½-inch chunks

1. Cut the shrimp in half lengthwise. In a large glass bowl, combine the shrimp, bell pepper, cucumber, onion, and cilantro.
2. In a small bowl, whisk together the lime, lemon, and clementine juices, olive oil, salt, and pepper. Pour the mixture over the shrimp and veggies and toss to coat. Cover and refrigerate for at least 2 hours, or up to 8 hours. Give the mixture a toss every 30 minutes for the first 2 hours to make sure all the shrimp "cook" in the juices.
3. Add the cut avocado just before serving and toss to combine.

**Per Serving**

calories: 497 | fat: 40g | protein: 25g
carbs: 14g | net carbs: 8g | fiber: 6g

## Lime Squid and Veggies Salad

**Prep time: 15 minutes | Cook time: 5 minutes | Serves 4**

4 medium squid tubes, cut into strips
½ cup mint leaves
2 medium cucumbers, halved and cut in strips
½ cup coriander leaves, reserve the stems
½ red onion, finely sliced

Salt and black pepper, to taste
1 teaspoon fish sauce
1 red chili, roughly chopped
1 clove garlic
2 limes, juiced
1 tablespoon chopped coriander
1 teaspoon olive oil

1. In a salad bowl, mix mint leaves, cucumber strips, coriander leaves, and red onion. Season with salt, black pepper and some olive oil; set aside. In the mortar, pound the coriander stems, and red chili to form a paste using the pestle. Add the fish sauce and lime juice, and mix with the pestle.
2. Heat a skillet over high heat on a stovetop and sear the squid on both sides to lightly brown, about 5 minutes. Pour the squid on the salad and drizzle with the chili dressing. Toss the ingredients with two spoons, garnish with coriander, and serve the salad as a single dish or with some more seafood.

**Per Serving**

calories: 318 | fat: 23g | protein: 25g
carbs: 3g | net carbs: 2g | fiber: 1g

## Dijon Cauliflower Salad

**Prep time: 10 minutes | Cook time: 10 minutes | Serves 6**

1 large cauliflower
Sea salt and freshly ground black pepper, to taste
3 hard-boiled eggs, diced
¾ cup avocado oil mayonnaise
2 tablespoons Dijon mustard
¼ cup dill pickle, diced
3 celery stalks, diced
1 tablespoon apple cider vinegar
1 teaspoon garlic powder

1. Remove the stem and cut the cauliflower into florets.
2. Put 1 to 2 inches water in a large pot, add a pinch of salt, and bring to a boil. Add the cauliflower, reduce the heat to low, and cover the pot. Steam the cauliflower for 10 minutes, or until fork-tender.
3. Drain the cauliflower and let it cool for 15 minutes.
4. Mix the remaining ingredients in a large bowl. When cooled, add the cauliflower and mix together.
5. Cover and refrigerate for 1 to 2 hours, until chilled. Serve cold.

**Per Serving**

calories: 305 | fat: 30g | protein: 6g
carbs: 4g | net carbs: 3g | fiber: 1g

## Bacon Salad with Walnuts

**Prep time: 5 minutes | Cook time: 10 minutes | Serves 4**

½ pound bacon, diced
1 (8-ounce) log fresh goat cheese
½ cup pork dust (or pork rinds crushed into a powder)
3 tablespoons plus 2 teaspoons coconut vinegar or red wine vinegar
3 tablespoons avocado oil, MCT oil, or extra-virgin olive oil
1 teaspoon Dijon
mustard
½ teaspoon fine sea salt
¼ teaspoon ground black pepper
2 drops stevia glycerite (optional)
4 cups leafy greens
½ avocado, sliced (optional)
½ cup raw walnuts, for garnish (optional; omit for nut-free)

1. Sauté the diced bacon in a skillet over medium heat until crisp, about 5 minutes. Using a slotted spoon, remove the bacon to a bowl, leaving the drippings in the pan.

2. Meanwhile, cut the goat cheese log into 8 medallions that are about ¼ inch thick.
3. Place the pork dust in a shallow bowl. Gently roll each goat cheese medallion in the pork dust to cover the medallions.
4. In batches, fry the medallions in the hot skillet with the bacon drippings over medium heat for 1 minute or until golden brown, then flip and fry for another minute. Remove the medallions from the skillet and set aside on a plate.
5. Add the vinegar, oil, mustard, salt, pepper, and stevia, if using, to the skillet and stir well to combine. Stir in the cooked bacon.
6. Plate the greens and avocado slices, if using, on a serving platter and top with the fried goat cheese medallions. Drizzle the bacon vinaigrette over the greens and garnish with walnuts and freshly ground pepper, if desired.

**Per Serving**

calories: 766 | fat: 67g | protein: 36g
carbs: 8g | net carbs: 4g | fiber: 4g

## Classic Caprese Salad

**Prep time: 10 minutes | Cook time: 0 minutes | Serves 8**

8 ounces (227 g) fresh mozzarella cheese
4 tomatoes
¼ cup balsamic vinegar
¼ cup extra virgin
olive oil
1 cup fresh basil
1 teaspoon sea salt
½ teaspoon freshly ground black pepper

1. Cut the mozzarella and tomatoes into ¼-inch-thick slices and arrange in an alternating pattern on a plate.
2. In a small bowl, mix the balsamic vinegar and olive oil. Drizzle on top of the mozzarella and tomatoes.
3. Stack the fresh basil and roll it into a tight log. Carefully cut into thin julienne slices, and toss over the salad.
4. Sprinkle the salt and pepper on top and enjoy.

**Per Serving**

calories: 148 | fat: 11g | protein: 9g
carbs: 4g | net carbs: 3g | fiber: 1g

## Egg and Avocado Salad in Lettuce Cups

**Prep time: 15 minutes | Cook time: 15 minutes | Serves 2**

4 large eggs
1 avocado, halved
Pink Himalayan salt
Freshly ground black pepper

½ teaspoon freshly squeezed lemon juice
4 butter lettuce cups, washed and patted dry with paper towels or a clean dish towel
2 radishes, thinly sliced

1.  In a medium saucepan, cover the eggs with water. Place over high heat, and bring the water to a boil. Once it is boiling, turn off the heat, cover, and leave on the burner for 10 to 12 minutes.
2.  Remove the eggs with a slotted spoon and run them under cold water for 1 minute or submerge them in an ice bath.
3.  Then gently tap the shells and peel. Run cold water over your hands as you remove the shells.
4.  In a medium bowl, chop the hardboiled eggs.
5.  Add the avocado to the bowl, and mash the flesh with a fork. Season with pink Himalayan salt and pepper, add the lemon juice, and stir to combine.
6.  Place the 4 lettuce cups on two plates. Top the lettuce cups with the egg salad and the slices of radish and serve.

**Per Serving**

calories: 259 | fat: 20.1g | protein: 15.1g | carbs: 8.0g | net carbs: 2.9g | fiber: 5.1g


## Ritzy Chicken Salad with Tzatziki Sauce

**Prep time: 15 minutes | Cook time: 20 minutes | Serves 2**

**Chicken:**

3 tablespoons extra virgin olive oil, divided
Juice of ½ lemon
1 tablespoon organic apple cider vinegar

½ teaspoon garlic powder
1 pound (454 g) boneless, skinless chicken thighs

**Tzatziki Sauce:**

1 cup full-fat organic Greek yogurt
1 tablespoon extra virgin olive oil
½ cup deseeded and grated Persian cucumber

2 garlic cloves, minced
Juice of 1 lemon
¼ teaspoon sea salt

**Salad:**

3 to 4 cups baby spinach leaves
½ cup cherry tomatoes, sliced
½ red onion, sliced

¼ cup full-fat feta, crumbled
¼ cup Kalamata olives, sliced

1.  In a small bowl, mix together 2 tablespoons olive oil, lemon juice, cider vinegar, and garlic powder. Put the chicken thighs in a large bowl and pour the marinade over them. Put the chicken in the refrigerator to marinate for 30 minutes.
2.  While the chicken marinates, mix together the tzatziki ingredients in a small bowl and set aside.
3.  Heat the remaining 1 tablespoon olive oil in a large skillet over medium heat. Add the chicken, cooking the thighs on each side for 8 to 10 minutes, or until cooked through and the internal temperature reaches 165ºF (74ºC).
4.  Remove the chicken from the skillet and slice each thigh into four or five pieces.
5.  Combine the salad ingredients and serve in two bowls, topped with the chicken and tzatziki sauce.

**Per Serving**

calories: 899 | fat: 68g | protein: 61g | carbs: 19g | net carbs: 16g | fiber: 3g

# Chapter 5 Snacks and Appetizers

## Wrapped Shrimp with Bacon

**Prep time: 15 minutes | Cook time: 15 minutes | Serves 8**

24 medium shrimp, deveined
8 slices of thick-cut bacon, cut into thirds
1 teaspoon mustard powder
1 teaspoon onion powder
½ teaspoon granulated garlic
½ teaspoon red pepper flakes, crushed
Sea salt and ground black pepper, to taste

1. Start by preheating your oven to 400ºF (205ºC). Line a large-sized baking sheet with Silpat mat or aluminum foil.
2. Wrap each shrimp with a piece of bacon; secure with a toothpick. Place the wrapped shrimp on the prepared baking sheet.
3. Sprinkle with mustard, onion powder, garlic, red pepper, salt, and black pepper.
4. Bake for about 13 minutes or until the shrimp is thoroughly cooked. Bon appétit!

**Per Serving**

calories: 120 | fat: 10.4g | protein: 5.6g
carbs: 0.4g | net carbs: 0.4g | fiber: 0g

## Bacon Fat Bombs

**Prep time: 15 minutes | Cook time: 0 minutes | Serves 8**

½ stick butter, at room temperature
8 ounces (227 g) cottage cheese, at room temperature
8 ounces (227 g) Mozzarella cheese, crumbled
1 teaspoon shallot powder
1 teaspoon Italian seasoning blend
2 ounces (57 g) bacon bits

1. Mix the butter, cheese, shallot powder, and Italian seasoning blend until well combined.
2. Place the mixture in your refrigerator for about 60 minutes.
3. Shape the mixture into 18 balls. Roll each ball in the bacon bits until coated on all sides. Enjoy!

**Per Serving**

calories: 150 | fat: 9.4g | protein: 13.0g
carbs: 2.1g | net carbs: 1.6g | fiber: 0.5g

## Bakery Mini Almond Muffins

**Prep time: 15 minutes | Cook time: 20 minutes | Serves 9**

3 eggs
2 tablespoons coconut oil
3 ounces (85 g) double cream
1 cup almond meal
½ cup flax seed meal
½ teaspoon monk fruit powder
½ teaspoon baking soda
½ teaspoon baking powder
A pinch of salt
½ teaspoon ground cloves
1 teaspoon ground cinnamon
1 teaspoon vanilla essence

1. In a mixing bowl, whisk the eggs with the coconut milk and double cream.
2. In another bowl, mix the remaining ingredients. Now, add the wet mixture to the dry mixture. Mix again to combine well.
3. Spoon the batter into small silicone molds. Bake in the preheated oven at 360ºF (182ºC) for 13 to 17 minutes. Bon appétit!

**Per Serving**

calories: 86 | fat: 6.5g | protein: 4.2g
carbs: 3.2g | net carbs: 3.2g | fiber: 0g

## Deviled Eggs

**Prep time: 10 minutes | Cook time: 20 minutes | Serves 6**

6 eggs
1 tablespoon green tabasco
⅓ cup sugar-free mayonnaise

1. Place the eggs in a saucepan, and cover with salted water. Bring to a boil over medium heat. Boil for 8 minutes. Place the eggs in an ice bath and let cool for 10 minutes. Peel and slice them in. Whisk together the tabasco, mayonnaise, and salt in a small bowl. Spoon this mixture on top of every egg.

**Per Serving**

calories: 180 | fat: 17.0g | protein: 6.0g
carbs: 5.0g | net carbs: 5.0g | fiber: 0g

## Mediterranean Cheese Sticks

**Prep time: 10 minutes | Cook time: 15 minutes | Serves 4**

2 eggs, beaten
1½ cups Romano cheese, grated
2 cups Mozzarella, shredded
2 garlic cloves,

crushed
1 teaspoon dried rosemary
1 teaspoon dried parsley flakes

1. Mix all of the ingredients until everything is well incorporated. Roll the dough out on a parchment-lined baking pan.
2. Bake in the preheated oven at 360ºF (182ºC) for about 13 minutes until golden brown.
3. Cut into sticks and serve at room temperature. Enjoy!

**Per Serving**

calories: 257 | fat: 12.3g | protein: 32.7g
carbs: 4.0g | net carbs: 3.0g | fiber: 1.0g


## Onions Rings

**Prep time: 15 minutes | Cook time: 20 minutes | Serves 4**

½ cup coconut flour
3 eggs
2 tablespoons water
2 tablespoons double cream
4 ounces (113 g) pork

rinds
3 ounces (85 g) Parmesan cheese, grated
2 onions, cut into ½-inch thick rings

1. Place the coconut flour in a shallow dish. In another dish, mix the eggs, water, and cream; place the pork rinds and Parmesan in the third dish.
2. Dip the onion rings into the coconut flour; then, dip them into the egg mixture; lastly, roll the onion rings in the Parmesan mixture.
3. Place the coated rings on a lightly greased baking rack; bake at 420ºF (216ºC) for 13 to 16 minutes. Enjoy!

**Per Serving**

calories: 323 | fat: 27.7g | protein: 10.2g
carbs: 5.6g | net carbs: 4.5g | fiber: 1.1g


## Cheese Biscuits

**Prep time: 15 minutes | Cook time: 20 minutes | Serves 10**

1 cup coconut flour
½ cup flaxseed meal
1½ cups almond meal
½ teaspoon baking soda
1 teaspoon baking powder
½ teaspoon salt

1 teaspoon paprika
2 eggs
1 stick butter
1 cup Romano cheese, grated
1½ cups Colby cheese, grated

1. Mix the flour with the baking soda, baking powder, salt, and paprika. In a separate bowl, beat the eggs and butter. Stir the wet mixture into the flour mixture. Fold in the grated cheese. Mix again until everything is well incorporated.
2. Roll the batter into 16 balls and place them on a lightly greased cookie sheet. Flatten them slightly with the palms of your hands.
3. Bake at 350ºF (180ºC) for about 17 minutes. Bon appétit!

**Per Serving**

calories: 380 | fat: 33.6g | protein: 14.0g
carbs: 6.6g | net carbs: 1.6g | fiber: 5.0g


## Chicken Wrapped Provolone and Prosciutto

**Prep time: 10 minutes | Cook time: 10 minutes | Serves 8**

¼ teaspoon garlic powder
8 ounces (227 g) provolone cheese

8 raw chicken tenders
Black pepper to taste
8 prosciutto slices

1. Pound the chicken until half an inch thick. Season with salt, pepper, and garlic powder. Cut the provolone cheese into 8 strips. Place a slice of prosciutto on a flat surface. Place one chicken tender on top. Top with a provolone strip. Roll the chicken, and secure with previously soaked skewers. Preheat the grill. Grill the wraps for about 3 minutes per side.

**Per Serving**

calories: 175 | fat: 10.1g | protein: 16.9g
carbs: 0g | net carbs: 0.7g | fiber: 0g

## Spanish Sausage and Cheese Stuffed Mushrooms

**Prep time: 15 minutes | Cook time: 25 minutes | Serves 6**

30 button mushrooms, stalks removed and cleaned
8 ounces (227 g) Chorizo sausage, crumbled
2 scallions, chopped
2 green garlic stalks, chopped
2 tablespoons fresh parsley, chopped
10 ounces (283 g) goat cheese, crumbled
Sea salt and ground black pepper, to season
½ teaspoon red pepper flakes, crushed

1. Place the mushroom caps on a lightly greased baking sheet.
2. Mix the remaining ingredients until well combined. Divide this stuffing between the mushroom caps.
3. Bake in the preheated oven at 340ºF (171ºC) for 25 minutes or until thoroughly cooked. Serve with cocktail sticks. Bon appétit!

**Per Serving**

calories: 325 | fat: 23.6g | protein: 23.0g
carbs: 5.0g | net carbs: 3.8g | fiber: 1.2g

## Cauliflower Fritters

**Prep time: 15 minutes | Cook time: 15 minutes | Serves 4**

1 pound (454 g) cauliflower, grated
½ cup Parmesan cheese
3 ounces (85 g) onion, finely chopped
½ teaspoon baking powder
½ cup almond flour
3 eggs
½ teaspoon lemon juice
Olive oil, for frying

1. Sprinkle the salt over the cauliflower in a bowl, and let it stand for 10 minutes. Place the other ingredients in the bowl. Mix with your hands to combine. Put a skillet over medium heat, and heat some olive oil in it. Shape fritters out of the cauliflower mixture. Fry for 3 minutes per side. Serve.

**Per Serving**

calories: 70 | fat: 5.3g | protein: 4.5g
carbs: 6.0g | net carbs: 3.0g | fiber: 3.0g

## Italian Sausage and Eggplant Pie

**Prep time: 15 minutes | Cook time: 40 minutes | Serves 6**

6 eggs
12 ounces (340 g) raw sausage rolls
10 cherry tomatoes, halved
2 tablespoons heavy cream
2 tablespoons Parmesan cheese
Salt and black pepper to serve
2 tablespoons parsley, chopped
5 eggplant slices

1. Preheat your oven to 375ºF (190ºC). Grease a pie dish with cooking spray.
2. Press the sausage roll at the bottom of a pie dish. Arrange the eggplant slices on top of the sausage. Top with cherry tomatoes.
3. Whisk together the eggs along with the heavy cream, salt, Parmesan cheese, and black pepper. Spoon the egg mixture over the sausage. Bake for about 40 minutes until it is browned around the edges. Serve warm, and scatter with chopped parsley.

**Per Serving**

calories: 341 | fat: 28.0g | protein: 1.7g
carbs: 5.9g | net carbs: 3.0g | fiber: 2.9g

## Parsnip Chips

**Prep time: 15 minutes | Cook time: 15 minutes | Serves 4**

3 tablespoons olive oil
⅓ cup natural yogurt
1 teaspoon lime juice
1 tablespoon parsley, chopped
Salt and black pepper, to taste
1 garlic clove, minced
2 cups parsnips, sliced

1. Preheat the oven to 300ºF (150ºC). Set parsnip on a baking sheet; toss with garlic powder, 1 tablespoon of olive oil, and salt. Bake for 15 minutes, tossing once halfway through, until slices are crisp and browned.
2. In a bowl, mix yogurt, lime juice, black pepper, 2 tablespoons of olive oil, garlic, and salt until well combined. Serve the chips with yogurt dip.

**Per Serving**

calories: 175 | fat: 12.6g | protein: 2.0g
carbs: 11.9g | net carbs: 8.6g | fiber: 3.3g

## Cheese and Ham Egg Cakes

**Prep time: 15 minutes | Cook time: 25 minutes | Serves 8**

2 cups ham, chopped
$^1/_3$ cup Parmesan cheese, grated
1 tablespoon parsley, chopped
¼ cup almond flour
9 eggs
$^1/_3$ cup mayonnaise, sugar-free
¼ teaspoon garlic powder
¼ cup onion, chopped
Sea salt to taste
Cooking spray

1. Preheat your oven to 375ºF (190ºC). Lightly grease nine muffin pans with cooking spray, and set aside.
2. Place the onion, ham, garlic powder, and salt, in a food processor, and pulse until ground.
3. Stir in the mayonnaise, almond flour, and Parmesan cheese. Press this mixture into the muffin cups.
4. Bake for 5 minutes. Crack an egg into each muffin cup. Return to the oven and bake for 20 more minutes or until the tops are firm to the touch and eggs are cooked. Leave to cool slightly before serving.

**Per Serving**
calories: 266 | fat: 18.0g | protein: 13.5g
carbs: 1.6g | net carbs: 1.0g | fiber: 0.6g

## Liverwurst Truffles

**Prep time: 10 minutes | Cook time: 0 minutes | Serves 8**

8 bacon slices, cooked and chopped
8 ounces (227 g) Liverwurst
¼ cup pistachios, chopped
1 teaspoon Dijon mustard
6 ounces (170 g) cream cheese

1. Combine liverwurst and pistachios in the bowl of your food processor. Pulse until smooth.
2. Whisk the cream cheese and mustard in another bowl. Make 12 balls out of the liverwurst mixture. Make a thin cream cheese layer over. Coat with bacon pieces. Arrange on a plate and refrigerate for 30 minutes.

**Per Serving**
calories: 146 | fat: 11.9g | protein: 7.1g
carbs: 2.7g | net carbs: 1.6g | fiber: 1.1g

## Simple Butter Broccoli

**Prep time: 5 minutes | Cook time: 5 minutes | Serves 6**

1 broccoli head, florets only
¼ cup butter
Salt to taste

1. Place the broccoli in a pot filled with salted water, and bring to a boil. Cook for about 3 minutes, or until tender. Melt the butter in a microwave. Drain the broccoli and transfer to a plate. Drizzle the butter over and season with some salt and pepper.

**Per Serving**
calories: 115 | fat: 7.8g | protein: 4.0g
carbs: 5.7g | net carbs: 5.6g | fiber: 0.1g

## Bacon and Avocado Muffin Sandwiches

**Prep time: 10 minutes | Cook time: 5 minutes | Serves 2**

¼ cup flax meal
1 egg
2 tablespoons heavy cream
2 tablespoons pesto
**Filling:**
2 tablespoons cream cheese
4 slices of bacon
¼ cup almond flour
¼ teaspoon baking soda
Salt and black pepper to taste

½ medium avocado, sliced

1. Mix together the dry muffin ingredients in a bowl. Add egg, heavy cream, and pesto, and whisk well with a fork. Season with salt and pepper. Divide the mixture between two ramekins. Place in the microwave and cook for 60-90 seconds. Leave to cool before filling.
2. Meanwhile, in a nonstick skillet, over medium heat, cook the bacon slices until crispy.
3. Transfer to paper towels to soak up excess fat. Set aside.Invert the muffins onto a plate and cut in half, crosswise. Make sandwiches by spreading cream cheese and topping with bacon and avocado.

**Per Serving**
calories: 512 | fat: 38.1g | protein: 16.5g
carbs: 8.7g | net carbs: 4.6g | fiber: 4.1g

## Blue Cheese and Ranch Dip

**Prep time: 5 minutes | Cook time: 0 minutes | Serves 10**

½ cup Greek-style yogurt
1 cup blue cheese, crumbled
½ cup mayonnaise
1 tablespoon lime juice
Freshly ground black pepper, to taste
2 tablespoons ranch seasoning

1. In a mixing bowl, thoroughly combine all ingredients until well incorporated.
2. Serve well chilled with your favorite keto dippers. Bon appétit!

**Per Serving**

calories: 94 | fat: 8g | protein: 4g
carbs: 1g | net carbs: 1g | fiber: 0g

## Chicken Wings with Ranch Dressing

**Prep time: 10 minutes | Cook time: 50 minutes | Serves 6**

2 pounds (907 g) chicken wings, pat dry
Nonstick cooking spray
**Ranch Dressing:**
¼ cup sour cream
¼ cup coconut milk
½ cup mayonnaise
½ teaspoon lemon juice
1 tablespoon fresh parsley, minced
Sea salt and cayenne pepper, to taste

1 clove garlic, minced
2 tablespoons onion, finely chopped
¼ teaspoon dry mustard
Sea salt and ground black pepper, to taste

1. Start by preheating your oven to 420ºF (216ºC).
2. Spritz the chicken wings with a cooking spray. Sprinkle the chicken wings with salt and cayenne pepper. Arrange the chicken wings on a parchment-lined baking pan. Bake in the preheated oven for 50 minutes or until the wings are golden and crispy.
3. In the meantime, make the dressing by mixing all of the above ingredients. Serve with warm wings.

**Per Serving**

calories: 466 | fat: 37g | protein: 27g
carbs: 2g | net carbs: 2g | fiber: 0g

## Mozzarella Meatballs

**Prep time: 10 minutes | Cook time: 18 to 25 minutes | Serves 8**

½ pound (227 g) ground pork
1 pound (454 g) ground turkey
1 garlic clove, minced
4 tablespoons pork rinds, crushed
2 tablespoons shallots, chopped
4 ounces (113 g) Mozzarella string cheese, cubed
1 ripe tomato, puréed
Salt and ground black pepper, to taste

1. In a mixing bowl, thoroughly combine all ingredients, except for the cheese. Shape the mixture into bite-sized balls.
2. Press 1 cheese cube into the center of each ball.
3. Place the meatballs on a parchment-lined baking sheet. Bake in the preheated oven at 350ºF (180ºC) for 18 to 25 minutes. Bon appétit!

**Per Serving**

calories: 389 | fat: 31g | protein: 24g
carbs: 2g | net carbs:1 g | fiber: 1g

## Italian Cheddar Cheese Crisps

**Prep time: 5 minutes | Cook time: 8 minutes | Serves 4**

1 cup sharp Cheddar cheese, grated
¼ teaspoon ground black pepper
½ teaspoon cayenne pepper
1 teaspoon Italian seasoning

1. Start by preheating an oven to 400ºF (205ºC). Line a baking sheet with a parchment paper.
2. Mix all of the above ingredients until well combined.
3. Then, place tablespoon-sized heaps of the mixture onto the prepared baking sheet.
4. Bake at the preheated oven for 8 minutes, until the edges start to brown. Allow the cheese crisps to cool slightly; then, place them on paper towels to drain the excess fat. Enjoy!

**Per Serving**

calories: 134 | fat: 11g | protein: 5g
carbs: 1g | net carbs: 1g | fiber: 0g

## Fried Baby Artichoke

**Prep time: 10 minutes | Cook time: 10 minutes | Serves 4**

| | |
|---|---|
| 12 fresh baby artichokes | juice |
| 2 tablespoons lemon | 2 tablespoons olive oil |
| | Salt to taste |

1. Slice the artichokes vertically into narrow wedges. Drain them on paper towels before frying.
2. Heat the olive oil in a cast-iron skillet over high heat. Fry the artichokes until browned and crispy. Drain excess oil on paper towels. Sprinkle with salt and lemon juice.

**Per Serving**

calories: 36 | fat: 2.5g | protein: 2.0g
carbs: 23.8g | net carbs: 3.0g | fiber: 20.8g

## Deviled Eggs with Chives

**Prep time: 5 minutes | Cook time: 15 minutes | Serves 8**

| | |
|---|---|
| 8 eggs | 1 teaspoon balsamic vinegar |
| 2 tablespoons cream cheese | Sea salt and freshly ground black pepper, to taste |
| 1 teaspoon Dijon mustard | |
| 1 tablespoon mayonnaise | ¼ teaspoon cayenne pepper |
| 1 tablespoon tomato purée, no sugar added | 2 tablespoons chives, chopped |

1. Place the eggs in a single layer in a saucepan. Add water to cover the eggs and bring to a boil.
2. Cover, turn off the heat, and let the eggs stand for 15 minutes. Drain the eggs and peel them under cold running water.
3. Slice the eggs in half lengthwise; remove the yolks and thoroughly combine them with cream cheese, mustard, mayo, tomato purée, vinegar, salt, black, and cayenne pepper.
4. Next, divide the yolk mixture among egg whites. Garnish with fresh chives and enjoy!

**Per Serving**

calories: 149 | fat: 11g | protein: 10g
carbs: 2g | net carbs: 2g | fiber: 0g

## Jalapeño and Zucchini Frittata Cups

**Prep time: 15 minutes | Cook time: 30 minutes | Serves 4**

| | |
|---|---|
| 2 tablespoons olive oil | 2 tablespoons Mozzarella cheese, shredded |
| 2 green onions, chopped | |
| 1 garlic clove, minced | 8 eggs, whisked |
| ½ jalapeño pepper, chopped | Salt and black pepper, to taste |
| ½ carrot, chopped | ½ teaspoon dried oregano |
| 1 zucchini, shredded | |

1. Sauté green onions and garlic in warm olive oil over medium heat for 3 minutes. Stir in carrot, zucchini, and jalapeño pepper, and cook for 4 more minutes. Remove the mixture to a lightly greased baking pan with a nonstick cooking spray. Top with Mozzarella cheese.
2. Cover with the whisked eggs; season with oregano, black pepper, and salt. Bake in the oven for about 20 minutes at 360ºF (182ºC).

**Per Serving**

calories: 336 | fat: 27.9g | protein: 14.1g
carbs: 5.3g | net carbs: 4.8g | fiber: 0.5g

## Lettuce Wraps with Ham and Tomato

**Prep time: 10 minutes | Cook time: 0 minutes | Serves 5**

| | |
|---|---|
| 10 Boston lettuce leaves, washed and rinsed well | cheese |
| | 10 thin ham slices |
| 1 tablespoon lemon juice, freshly squeezed | 1 tomato, chopped |
| | 1 red chili pepper, chopped |
| 10 tablespoons cream | |

1. Drizzle lemon juice over the lettuce leaves. Spread cream cheese over the lettuce leaves. Add a ham slice on each leaf.
2. Divide chopped tomatoes between the lettuce leaves. Top with chili peppers and arrange on a nice serving platter. Bon appétit!

**Per Serving**

calories: 148 | fat: 10g | protein: 11g
carbs: 4g | net carbs: 3g | fiber: 1g

## Baked Romano Zucchini Rounds

**Prep time: 5 minutes | Cook time: 15 minutes | Serves 6**

2 tablespoons olive oil
2 eggs
½ teaspoon smoked paprika
Sea salt and ground black pepper, to taste

2 pounds (907 g) zucchini, sliced into rounds
½ cup Romano cheese, shredded

1. Begin by preheating an oven to 420ºF (216ºC). Coat a rimmed baking sheet with Silpat mat or parchment paper.
2. In a mixing bowl, whisk the olive oil with eggs. Add in the paprika, salt, and black pepper. Now, dip the zucchini slices into the egg mixture.
3. Top with the shredded Romano cheese.
4. Arrange the zucchini rounds on the baking sheet; bake for 15 minutes until they are golden. Serve at room temperature.

**Per Serving**

calories: 137 | fat: 10g | protein: 9g
carbs: 6g | net carbs: 4g | fiber: 2g

## Fresh Homemade Guacamole

**Prep time: 15 minutes | Cook time: 0 minutes | Serves 4**

2 ripe avocados
½ tomato, chopped
¼ cup minced red onions
2 tablespoons finely chopped fresh cilantro
1 tablespoon fresh

lime juice
½ teaspoon minced garlic
½ teaspoon salt
1 tablespoon sour cream (optional)

1. Slice the avocados in half lengthwise, remove the pits, and scoop the flesh into a medium-sized serving bowl. Mash the avocado flesh.
2. Stir in the tomato, onions, cilantro, lime juice, garlic, and salt. Fold in the sour cream, if using.
3. Serve right away or place in the refrigerator to chill until ready to serve.

**Per Serving**

calories: 133 | fat: 12g | protein: 2g
carbs: 8g | net carbs: 3g | fiber: 5g

## Chorizo and Asparagus Traybake

**Prep time: 15 minutes | Cook time: 15 minutes | Serves 4**

2 tablespoons olive oil
A bunch of asparagus, ends trimmed and chopped
4 ounces (113 g)

Spanish chorizo, sliced
Salt and black pepper to taste
¼ cup chopped parsley

1. Preheat your oven to 325ºF (163ºC) and grease a baking dish with olive oil.
2. Add in the asparagus and season with salt and black pepper. Stir in the chorizo slices. Bake for 15 minutes until the chorizo is crispy. Arrange on a serving platter and serve sprinkled with parsley.

**Per Serving**

calories: 412 | fat: 36.6g | protein: 14.6g
carbs: 4.3g | net carbs: 3.3g | fiber: 1.0g

## Herbed Prawn and Veggie Skewers

**Prep time: 10 minutes | Cook time: 8 to 9 minutes | Serves 4**

2 tablespoons olive oil
1 pound (454 g) king prawns, deveined and cleaned
Sea salt and ground black pepper, to taste
1 teaspoon garlic powder
1 tablespoon fresh

sage, minced
1 teaspoon fresh rosemary
2 tablespoons fresh lime juice
2 tablespoons cilantro, chopped
2 bell peppers, diced
1 cup cherry tomatoes

1. Heat the olive oil in a wok over a moderately high heat.
2. Now, cook the prawns for 7 to 8 minutes, until they have turned pink. Stir in the seasonings and cook an additional minute, stirring frequently.
3. Remove from the heat and toss with the lime juice and fresh cilantro. Tread the prawns onto bamboo skewers, alternating them with peppers and cherry tomatoes.
4. Serve on a serving platter. Bon appétit!

**Per Serving**

calories: 179 | fat: 8g | protein:20 g
carbs: 5g | net carbs: 4g | fiber: 1g

## Deviled Eggs with Roasted Peppers

**Prep time: 5 minutes | Cook time: 9 t0 10 minutes | Serves 10**

10 eggs
¼ cup sour cream
¼ cup roasted red pepper, chopped
2 tablespoons olive oil
1 teaspoon stone-

ground mustard
1 garlic clove, minced
Sea salt, to taste
1 teaspoon red pepper flakes

1. Arrange the eggs in a saucepan. Pour in water (1-inch above the eggs) and bring to a boil. Heat off and let it sit, covered, for 9 to 10 minutes.
2. When the eggs are cool enough to handle, peel away the shells; rinse the eggs under running water. Separate egg whites and yolks.
3. Mix the egg yolks with the sour cream, roasted pepper, olive oil, mustard, garlic, and salt.
4. Stuff the eggs, arrange on a nice serving platter, and garnish with red pepper flakes. Enjoy!

**Per Serving**

calories: 97 | fat: 8g | protein: 6g
carbs: 1g | net carbs: 1g | fiber:0 g

## Greek-Style Ricotta Olive Dip

**Prep time: 5 minutes | Cook time: 0 minutes | Serves 8**

10 ounces (284 g) ricotta cheese
4 tablespoons Greek yogurt
½ teaspoon cayenne pepper
4 tablespoons olives, sliced

½ teaspoon shallot powder
½ teaspoon garlic salt
½ teaspoon black pepper
4 tablespoons cilantro, minced

1. Thoroughly combine the ricotta cheese, Greek yogurt, cayenne pepper, olives, shallot powder, garlic salt, and black pepper in a mixing bowl.
2. Transfer to a nice serving bowl.
3. Garnish with cilantro, serve and enjoy your party!

**Per Serving**

calories: 72 | fat: 6g | protein: 4g
carbs: 2g | net carbs: 2g | fiber: 0g

## Prosciutto Wrapped Basil Mozzarella

**Prep time: 10 minutes | Cook time: 0 minutes | Serves 6**

6 thin prosciutto slices
18 basil leaves
18 Mozzarella ciliegine

(about 8½ ounces / 241 g in total)

1. Cut the prosciutto slices into three strips. Place basil leaves at the end of each strip. Top with Mozzarella. Wrap the Mozzarella in prosciutto. Secure with toothpicks.

**Per Serving**

calories: 164 | fat: 12.0g | protein: 13.1g
carbs: 0.6g | net carbs: 0.6g | fiber: 0g

## Crispy Fried Dill Pickles

**Prep time: 5 minutes | Cook time: 5 minutes | Serves 2**

¼ cup avocado oil or coconut oil
3 tablespoons mayonnaise
¼ cup finely grated Parmesan cheese

3 tablespoons golden flaxseed meal
⅛ teaspoon garlic powder
12 dill pickle rounds

1. Heat the oil in a small skillet over medium-high heat.
2. Place the mayonnaise in a bowl. In another bowl, mix together the Parmesan cheese, flaxseed meal, and garlic powder.
3. Place the pickle slices on a paper towel and cover with another paper towel to dry the tops.
4. Dip each pickle slice into the mayonnaise and then into the Parmesan and flaxseed "breading," making sure to coat the slices evenly.
5. When the temperature of the oil reaches 400°F (205°C), gently place the breaded pickles in the hot oil and fry until golden and crispy, 1 to 2 minutes per side. Place the fried pickles on a paper towel-lined plate to absorb the excess oil before serving.

**Per Serving**

calories: 376 | fat: 38g | protein: 8g
carbs: 5g | net carbs: 1g | fiber: 4g

## Hearty Burger Dip

**Prep time: 10 minutes | Cook time: 1 hour 30 minutes | Serves 2**

¼ pound (113 g) ground pork
¼ pound (113 g) ground turkey
½ red onion, chopped
1 garlic clove, minced
1 serrano pepper, chopped
1 bell pepper, chopped
2 ounces (57 g) sour cream
½ cup Provolone cheese, grated
2 ounces (57 g) tomato purée
½ teaspoon mustard
½ teaspoon dried oregano
½ teaspoon dried basil
¼ teaspoon dried marjoram

1. Place all of the above ingredients, except for the sour cream and Provolone cheese in your slow cooker.
2. Cook for 1 hour 30 minutes at Low setting. Afterwards, fold in sour cream and cheese.
3. Serve warm with celery sticks if desired. Bon appétit!

**Per Serving**

calories: 423 | fat: 29g | protein: 32g
carbs: 5g | net carbs: 4g | fiber: 1g

## Lemony Bacon Chips

**Prep time: 5 minutes | Cook time: 10 minutes | Serves 12**

1½ pounds (680 g) bacon, cut into 1-inch squares
¼ cup lemon juice
1 teaspoon Ranch seasoning mix
1 tablespoon hot sauce

1. Toss the bacon squares with the lemon juice, Ranch seasoning mix, and hot sauce. Arrange the bacon squares on a parchment-lined baking sheet.
2. Roast in the preheated oven at 375ºF (190ºC) approximately 10 minutes or until crisp.
3. Let it cool completely before storing. Bon appétit!

**Per Serving**

calories: 232 | fat: 23g | protein: 7g
carbs: 1g | net carbs: 1g | fiber: 0g

## Ranch Chicken-Bacon Dip

**Prep time: 10 minutes | Cook time: 20 minutes | Serves 6**

3 slices bacon
1½ cups shredded cooked chicken
1 (8-ounce / 227-g) package cream
cheese, softened
½ cup Buffalo sauce
½ cup ranch dressing
Chopped green onions, for garnish (optional)

1. Preheat the oven to 375ºF (190ºC).
2. In a skillet over medium heat, fry the bacon until crispy. Set aside on a paper towel-lined plate to cool, then chop.
3. In a large bowl, combine the shredded chicken, cream cheese, Buffalo sauce, ranch dressing, and bacon; mix well. (If desired, reserve some of the bacon to sprinkle on top, as pictured.)
4. Transfer the chicken mixture to a shallow 1-quart baking dish and bake for 20 minutes, until warm throughout.
5. Garnish with chopped green onions, if desired.

**Per Serving**

calories: 286 | fat: 25g | protein: 11g
carbs: 3g | net carbs: 3g | fiber: 0g

## Creamy Herb Dip

**Prep time: 15 minutes | Cook time: 5 minutes | Serves 7**

1 (8-ounce / 227-g) package cream cheese
½ cup heavy whipping cream
¼ cup sour cream
3 tablespoons finely chopped fresh chives
2 tablespoons finely chopped onions
2 tablespoons finely chopped fresh parsley
½ teaspoon garlic powder

1. Place the cream cheese and heavy whipping cream in a microwave-safe bowl and microwave on high for 1 minute; stir and repeat until the texture is smooth.
2. Add the remaining ingredients and stir to combine.
3. Place in the refrigerator to chill for at least 30 minutes before serving.

**Per Serving**

calories: 156 | fat: 14g | protein: 3g
carbs: 2g | net carbs: 2g | fiber: 1g

## Classic Caprese Skewers

**Prep time: 15 minutes | Cook time: 0 minutes | Serves 6**

8 ounces (227 g) ciliegini Mozzarella balls, drained and halved
**Marinade:**
¼ cup extra-virgin olive oil
1 clove garlic, pressed or minced
1 tablespoon chopped fresh parsley

9 grape tomatoes, halved
18 fresh basil leaves

1 tablespoon dried ground oregano
1 tablespoon fresh lemon juice
Kosher salt and ground black pepper, to taste

1. In a medium-sized bowl, combine the Mozzarella balls with the marinade ingredients. Stir well and cover; place in the refrigerator to marinate for 1 hour.
2. To assemble, place a Mozzarella ball, a basil leaf (folded in half lengthwise if needed), and a grape tomato half on a toothpick.
3. Serve right away or store in the refrigerator until ready to serve.

**Per Serving**

calories: 174 | fat: 16g | protein: 8g | carbs: 2g | net carbs: 2g | fiber: 0g


## Cheesy Charcuterie Board

**Prep time: 15 minutes | Cook time: 0 minutes | Serves 6 to 8**

4 ounces (113 g) prosciutto, sliced
4 ounces (113 g) Calabrese salami, sliced
4 ounces (113 g) capicola, sliced
7 ounces (198 g) Parrano Gouda cheese
7 ounces (198 g) aged Manchego cheese
7 ounces (198 g) Brie cheese

½ cup roasted almonds
½ cup mixed olives
12 cornichons (small, tart pickles)
1 sprig fresh rosemary or other herbs of choice, for garnish

1. Arrange the meats, cheeses, and almonds on a large wooden cutting board.
2. Place the olives and pickles in separate bowls and set them on or alongside the cutting board. Garnish with a spring of rosemary or other fresh herbs of your choice.

**Per Serving**

calories: 445 | fat: 35g | protein: 31g | carbs: 3g | net carbs: 2g | fiber: 1g


## Cheese Crisps with Basil

**Prep time: 5 minutes | Cook time: 8 minutes | Serves 2**

½ cup shredded Cheddar cheese
½ cup shredded Parmesan cheese

½ teaspoon dried basil
¼ teaspoon garlic powder

1. Preheat the oven to 400ºF (205ºC). Line a baking sheet with parchment paper.
2. In a medium-sized bowl, mix together all the ingredients.
3. 3 Scoop up a heaping tablespoon of the mixture and place it on the parchment paper. Repeat, making a total of 8 small piles, spacing them 2 inches apart to prevent the cheese from running together.
4. Bake for 8 minutes, until golden brown. Let cool for 5 minutes before removing from the parchment paper.

**Per Serving**

calories: 195 | fat: 13g | protein: 15g | carbs: 3g | net carbs: 3g | fiber: 0g

# Chapter 6 Vegan and Vegetarian

## Spinach and Zucchini Chowder

**Prep time: 15 minutes | Cook time: 22 minutes | Serves 4**

1 tablespoon olive oil
1 clove garlic, chopped
½ cup scallions, chopped
4 cups water
2 zucchini, sliced
1 celery stalk, chopped
2 tablespoons vegetable bouillon
powder
4 ounces (113 g) baby spinach
Salt and ground black pepper, to taste
1 heaping tablespoon fresh parsley, chopped
1 tablespoon butter
1 egg, beaten

1. In a stockpot, heat the oil over medium-high heat. Now, cook the garlic and scallions until tender or about 4 minutes.
2. Add water, zucchini, celery, vegetable bouillon powder; cook for 13 minutes. Add spinach, salt, black pepper, parsley, and butter; cook for a further 5 minutes.
3. Then, stir in the egg and mix until well incorporated. Ladle into individual bowls and serve warm. Enjoy!

**Per Serving**

calories: 85 | fat: 6g | protein: 4g
carbs: 4g | net carbs: 3g | fiber: 1g

## Peanut Butter Crêpes with Coconut

**Prep time: 5 minutes | Cook time: 4 to 5 minutes | Serves 5**

4 eggs, well whisked
4 ounces (113 g) cream cheese
A pinch of salt
2 tablespoons coconut
oil
3 tablespoons peanut butter
2 tablespoons toasted coconut

1. Whisk the eggs, cream cheese, and salt in a mixing bowl.
2. Heat the oil in a pancake frying pan over medium-high heat.
3. Fry each pancake for 4 to 5 minutes. Serve topped with peanut butter and coconut. Enjoy!

**Per Serving**

calories: 248 | fat: 22g | protein: 9g
carbs: 6g | net carbs: 5g | fiber: 1g

## Coleslaw with Cauliflower

**Prep time: 5 minutes | Cook time: 0 minutes | Serves 5**

1 cup green cabbage, shredded
1 cup fresh cauliflower, chopped
4 tablespoons shallots, chopped
1 teaspoon garlic,
minced
1 teaspoon lime juice
1 teaspoon white wine vinegar
⅓ cup mayonnaise
Sea salt and ground black pepper, to taste

1. Add the cabbage, cauliflower, shallots, and garlic to a salad bowl.
2. In a small mixing dish, whisk the lime juice, vinegar, mayonnaise, salt, and pepper.
3. Dress the salad and serve immediately. Bon appétit!

**Per Serving**

calories: 121 | fat: 9g | protein: 3g
carbs: 7g | net carbs: 5g | fiber: 2g

## Balsamic Broccoli Salad

**Prep time: 10 minutes | Cook time: 22 minutes | Serves 6**

6 cups broccoli florets
1 red chili pepper, sliced
1 garlic clove, minced
1 shallot, sliced
½ cup mayonnaise
1 teaspoon Dijon mustard
2 tablespoons balsamic vinegar
1 tablespoon prepared horseradish
Kosher salt and ground black pepper, to taste

1. Brush the broccoli florets with nonstick cooking spray and roast at 425ºF (220ºC) for about 22 minutes until crisp-tender and little charred.
2. In a salad bowl, toss the roasted broccoli florets, chili pepper, garlic, and shallot.
3. In a small mixing dish, thoroughly combine the remaining ingredients.
4. Dress the salad and serve immediately. Bon appétit!

**Per Serving**

calories: 170 | fat: 14g | protein: 3g
carbs: 7g | net carbs: 4g | fiber: 3g

## Garlicky Creamed Swiss Chard

**Prep time: 10 minutes | Cook time: 10 minutes | Serves 6**

2 tablespoons butter
1 yellow onion, chopped
2 garlic cloves, minced
½ teaspoon kosher salt
¼ teaspoon ground black pepper
¼ teaspoon dried

oregano
¼ teaspoon dried dill
1½ pounds (680 g) Swiss chard
½ cup vegetable broth
2 tablespoons dry white wine
1 cup sour cream

1. Melt the butter in a saucepan over a moderate flame. Then, sauté the onion until tender and fragrant or about 4 minutes.
2. Stir in the garlic and continue to sauté for 1 minute or until aromatic. Add in the salt, black pepper, oregano, and basil.
3. Fold in the Swiss chard in batches. Pour in vegetable broth and cook for 5 minutes or until Swiss chard wilts. Stir in the wine and sour cream. Stir to combine well and serve.

**Per Serving**

calories: 149 | fat: 11g | protein: 5g
carbs: 7g | net carbs: 5g | fiber: 2g

## Hearty Veggie Stir-Fry

**Prep time: 20 minutes | Cook time: 15 minutes | Serves 3**

4 tablespoons sesame oil
½ cup shallot, chopped
2 cups white mushrooms, sliced
1 zucchini, spiralized
1 cup cauliflower rice
2 cloves garlic, minced
Kosher salt and ground black pepper,

to taste
½ teaspoon turmeric powder
½ teaspoon cayenne pepper
½ teaspoon mustard seeds
2 tomatoes, puréed
3 eggs
3 ounces (85 g) Asiago cheese, shredded

1. Heat 1 tablespoon of the sesame oil in a wok over medium-high heat. Now, cook the shallot and mushrooms until just tender and fragrant or about 3 minutes; reserve.
2. In the same wok, heat another tablespoon of the sesame oil. Fry the zucchini until crisp-tender about 2 minutes or so; reserve.
3. Heat another tablespoon of the sesame oil and cook the cauliflower rice for 3 to 4 minutes or until just tender and fragrant. Return the sautéed vegetables to the wok.
4. Add in the garlic, spices and tomatoes and stir for 2 minutes more or until heated through.
5. In a nonstick skillet, heat the remaining tablespoon of sesame oil. Fry the eggs over medium-high heat until they are set or about 5 minutes.
6. Divide the vegetables between three serving plates. Top each serving with the fried egg. Garnish with Asiago cheese and serve immediately.

**Per Serving**

calories: 378 | fat: 32g | protein: 15g
carbs: 7g | net carbs: 5g | fiber:2 g

## Mozzarella Creamed Salad with Basil

**Prep time: 20 minutes | Cook time: 0 minutes | Serves 4**

4 ounces (113 g) arugula
4 ounces (113 g) lettuce
4 scallions, sliced
2 green garlic stalks, sliced
½ cup celery rib, chopped
1 cucumber, sliced
1 tomato, sliced
½ cup olives, pitted

and halved
½ cup mayonnaise
1 teaspoon stone-ground mustard
2 tablespoons white vinegar
Sea salt and ground black pepper, to taste
½ cup Mozzarella cheese
2 tablespoons fresh basil leaves, snipped

1. Toss the arugula, lettuce, scallions, green garlic, celery, cucumber, tomato, and olives in a large-sized bowl.
2. In a small mixing dish, whisk the mayonnaise, mustard, vinegar, salt, and black pepper. Add the mayo mixture to the vegetables and toss to combine well.
3. Top with Mozzarella and serve garnished with fresh basil. Enjoy!

**Per Serving**

calories: 255 | fat: 23g | protein: 7g
carbs: 7g | net carbs: 4g | fiber: 3g

## Fried Veggies with Eggs

**Prep time: 10 minutes | Cook time: 23 minutes | Serves 4**

2 tablespoons olive oil
1 shallot, sliced
2 bell peppers, seeded and sliced
2 garlic cloves, minced
½ teaspoon ginger, peeled and minced
1 cup green cabbage, shredded
1 cup broccoli florets
1 cup cauliflower florets
½ cup cream of onion soup
4 eggs

1. Heat the olive oil in a large-sized frying pan over high heat. Now, fry the shallots and pepper for 3 minutes, until just tender. Add in the garlic and ginger; continue sautéing for 30 seconds more until aromatic.
2. Then, stir in the cabbage, broccoli, cauliflower, and onion soup. Turn the heat to medium-low. Continue to cook for 10 minutes or until tender and thoroughly cooked.
3. Next, make four indentations in the vegetable mixture using the back of a wooden spoon. Crack the eggs into the indentations.
4. Cover your frying pan with a lid. Cook for a further10 minutes or until the egg whites are firm but the yolks are a little runny. Serve immediately.

**Per Serving**

calories: 121 | fat: 7g | protein: 7g
carbs: 7g | net carbs: 5g | fiber: 2g

## Italian Pepper and Mushrooms Stew

**Prep time: 15 minutes | Cook time: 25 minutes | Serves 5**

3 tablespoons extra-virgin olive oil
1 red onion, chopped
2 sweet Italian peppers, chopped
1 poblano pepper, chopped
1 pound (454 g) cremini mushrooms, sliced
2 garlic cloves
2 cups water
1 cup cream of mushroom soup
½ teaspoon ground cumin
½ teaspoon mustard seeds
2 vine-ripe tomatoes, puréed
2 bay laurels
Sea salt and ground black pepper, to taste

1. Heat the oil in a heavy-bottomed soup pot over medium-high heat. Once hot, sauté the onion and peppers for 3 minutes, until crisp-tender and fragrant.
2. Stir in the mushrooms and garlic and continue to sauté an additional 2 minutes.
3. Add in the remaining ingredients and turn the heat to medium-low. Cook, partially covered, for 20 minutes or until thoroughly cooked.
4. Ladle into individual bowls and serve warm. Enjoy!

**Per Serving**

calories: 156 | fat: 12g | protein: 5g
carbs: 6g | net carbs: 4g | fiber: 2g

## Traditional Thai Tom Kha Soup

**Prep time: 20 minutes | Cook time: 22 minutes | Serves 2**

1 teaspoon coconut oil
1 shallot, chopped
1 clove garlic, minced
½ celery stalk, chopped
½ bell pepper, chopped
1 Bird's eye chili, divined and minced
1 cup vegetable broth
¼ teaspoon stone ground mustard
Sea salt and freshly cracked black pepper, to season
½ teaspoon ground cumin
½ teaspoon coriander seeds
2 cardamom pods
1 cup full-fat coconut milk
2 tablespoons Thai basil leaves, snipped

1. In a deep saucepan, heat the coconut oil until sizzling; now, sauté the shallot, garlic, celery, and peppers for 5 minutes, until just tender and fragrant; make sure to stir frequently.
2. Add a splash of broth to deglaze the pan. Add in the remaining broth, mustard, and spices and bring to a rolling boil.
3. Turn the heat to medium-low and let it simmer for 15 minutes or until heated through. After that, pour in the coconut milk and continue to simmer for 2 minutes more.
4. Ladle into soup bowls and serve garnished with fresh Thai basil. Enjoy!

**Per Serving**

calories: 273 | fat: 27g | protein: 5g
carbs: 6g | net carbs: 5g | fiber: 1g

## Roasted Eggplant with Avocado

**Prep time: 5 minutes | Cook time: 20 to 25 minutes | Serves 7**

2 pounds (907 g) eggplant, sliced
3 teaspoons avocado oil
2 tablespoons tahini
1 teaspoon garlic paste
1 tablespoon Dijon mustard
1 tablespoon lemon juice
½ teaspoon harissa
1 avocado, pitted, peeled and mashed

1. Brush the bottom of a roasting pan with nonstick cooking oil. Arrange the eggplant slices on the prepared roasting pan. Drizzle the eggplant with 2 teaspoons of the avocado oil.
2. Transfer the pan to the preheated oven. Roast in the preheated oven at 420ºF (216ºC) for 15 to 20 minutes.
3. Meanwhile, mix the remaining ingredients, except for the avocado, until everything is well incorporated. Divide this mixture between the eggplant slices.
4. Broil approximately 5 minutes. Top with the mashed avocado and serve warm. Bon appétit!

**Per Serving**

calories: 94 | fat: 6g | protein: 3g
carbs: 7g | net carbs: 3g | fiber: 4g

## Provolone Zucchini Lasagna

**Prep time: 20 minutes | Cook time: 56 minutes | Serves 2**

1 large-sized zucchini, sliced lengthwise
1 tablespoon olive oil
1 red bell pepper, chopped
1 shallot, chopped
½ pound (227 g) chestnut mushrooms, chopped
2 cloves garlic, pressed
Sea salt and ground black pepper, to season
¼ teaspoon red pepper flakes
¼ teaspoon dried oregano
½ teaspoon dried dill weed
1 vine-ripe tomato, puréed
1 egg, whisked
½ cup Greek-style yogurt
½ cup Provolone cheese, grated

1. Place the zucchini slices in a bowl with a colander; add 1 teaspoon of salt and let it stand for 12 to 15 minutes; gently squeeze to discard the excess water.
2. Grill the zucchini slices for 3 minutes per side until beginning to brown; reserve.
3. Heat the olive oil in a skillet over moderate flame. Now, sauté the pepper and shallot for 3 minutes, until they have softened.
4. Next, stir in the mushrooms and garlic; continue sautéing until they are just fragrant. Add in the spices and puréed tomatoes and let it cook until heated through or about 5 minutes.
5. Pour the mushroom/tomato purée on the bottom of a lightly greased baking pan. Arrange the zucchini slices on top.
6. Mix the egg with the Greek yogurt; add the mixture to the top. Top with the grated Provolone cheese and transfer to the preheated oven.
7. Bake at 370ºF (188ºC) approximately 45 minutes until the cheese is melted and the edges are bubbling.
8. Let your lasagna stand for about 8 minutes before slicing and serving. Bon appétit!

**Per Serving**

calories: 284 | fat: 18g | protein: 20g
carbs: 8g | net carbs: 5g | fiber: 3g

## Vegetable Stir-Fry with Seeds

**Prep time: 10 minutes | Cook time: 11 minutes | Serves 3**

2 tablespoons sesame oil
1 yellow onion, sliced
1 red bell pepper, seeded and sliced
2 garlic cloves, minced
1 tomato, chopped
½ cup cream of mushroom soup
Sea salt and ground black pepper, to taste
½ teaspoon cayenne pepper
½ teaspoon celery seeds
½ teaspoon fennel seeds

1. Heat the sesame oil in a wok over medium-high heat. Stir fry the onion and peppers for 3 to 4 minutes.
2. Add in the garlic and continue to cook for 30 seconds more. Add in the remaining ingredients and cook for a further 8 minutes.
3. Taste, adjust seasonings and serve warm. Enjoy!

**Per Serving**

calories: 118 | fat: 10g | protein: 2g
carbs: 6g | net carbs: 5g | fiber: 1g

## Balsamic Zucchini Salad

**Prep time: 15 minutes | Cook time: 9 minutes | Serves 5**

| | |
|---|---|
| 1½ pounds (680 g) zucchini, sliced | 1 red onion, sliced |
| 4 tablespoons extra-virgin olive oil, divided | 1 garlic clove, pressed |
| Sea salt and ground black pepper, to taste | 2 tomatoes, sliced |
| ½ teaspoon cayenne pepper | 1 teaspoon Dijon mustard |
| ½ teaspoon dried dill weed | 1 tablespoon balsamic vinegar |
| ½ teaspoon dried basil | 1 tablespoon fresh lime juice |
| | 4 ounces (113 g) goat cheese, crumbled |

1. Toss the zucchini with 2 tablespoons of olive oil and spices. Arrange them on a rimmed baking sheet.
2. Roast in the preheated oven at 425ºF (220ºC) until tender about 9 minutes. Toss roasted zucchini with red onion, garlic, and tomatoes.
3. Add the remaining tablespoons of olive oil, mustard, vinegar, and lime juice. Toss to combine and top with goat cheese. Enjoy!

**Per Serving**

calories: 186 | fat: 14g | protein: 11g
carbs: 7g | net carbs: 5g | fiber: 2g

## Broccoli and Spinach Soup

**Prep time: 15 minutes | Cook time: 10 to 13 minutes | Serves 2**

| | |
|---|---|
| 1 tablespoon butter, at room temperature | 1 bay laurel |
| ½ small-sized leek, chopped | 1 thyme sprig, chopped |
| ¼ cup celery rib, chopped | 1 cup spinach leaves |
| ½ teaspoon ginger garlic paste | Kosher salt and ground black pepper, to taste |
| 1½ cups broccoli florets | 2 tablespoons cream cheese |
| 1½ cups roasted vegetable broth | 1 tablespoon tahini butter |
| | $^1/_3$ cup yogurt |

1. In a Dutch pot, melt the butter over medium-high heat. Now, sauté the leeks and celery for 3 minutes until just tender and fragrant.

2. Add the ginger-garlic paste and continue cooking an additional 30 seconds or until aromatic.
3. Now, stir in the broccoli, broth, bay laurel, and thyme, and bring it to a rapid boil. Then, turn the heat to low and let it simmer, covered, for a further 5 to 8 minutes.
4. After that, stir in the spinach, salt, and black pepper; let it simmer for 2 minutes more or until the leaves have wilted.
5. Transfer the soup to a food processor; add the cream cheese and tahini butter; process until everything is smooth and uniform. Swirl the yogurt into the soup and serve warm. Bon appétit!

**Per Serving**

calories: 208 | fat: 16g | protein: 9g
carbs: 6g | net carbs: 3g | fiber: 3g

## Lebanese Tabbouleh Salad

**Prep time: 15 minutes | Cook time: 8 minutes | Serves 2**

| | |
|---|---|
| 1 cup cauliflower florets | 1 Lebanese cucumber, diced |
| 1 tablespoon fresh mint leaves, roughly chopped | Pink salt and freshly cracked black pepper, to taste |
| 1 tablespoon fresh parsley leaves, roughly chopped | 1 tablespoon hulled hemp seeds |
| ½ white onion, thinly sliced | 1 tablespoon fresh lemon juice |
| ½ cup cherry tomatoes, halved | 2 tablespoons extra-virgin olive oil |

1. Pulse the cauliflower florets in your food processor until they're broken into tiny chunks (just bigger than rice).
2. Pat dry with paper towels. Cook in a lightly greased nonstick skillet over medium heat until the cauliflower rice is turning golden or about 8 minutes; transfer to a serving bowl.
3. Add the remaining ingredients and toss to combine well.
4. Adjust the seasonings and serve. Enjoy!

**Per Serving**

calories: 180 | fat: 16g | protein: 3g
carbs: 7g | net carbs: 4g | fiber: 3g

## Stuffed Peppers with Olives

**Prep time: 10 minutes | Cook time: 32 minutes | Serves 2**

1 garlic clove, minced
2 scallions, chopped
3 ounces (85 g) cream cheese
3 eggs
3 ounces (85 g) Provolone cheese, grated
Sea salt and ground
black pepper, to taste
½ teaspoon hot paprika
1 teaspoon coriander
3 bell peppers, seeded and sliced in half
4 Kalamata olives, pitted and sliced

1. In a mixing bowl, thoroughly combine the garlic, scallions, cream cheese, eggs, provolone cheese, salt, black pepper, paprika, and coriander.
2. Stuff the peppers and place them on a parchment lined baking sheet.
3. Bake in the preheated oven at 370°F (188°C) approximately 30 minutes until the peppers are tender. If you want your peppers nicely charred, just place them under the broiler for 2 minutes.
4. Garnish with olives and serve immediately. Bon appétit!

**Per Serving**

calories: 387 | fat: 30g | protein: 23g
carbs: 5g | net carbs: 4g | fiber: 1g

## Spiced Mashed Cauliflower

**Prep time: 5 minutes | Cook time: 5 minutes | Serves 8**

½ pound (227 g) cauliflower florets
Sea salt and ground black pepper, to taste
½ teaspoon cayenne pepper
½ teaspoon dried
oregano
½ teaspoon dried basil
1 cup heavy whipping cream
5 ounces (142 g) Swiss cheese, grated

1. Steam the cauliflower for 5 minutes, until tender; pulse in your food processor until it resembles mashed potatoes.
2. Season the mashed cauliflower with salt, black pepper, cayenne pepper, oregano, and basil.
3. In a saucepan, warm the cream and stir in the cheese. Whisk until the cheese is melted.
4. Fold in the mashed cauliflower and stir again. Serve with your favorite keto veggies. Bon appétit!

**Per Serving**

calories: 129 | fat: 10g | protein: 6g
carbs: 3g | net carbs: 2g | fiber: 1g

## Button Mushroom Stroganoff

**Prep time: 20 minutes | Cook time: 22 minutes | Serves 5**

2 tablespoons olive oil
½ cup onion, minced
1 tablespoon butter
1½ pounds (680 g) button mushrooms, sliced
1 teaspoon garlic paste
½ teaspoon red curry paste
Sea salt and ground black pepper, to taste
1 teaspoon dried parsley flakes
½ teaspoon celery seeds
½ teaspoon mustard seeds
½ teaspoon red pepper flakes
2 tablespoons tomato purée
4 cups vegetable stock
1 cup sour cream

1. Heat the olive oil in a heavy-bottomed soup pot until sizzling. Then, sauté the onion until tender and translucent or about 4 minutes.
2. Then, melt the butter in the same pot and cook the mushrooms for 3 to 4 minutes until just tender. Add in the garlic paste, curry paste, spices, tomato purée, and stock.
3. Bring the mixture to just below boiling point. Turn the heat to simmer and let it cook for 15 minutes longer.
4. Fold in the sour cream and stir it all together. Taste, adjust the seasonings and serve warm. Enjoy!

**Per Serving**

calories: 166 | fat: 13g | protein: 6g
carbs: 7g | net carbs: 5g | fiber: 2g

## Parmesan Zoodles with Avocado Sauce

**Prep time: 10 minutes | Cook time: 0 minutes | Serves 2**

½ avocado, pitted and peeled
2 tablespoons sunflower seeds, hulled
1 ripe tomato, quartered
2 tablespoons water
Sea salt and ground

black pepper, to taste
¼ teaspoon dried dill weed
1 medium-sized zucchini, sliced
2 tablespoons Parmesan cheese, preferably freshly grated

1. In your blender or food processor, purée the avocado, sunflower seeds, tomato, water, salt, black pepper, and dill until creamy and uniform.
2. Prepare your zoodles using a spiralizer.
3. Top the zoodles with the sauce; serve garnished with parmesan cheese. Bon appétit!

**Per Serving**

calories: 164 | fat: 14g | protein: 6g
carbs: 9g | net carbs: 4g | fiber: 5g

## Broccoli Salad with Tahini Dressing

**Prep time: 15 minutes | Cook time: 0 minutes | Serves 2**

½ cup broccoli florets
1 bell pepper, seeded and sliced
1 shallot, thinly sliced
½ cup arugula

2 ounces (57 g) Mozzarella cheese
2 tablespoons toasted sunflower seeds

**Tahini Dressing:**

1 tablespoon freshly squeezed lemon juice
¼ cup tahini (sesame butter)
1 garlic clove, minced

½ teaspoon yellow mustard
½ teaspoon ground black pepper
Pink salt, to taste

1. Place the cabbage, pepper, shallot, and arugula in a nice salad bowl. Mix all ingredients for the dressing.
2. Now, dress your salad and top with the Mozzarella cheese and sunflower seeds.
3. Serve at room temperature or well chilled. Bon appétit!

**Per Serving**

calories: 323 | fat: 25g | protein: 16g
carbs: 7g | net carbs: 3g | fiber: 4g

## Asparagus with Mayonnaise

**Prep time: 10 minutes | Cook time: 9 to 11 minutes | Serves 5**

1½ pounds (680 g) asparagus, trimmed
4 tablespoons olive oil
Sea salt and ground black pepper, to taste
4 tablespoons shallots, minced

½ cup mayonnaise
4 tablespoons sour cream
2 tablespoons coriander, chopped
1 teaspoon fresh garlic, minced

1. Begin by preheating your oven to 390ºF (199ºC). Brush the asparagus spears with olive oil. Add the salt, black pepper, and shallots and roast for 9 to 11 minutes in the preheated oven.
2. Meanwhile, mix the remaining ingredients to make the dipping sauce.
3. Serve the asparagus with the mayo sauce on the side and enjoy!

**Per Serving**

calories: 296 | fat: 28g | protein: 4g
carbs: 7g | net carbs: 4g | fiber: 3g

## Broccoli and Zucchini Soup

**Prep time: 10 minutes | Cook time: 25 minutes | Serves 4**

3 tablespoons olive oil
2 cups broccoli florets
1 green bell pepper, chopped
1 jalapeño pepper, chopped
1 medium zucchini, cut into chunks

4 cups vegetable broth
Kosher salt and ground black pepper, to taste
½ teaspoon dried dill weed
1 bay laurel

1. Heat the olive oil in a heavy-bottomed pot over medium-high heat. Now, sauté the broccoli, peppers, and zucchini for 5 minutes, until they have softened.
2. Add in the remaining ingredients and stir to combine. Cook until the soup comes to a boil. Turn the heat to simmer.
3. Partially cover and let it simmer for a further 20 minutes or until heated through. Purée with an immersion blender and serve warm. Bon appétit!

**Per Serving**

calories: 111 | fat: 10g | protein: 2g
carbs: 4g | net carbs: 2g | fiber: 2g

## Greek Roasted Cauliflower with Feta Cheese

**Prep time: 5 minutes | Cook time: 40 minutes | Serves 4**

1 pound (454 g) cauliflower, halved
1 medium-sized leek, cut into 2-inch pieces
2 tablespoons olive oil
1 tablespoon Greek seasoning blend
Sea salt and ground black pepper, to taste
1 cup feta cheese, crumbled

1. Begin by preheating your oven to 390ºF (199ºC). Toss cauliflower and leek with olive oil, Greek seasoning blend, salt, and black pepper.
2. Arrange vegetables on a parchment-lined roasting pan. Transfer to the preheated oven.
3. Roast approximately 20 minutes; turn them over and roast an additional 20 minutes. Top with feta cheese and serve immediately. Enjoy!

**Per Serving**

calories: 194 | fat: 15g | protein: 7g
carbs: 6g | net carbs: 3g | fiber: 3g

## Mediterranean Cauliflower Quiche

**Prep time: 15 minutes | Cook time: 45 minutes | Serves 2**

½ pound (227 g) small cauliflower florets
½ cup vegetable broth
2 scallions, chopped
1 teaspoon garlic, crushed
½ cup almond milk
2 eggs, whisked
Sea salt and ground
black pepper, to taste
½ teaspoon paprika
½ teaspoon basil
½ teaspoon oregano
1 ounce (28 g) sour cream
3 ounces (85 g) Provolone cheese, freshly grated

1. Cook the cauliflower with the vegetable broth over medium-low flame until tender but crispy. Transfer the cauliflower florets to a lightly greased casserole dish.
2. Then, preheat your oven to 360ºF (182ºC). In a mixing dish, thoroughly combine the scallions, garlic, milk, eggs, salt, black pepper, paprika, basil, and oregano.
3. Pour the scallion mixture over the cauliflower florets. Mix the sour cream and Provolone cheese; add the cheese mixture to the top. Cover with foil.

4. Bake in the preheated oven for about 45 minutes, until topping is lightly golden and everything is heated through.
5. Transfer to a cooling rack for 10 minutes before serving. Bon appétit!

**Per Serving**

calories: 309 | fat: 21g | protein: 21g
carbs: 8g | net carbs: 5g | fiber: 3g

## Brown Mushrooms and Cabbage

**Prep time: 15 minutes | Cook time: 13 minutes | Serves 3**

2 tablespoons extra-virgin olive oil
½ cup onion, chopped
2 cups brown mushrooms, sliced
1 garlic clove, pressed
¾ pound (340 g) green cabbage, shredded
½ cup cream of mushroom soup
1 bay laurel
Kosher salt, to season
½ teaspoon caraway seeds
½ teaspoon ground black pepper, to taste
1 teaspoon smoked paprika
1 tablespoon apple cider vinegar

1. Heat the oil in a heavy-bottomed pot over medium-high heat. Now, sweat the onion for 3 minutes, until tender and translucent.
2. Next, stir in the mushrooms; continue to sauté until the mushrooms are caramelized or about 3 minutes. Don't crowd the mushrooms.
3. Stir in the garlic and sauté for 30 seconds longer or until aromatic. Add in the green cabbage, soup, bay laurel, salt, caraway seeds, black pepper, and paprika.
4. Continue cooking for 7 to 8 minutes more or until the cabbage leaves wilt. Ladle into three serving bowls.
5. Drizzle vinegar over each serving and serve warm. Bon appétit!

**Per Serving**

calories: 133 | fat: 9g | protein: 4g
carbs: 7g | net carbs: 3g | fiber: 4g

## Broccoli-Cabbage Soup

**Prep time: 10 minutes | Cook time: 29 minutes | Serves 6**

2 tablespoons extra-virgin olive oil
2 bell peppers, chopped
1 cup broccoli florets
1 shallot, chopped
1 teaspoon garlic, minced
1 pound (454 g) cabbage, shredded

1 cup tomato purée
5 cups vegetable broth
Sea salt and ground black pepper, to taste
½ teaspoon cayenne pepper
½ teaspoon dried dill weed
1 bay laurel

1. Heat the oil in a heavy-bottomed pot over the highest setting. Now, sauté the bell peppers, broccoli and shallot for about 4 minutes or until they have softened.
2. Add in the remaining ingredients and gently stir to combine well.
3. Turn the heat to medium-low; let it simmer, partially covered, for 25 minutes.
4. Ladle into individual bowls and serve warm. Enjoy!

**Per Serving**

calories: 82 | fat: 4g | protein: 2g | carbs: 6g | net carbs: 3g | fiber: 3g

## Spinach and Egg Salad

**Prep time: 10 minutes | Cook time: 8 minutes | Serves 3**

4 eggs
Sea salt and red pepper flakes, to taste
½ pound (227 g) spinach
1 roasted pepper in oil, drained and chopped
1 tomato, diced

2 scallions, sliced
¼ teaspoon dried oregano
½ teaspoon dried basil
2 tablespoons white vinegar
2 tablespoons extra-virgin olive oil

1. Cook the eggs in a saucepan for about 8 minutes; peel the eggs under running water and carefully slice them. Season the eggs with salt and red pepper.
2. Add the spinach, red pepper, tomato, scallions, oregano, and basil to a nice serving bowl.
3. Drizzle vinegar and olive oil over your vegetables. Top with the boiled eggs. Serve at room temperature or well chilled. Bon appétit!

**Per Serving**

calories: 156 | fat: 10g | protein: 10g | carbs: 7g | net carbs: 4g | fiber: 3g

## Chinese Cabbage Stir-Fry

**Prep time: 10 minutes | Cook time: 7 minutes | Serves 5**

3 tablespoons sesame oil
1 shallot, sliced
2 garlic cloves, minced
1 tablespoon Shaoxing wine
Sea salt and ground black pepper, to taste

½ teaspoon chili sauce, sugar-free
¼ teaspoon rougui (Chinese cinnamon)
½ teaspoon fennel seeds
½ teaspoon Sichuan peppercorns, crushed
1½ pounds (680 g) Chinese cabbage, shredded

1. Heat the sesame oil in a wok over medium-high heat.
2. Once hot, sauté the shallot and garlic until tender and translucent or about 2 minutes. Add the Shaoxing wine to deglaze the pan.
3. Add in the remaining ingredients.
4. Cook, stirring continuously, until the cabbage leaves are wilted about 5 minutes. Serve with some extra toasted sesame seeds if desired. Enjoy!

**Per Serving**

calories: 108 | fat: 9g | protein: 2g | carbs: 8g | net carbs: 6g | fiber: 2g

# Chapter 7 Vegetables and Sides

## Mushroom and Bell Pepper Omelet

**Prep time: 5 minutes | Cook time: 5 minutes | Serves 4**

2 tablespoons olive oil
1 cup Chanterelle mushrooms, chopped
2 bell peppers,
chopped
1 white onion, chopped
6 eggs

1. Heat the olive oil in a nonstick skillet over moderate heat. Now, cook the mushrooms, peppers, and onion until they have softened.
2. In a mixing bowl, whisk the eggs until frothy. Add the eggs to the skillet, reduce the heat to medium-low, and cook approximately 5 minutes until the center starts to look dry. Do not overcook.
3. Taste and season with salt to taste. Bon appétit!

**Per Serving**

calories: 240 | fat: 17.5g | protein: 12.3g
carbs: 6.1g | net carbs: 4.3g | fiber: 1.8g

## Leek, Mushroom, and Zucchini Stew

**Prep time: 5 minutes | Cook time: 15 minutes | Serves 4**

½ cup leeks, chopped
1 pound (454 g) brown mushrooms, chopped
1 teaspoon garlic,
minced
1 medium-sized zucchini, diced
2 ripe tomatoes, puréed

1. Heat up a lightly greased soup pot over medium-high heat. Now, sauté the leeks until just tender about 3 minutes.
2. Stir in the mushrooms, garlic, and zucchini. Continue to sauté an additional 2 minutes or until tender and aromatic.
3. Add in the tomatoes and 2 cups of water. Season with Sazón spice, if desired. Reduce the temperature to simmer and continue to cook, covered, for 10 to 12 minutes more. Bon appétit!

**Per Serving**

calories: 108 | fat: 7.5g | protein: 3.1g
carbs: 7.0g | net carbs: 4.5g | fiber: 2.5g

## Liverwurst and Pistachio Balls

**Prep time: 10 minutes | Cook time: 0 minutes | Serves 8**

8 bacon slices, cooked and chopped
8 ounces (227 g) Liverwurst
¼ cup chopped
pistachios
1 teaspoon Dijon mustard
6 ounces (170 g) cream cheese

1. Combine the liverwurst and pistachios in the bowl of food the processor. Pulse until smooth. Whisk the cream cheese and mustard in another bowl. Make 12 balls out of the liverwurst mixture.
2. Make a thin cream cheese layer over. Coat with bacon, arrange on a plate and chill for 30 minutes.

**Per Serving**

calories: 227 | fat: 25g | protein: 9g
carbs: 4g | net carbs: 3g | fiber: 1g

## Mozzarella Italian Peppers

**Prep time: 7 minutes | Cook time: 13 minutes | Serves 5**

4 tablespoons canola oil
1 yellow onion, sliced
1⅓ pounds (605 g) Italian peppers, deveined and sliced
1 teaspoon Italian
seasoning mix
Sea salt and cayenne pepper, to season
2 balls buffalo Mozzarella, drained and halved

1. Heat the canola oil in a saucepan over a medium-low flame. Now, sauté the onion until just tender and translucent.
2. Add in the peppers and spices. Cook for about 13 minutes, adding a splash of water to deglaze the pan.
3. Divide between serving plates; top with cheese and serve immediately. Enjoy!

**Per Serving**

calories: 175 | fat: 11.0g | protein: 10.4g
carbs: 7.0g | net carbs: 5.1g | fiber: 1.9g

## Gruyere Crisps

**Prep time: 5 minutes | Cook time: 6 minutes | Serves 4**

| | |
|---|---|
| 2 cups Gruyere cheese, shredded | powder |
| ½ teaspoon garlic powder | 1 rosemary sprig, minced |
| ¼ teaspoon onion | ½ teaspoon chili powder |

1. Set oven to 400ºF (205ºC). Coat two baking sheets with parchment paper.
2. Mix Gruyere cheese with the seasonings. Take 1 tablespoon of cheese mixture and form small mounds on the baking sheets. Bake for 6 minutes. Leave to cool. Serve.

**Per Serving**

calories: 276 | fat: 21g | protein: 20g
carbs: 1g | net carbs: 1g | fiber: 0g

## Mushroom Red Wine Chili

**Prep time: 10 minutes | Cook time: 15 minutes | Serves 3**

| | |
|---|---|
| 3 ounces (85 g) bacon, diced | 3 tablespoons dry red wine |
| 1 brown onion, chopped | ½ teaspoon freshly ground black pepper |
| 2 cloves garlic, minced | 1 teaspoon chili powder |
| ¾ pound (340 g) brown mushrooms, sliced | 2 bay laurels |
| | Sea salt, to taste |

1. Heat a soup pot over a medium-high flame and fry the bacon; once the bacon is crisp, remove from the pot and reserve.
2. Now, cook the brown onion and garlic until they have softened or about 6 minutes. Stir in the mushrooms and sauté them for 3 to 4 minutes longer.
3. Turn the heat to simmer; add the other ingredients and continue to cook for 10 minutes more, until most of the cooking liquid has evaporated.
4. Ladle into bowls and top with the reserved bacon. Bon appétit!

**Per Serving**

calories: 160 | fat: 11.3g | protein: 6.9g
carbs: 6.0g | net carbs: 4.7g | fiber: 1.3g

## Fried Cabbage

**Prep time: 10 minutes | Cook time: 15 minutes | Serves 3**

| | |
|---|---|
| 4 ounces (113 g) bacon, diced | ½ teaspoon cayenne pepper |
| 1 medium-sized onion, chopped | 1 pound (454 g) red cabbage, shredded |
| 2 cloves garlic, minced | ¼ teaspoon ground black pepper, to season |
| ½ teaspoon caraway seeds | 1 cup beef bone broth |
| 1 bay laurel | |

1. Heat up a nonstick skillet over a moderate flame. Cook the bacon for 3 to 4 minutes, stirring continuously; set aside.
2. In the same skillet, sauté the onion for 2 to 3 minutes or until it has softened. Now, sauté the garlic and caraway seeds for 30 seconds more or until aromatic.
3. Then, add in the remaining ingredients and stir to combine. Reduce the temperature to medium-low, cover, and cook for 10 minutes longer; stirring periodically to ensure even cooking.
4. Serve in individual bowls, garnished with the reserved bacon. Enjoy!

**Per Serving**

calories: 242 | fat: 22.2g | protein: 6.5g
carbs: 6.8g | net carbs: 4.9g | fiber: 1.9g

## String Beans and Mushrooms

**Prep time: 10 minutes | Cook time: 20 to 25 minutes | Serves 4**

| | |
|---|---|
| 2 cups string beans, cut in halves | 3 tablespoons olive oil |
| 1 pound (454 g) cremini mushrooms, quartered | 3 shallots, julienned |
| 3 tomatoes, quartered | ½ teaspoon dried thyme |
| 2 cloves garlic, minced | Salt and black pepper, to season |

1. Preheat oven to 450ºF (235ºC). In a bowl, mix the strings beans, mushrooms, tomatoes, garlic, olive oil, shallots, thyme, salt, and pepper. Pour the vegetables in a baking sheet and spread them all around.
2. Place the baking sheet in the oven and bake the veggies for 20 to 25 minutes.

**Per Serving**

calories: 154 | fat: 11g | protein: 4g
carbs: 13g | net carbs: 9g | fiber: 4g

## Spinach and Butternut Squash Stew

**Prep time: 10 minutes | Cook time: 30 minutes | Serves 4**

2 tablespoons olive oil
1 Spanish onion, peeled and diced
1 garlic clove, minced
½ pound (227 g) butternut squash, diced
1 celery stalk, chopped
3 cups vegetable broth
Kosher salt and freshly cracked black pepper, to taste
4cups baby spinach
4 tablespoons sour cream

1. Heat the olive oil in a soup pot over a moderate flame. Now, sauté the Spanish onion until tender and translucent.
2. Then, cook the garlic until just tender and aromatic.
3. Stir in the butternut squash, celery, broth, salt, and black pepper. Turn the heat to simmer and let it cook, covered, for 30 minutes.
4. Fold in the baby spinach leaves and cover with the lid; let it sit in the residual heat until the baby spinach wilts completely.
5. Serve dolloped with cold sour cream. Enjoy!

**Per Serving**

calories: 150 | fat: 11.6g | protein: 2.5g
carbs: 6.8g | net carbs: 4.5g | fiber: 2.3g

## Cauliflower Soup

**Prep time: 4 minutes | Cook time: 15 minutes | Serves 4**

2 green onions, chopped
½ teaspoon ginger-garlic paste
1 celery stalk, chopped
1 pound (454 g) cauliflower florets
3 cups vegetable broth

1. Heat up a lightly oiled soup pot over a medium-high flame. Now, sauté the green onions until they have softened.
2. Stir in the ginger-garlic paste, celery, cauliflower, and vegetable broth; bring to a rapid boil. Turn the heat to medium-low.
3. Continue to simmer for 13 minutes more or until heated through; heat off.
4. Puree the soup in your blender until creamy and uniform. Enjoy!

**Per Serving**

calories: 70 | fat: 1.6g | protein: 6.2g
carbs: 7.0g | net carbs: 4.0g | fiber: 3.0g

## Mozzarella Roasted Peppers

**Prep time: 5 minutes | Cook time: 15 minutes | Serves 4**

2 teaspoons olive oil
4 Italian sweet peppers, deveined and halved
Sat and black pepper,
to taste
¼ teaspoon red pepper flakes
8 ounces (227 g) Mozzarella cheese

1. Put your oven on broil. Drizzle the pepper halves with olive oil. Season the peppers with salt, black pepper, and red pepper flakes.
2. Top the pepper halves with Mozzarella cheese. Arrange the stuffed peppers on a parchment-lined baking tray.
3. Roast for 12 to 15 until the cheese is browned on top and the peppers are tender and blistered. Bon appétit!

**Per Serving**

calories: 215 | fat: 15.1g | protein: 13.5g
carbs: 6.7g | net carbs: 4.7g | fiber: 2.0g

## Wax Beans with Tomato-Mustard Sauce

**Prep time: 9 minutes | Cook time: 6 minutes | Serves 4**

1 tablespoon butter
2 garlic cloves, thinly sliced
½ pound (227 g) wax beans, trimmed
½ cup tomato sauce
2 tablespoons dry white wine
½ teaspoon mustard seeds
Sea salt and ground black pepper, to taste

1. Melt the butter in a saucepan over a medium-high flame. Now, sauté the garlic until aromatic but not browned.
2. Stir in the wax beans, tomato sauce, wine, and mustard seeds. Season with salt and black pepper to taste.
3. Turn the heat to medium-low, partially cover and continue to cook for 6 minutes longer or until everything is heated through. Bon appétit!

**Per Serving**

calories: 56 | fat: 3.5g | protein: 1.5g
carbs: 6.0g | net carbs: 3.8g | fiber: 2.2g

## White Wine-Dijon Brussels Sprouts

**Prep time: 10 minutes | Cook time: 10 minutes | Serves 3**

6 ounces (170 g) smoked bacon, diced
12 Brussels sprouts, trimmed and halved
¼ teaspoon ground bay leaf
¼ teaspoon dried oregano

¼ teaspoon dried sage
¼ teaspoon freshly cracked black pepper, or more to taste
Sea salt, to taste
½ cup dry white wine
1 teaspoon Dijon mustard

1. Heat up a nonstick skillet over medium-high heat. Once hot, cook the bacon for 1 minute.
2. Add the Brussels sprouts and seasoning and continue sautéing, adding white wine and stirring until the bacon is crisp and the Brussels sprouts are tender. It will take about 9 minutes.
3. Then, stir in the mustard, remove from the heat, and serve immediately. Enjoy!

**Per Serving**

calories: 298 | fat: 22.4g | protein: 9.6g
carbs: 6.4g | net carbs: 3.4g | fiber: 3.0g

## Fennel Avgolemono

**Prep time: 10 minutes | Cook time: 20 minutes | Serves 6**

2 tablespoons olive oil
1 celery stalk, chopped
1 pound (454 g) fennel bulbs, sliced
1 garlic clove, minced
1 bay laurel
1 thyme sprig

5 cups chicken stock
Sea salt and ground black pepper, to season
2 eggs
1 tablespoon freshly squeezed lemon juice

1. Heat the olive oil in a heavy-bottomed pot over a medium-high flame. Now, sauté the celery and fennel until they have softened but not browned, about 8 minutes.
2. Add in the garlic, bay laurel, and thyme sprig; continue sautéing until aromatic an additional minute or so.
3. Add the chicken stock, salt, and black pepper to the pot. Bring to a boil. Reduce the heat to medium-low and let it simmer, partially covered, approximately 13 minutes.
4. Discard the bay laurel and then, blend your soup with an immersion blender.

5. Whisk the eggs and lemon juice; gradually pour 2 cups of the hot soup into the egg mixture, whisking constantly.
6. Return the soup to the pot and continue stirring for a few minutes or just until thickened. Serve warm.

**Per Serving**

calories: 85 | fat: 6.2g | protein: 2.8g
carbs: 6.0g | net carbs: 3.5g | fiber: 2.5g

## Za'atar Chanterelle Stew

**Prep time: 15 minutes | Cook time: 50 minutes | Serves 4**

½ teaspoon Za'atar spice
4 tablespoons olive oil
½ cup shallots, chopped
2 bell peppers, chopped
1 poblano pepper, finely chopped
8 ounces (227

g) Chanterelle mushroom, sliced
½ teaspoon garlic, minced
Sea salt and freshly cracked black pepper, to taste
1 cup tomato purée
3 cups vegetable broth
1 bay laurel

1. Combine the Za'atar with 3 tablespoons of olive oil in a small saucepan. Cook over a moderate flame until hot; make sure not to burn the zaatar. Set aside for 1 hour to cool and infuse.
2. In a heavy-bottomed pot, heat the remaining tablespoon of olive oil. Now, sauté the shallots and bell peppers until just tender and fragrant.
3. Stir in the poblano pepper, mushrooms, and garlic; continue to sauté until the mushrooms have softened.
4. Next, add in the salt, black pepper, tomato purée, broth, and bay laurel. Once your stew begins to boil, turn the heat down to a simmer.
5. Let it simmer for about 40 minutes until everything is thoroughly cooked. Ladle into individual bowls and drizzle each serving with Za'atar oil. Bon appétit!

**Per Serving**

calories: 156 | fat: 13.8g | protein: 1.4g
carbs: 6.0g | net carbs: 3.1g | fiber: 2.9g

## Romaine Lettuce Boats

**Prep time: 10 minutes | Cook time: 3 minutes | Serves 4**

½ pound (227 g) pork sausage, sliced
1 green bell pepper, deveined and chopped
1 garlic clove, minced
½ cup tomato purée
¼ teaspoon ground black pepper
½ teaspoon fennel seeds
Himalayan salt, to taste
1 head romaine lettuce, separated into leaves
2 scallions, chopped

1. Preheat a nonstick frying pan over a moderate flame. Then, sear the pork sausage until no longer pink, crumbling with a fork.
2. Stir in the bell pepper and garlic, and continue sautéing an additional minute or so or until fragrant.
3. Fold in the tomato purée. Season with black pepper, fennel seeds, and salt. Stir well and continue to cook for 2 minutes more; remove from the heat.
4. Arrange the lettuce boats on a serving platter. Then, top each boat with the sausage mixture. Garnish with scallions and serve immediately. Bon appétit!

**Per Serving**

calories: 231 | fat: 18.1g | protein: 10.2g
carbs: 5.6g | net carbs: 3.5g | fiber: 2.1g

## Mushroom Mélange

**Prep time: 10 minutes | Cook time: 15 minutes | Serves 6**

4 tablespoons olive oil
1 bell pepper, sliced
½ cup leeks, finely diced
2 cloves garlic, smashed
2 pounds (907 g) brown mushrooms, sliced
2 cups chicken broth
1 cup tomato sauce
½ teaspoon dried oregano
½ teaspoon chili powder
½ teaspoon paprika
½ teaspoon ground black pepper
Sea salt, to taste

1. Heat the oil in a heavy-bottomed pot over medium-high flame. Now, sauté bell pepper along with the leeks for about 5 minutes.
2. Stir in the garlic and mushrooms, and continue sautéing an additional minute or so. Add in a splash of chicken broth to deglaze the bottom of the pan.

3. After that, add in the tomato sauce and seasonings. Bring to a boil and immediately reduce the heat to simmer.
4. Partially cover and cook for 8 to 10 minutes more or until the mushrooms are cooked through.
5. Ladle into individual bowls and serve with cauli rice if desired. Bon appétit!

**Per Serving**

calories: 124 | fat: 9.2g | protein: 4.6g
carbs: 5.8g | net carbs: 4.3g | fiber: 1.5g

## Cheesy Ham Pizza Rolls

**Prep time: 15 minutes | Cook time: 30 minutes | Serves 5**

**Dough:**
½ cup Parmesan cheese
1 cup Mozzarella cheese
3 egg whites
¾ cup coconut flour
1 cup heavy cream

**Filling:**
2 cups cooked ham, sliced
1 cup Gouda cheese, sliced
5 tablespoons tomato
purée
1 teaspoon crushed black pepper, for topping

1. Preheat the oven to 400ºF (205ºC), and line a baking sheet with parchment paper.
2. In a food processor, combine the ingredients for the crust and process until a smooth dough forms. You may need to add water, a tablespoon at a time, to achieve this result.
3. Flatten the dough into a rectangular shape onto the prepared baking sheet. Bake for about 15 minutes. Remove from the oven and allow to cool slightly.
4. Spread the tomato purée evenly across the dough. Top with the sliced ham and Gouda cheese.
5. Roll the dough carefully into a log. Slice the log into 5 even pieces and place each one back onto the baking sheet. Sprinkle with crushed black pepper.
6. Bake again for about 10 minutes until the dough is golden brown and the cheese is bubbly.

**Per Serving**

calories: 492 | fat: 35g | protein: 35g
carbs: 6g | net carbs: 4g | fiber: 2g

## Queso Fresco Avocado Salsa

**Prep time: 5 minutes | Cook time: 0 minutes | Serves 4**

2 tomatoes, diced
3 scallions, chopped
1 poblano pepper, chopped
1 garlic clove, minced
2 ripe avocados, peeled, pitted and diced
1 tablespoon extra-

virgin olive oil
2 tablespoons fresh lime juice
Sea salt and ground black pepper, to season
¼ cup queso fresco, crumbled

1. Place the tomatoes, scallions, poblano pepper, garlic and avocado in a serving bowl. Drizzle olive oil and lime juice over everything.
2. Season with salt and black pepper.
3. To serve, top with crumbled queso fresco and enjoy!

**Per Serving**

calories: 189 | fat: 16.0g | protein: 3.6g
carbs: 6.9g | net carbs: 2.7g | fiber: 4.2g

## Parmigiano-Reggiano Cheese Broiled Avocados

**Prep time: 10 minutes | Cook time: 5 minutes | Serves 6**

3 avocados, pitted and halved
½ teaspoon red pepper flakes, crushed
½ teaspoon Himalayan salt

3 tablespoons extra-virgin olive oil
6 tablespoons Parmigiano-Reggiano cheese, grated

1. Begin by preheating your oven for broil.
2. Then, cut a crisscross pattern about ¾ of the way through on each avocado half with a sharp knife.
3. Sprinkle red pepper and salt over the avocado halves. Drizzle olive oil over them and top with the grated Parmigiano-Reggiano cheese.
4. Transfer the avocado halves to a roasting pan and cook under the broiler approximately 5 minutes. Enjoy!

**Per Serving**

calories: 196 | fat: 18.8g | protein: 2.6g
carbs: 6.4g | net carbs: 1.9g | fiber: 4.5g

## Baked Eggplant Rounds

**Prep time: 10 minutes | Cook time: 35 minutes | Serves 6**

1 pound (454 g) eggplant, peeled and sliced
2 teaspoons Italian seasoning blend
½ teaspoon cayenne pepper

½ teaspoon salt
1½ cups marinara sauce
1 cup Mozzarella cheese
2 tablespoons fresh basil leaves, snipped

1. Begin by preheating your oven to 380ºF (193ºC). Line a baking pan with parchment paper.
2. Now, arrange the eggplant rounds on the baking pan. Season with the Italian blend, cayenne pepper, and salt.
3. Bake for 25 to 28 minutes, flipping the rounds half-way through baking time.
4. Next, remove from the oven and top with the marinara sauce and Mozzarella cheese.
5. Bake for 6 to 8 minutes more until Mozzarella is bubbling. Garnish with fresh basil leaves just before serving.

**Per Serving**

calories: 92 | fat: 4.8g | protein: 5.2g
carbs: 5.2g | net carbs: 2.3g | fiber: 2.9g

## Green Cabbage with Tofu

**Prep time: 5 minutes | Cook time: 15 minutes | Serves 3**

6 ounces (170 g) tofu, diced
½ shallot, chopped
2 garlic cloves, finely chopped

1 (1½-pound / 680-g) head green cabbage, cut into strips
½ cup vegetable broth

1. Heat up a lightly oiled sauté pan over moderate heat. Now, cook the tofu until brown and crisp; set aside.
2. Then, sauté the shallot and garlic until just tender and fragrant. Add in the green cabbage and beef bone broth; stir to combine.
3. Reduce the heat to medium-low and continue cooking an additional 13 minutes. Season with salt to taste, top with reserved tofu and serve warm. Bon appétit!

**Per Serving**

calories: 168 | fat: 11.7g | protein: 10.5g
carbs: 5.2g | net carbs: 2.9g | fiber: 2.3g

## Peasant Stir-Fry

**Prep time: 10 minutes | Cook time: 20 minutes | Serves 5**

2 tablespoons olive oil
1 yellow onion, sliced
3 garlic cloves, halved
8 bell peppers, deveined and cut into strips
1 tomato, chopped
½ teaspoon ground black pepper
½ teaspoon paprika
½ teaspoon kosher salt
2 eggs

1. Heat the olive oil in a frying pan over medium-low heat. Now, sweat the onion for 3 to 4 minutes or until tender.
2. Now, stir in the garlic and peppers; continue sautéing for 5 minutes. Then, add in the tomato, black pepper, paprika, and kosher salt.
3. Partially cover and continue to cook for a further 6 to 8 minutes.
4. Fold in the eggs and stir fry for another 5 minutes. Serve warm and enjoy!

**Per Serving**

calories: 115 | fat: 7.5g | protein: 3.4g
carbs: 6.0g | net carbs: 4.5g | fiber: 1.5g

## Avocado Sauced Cucumber Noodles

**Prep time: 15 minutes | Cook time: 0 minutes | Serves 2**

½ teaspoon sea salt
1 cucumber, spiralized
1 California avocado, pitted, peeled and mashed
1 tablespoon olive oil
½ teaspoon garlic powder
½ teaspoon paprika
1 tablespoon fresh lime juice

1. Toss your cucumber with salt and let it sit for 30 minutes; discard the excess water and pat dry.
2. In a mixing bowl, thoroughly combine the avocado with the olive oil, garlic powder, paprika, and lime juice.
3. Add the sauce to the cucumber noodles and serve immediately. Bon appétit!

**Per Serving**

calories: 195 | fat: 17.2g | protein: 2.6g
carbs: 7.6g | net carbs: 3.0g | fiber: 4.6g

## Gruyère Celery Boats

**Prep time: 10 minutes | Cook time: 35 minutes | Serves 2**

1 jalapeño pepper, deveined and minced
¼ teaspoon sea salt
¼ teaspoon ground black pepper
1 teaspoon granulated garlic
3 tablespoons scallions, minced
½ teaspoon caraway seeds
2 ounces (57 g) Gruyère cheese
3 celery stalks, halved

1. In a mixing bowl, thoroughly combine the minced jalapeño with sea salt, black pepper, garlic, scallions, caraway seeds, and Gruyère cheese.
2. Spread this mixture over the celery stalks. Then, arrange them on a parchment-lined baking tray.
3. Roast in the preheated oven at 360°F (182°C) for 35 minutes or until cooked through.

**Per Serving**

calories: 195 | fat: 17.1g | protein: 2.5g
carbs: 7.0g | net carbs: 2.0g | fiber: 5.0g

## Roasted Brussels Sprouts with Balsamic Glaze

**Prep time: 5 minutes | Cook time: 20 to 30 minutes | Serves 8**

¼ cup olive oil
2 tablespoons balsamic vinegar
½ teaspoon garlic powder
1 teaspoon sea salt
¼ teaspoon black pepper
1 pound (454 g) Brussels sprouts, trimmed and halved

1. Preheat the oven to 450°F (235°C). Line a large baking sheet with foil.
2. In a large bowl, whisk together the oil, balsamic vinegar, garlic powder, sea salt, and black pepper, until smooth. Add the Brussels sprouts and toss to coat.
3. Spread the Brussels sprouts over the baking sheet in a single layer, so that all the sprouts touch the pan. Roast for 10 to 15 minutes, until browned on the bottom. Flip and repeat for another 10 to 15 minutes.

**Per Serving**

calories: 88 | fat: 6g | protein: 1g
carbs: 5g | net carbs: 3g | fiber: 2g

## Goat Cheese Eggplant Casserole

**Prep time: 10 minutes | Cook time: 25 minutes | Serves 3**

1 (1-pound / 454-g) eggplant, cut into rounds
2 bell peppers, deveined and quartered
2 vine-ripe tomatoes, sliced
3 tablespoons olive oil
Sea salt and freshly
ground black pepper, to taste
½ teaspoon red pepper flakes, crushed
½ teaspoon sumac
½ cup sour cream
1½ cups goat cheese
2 tablespoons green onions, chopped

1. Place your eggplant and peppers in a baking pan. Top with the sliced tomatoes. Drizzle olive oil over the vegetables.
2. Season with salt, black pepper, crushed red pepper, and sumac. Bake in the preheated oven at 420ºF (216ºC) for 15 minutes. Rotate the pan and bake an additional 10 minutes.
3. Top with sour cream and goat cheese. Garnish with green onions and serve. Enjoy!

**Per Serving**

calories: 476 | fat: 41.4g | protein: 18.4g
carbs: 7.2g | net carbs: 3.6g | fiber: 3.6g

## Provençal Ratatouille

**Prep time: 15 minutes | Cook time: 35 minutes | Serves 6**

2 tablespoons olive oil
2 garlic cloves, finely minced
1 red pepper, sliced
1 yellow pepper, sliced
1 green pepper, sliced
1 shallot, sliced
1 large-sized zucchini, sliced
3 tomatoes, sliced
1 cup vegetable broth
Sea salt, to taste
½ teaspoon dried oregano
½ teaspoon dried parsley flakes
½ teaspoon paprika
½ teaspoon ground black pepper
6 eggs

1. Start by preheating your oven to 400ºF (205ºC). Brush the sides and bottom of a baking pan with olive oil.
2. Layer all vegetables into the prepared pan and cover tightly with foil. Pour in the vegetable broth. Season with salt, oregano, parsley, paprika, and ground black pepper.
3. Bake for about 25 minutes.

4. Create six indentations in the hot ratatouille. Break an egg into each indentation. Bake until the eggs are set or about 9 minutes. Enjoy!

**Per Serving**

calories: 440 | fat: 45.0g | protein: 6.4g
carbs: 5.6g | net carbs: 4.6g | fiber: 1.0g

## Buttered Mushrooms with Sage

**Prep time: 5 minutes | Cook time: 14 to 19 minutes | Serves 8**

5 tablespoons butter, divided
¼ teaspoon ground sage
2 cloves garlic, minced
1 pound (454 g) baby portobello
mushrooms, cut into quarters
½ teaspoon sea salt
⅛ teaspoon black pepper
8 medium fresh sage leaves

1. In a large sauté pan, melt 4 tablespoons of the butter over medium heat. Add the dried sage and heat for 2 to 3 minutes, stirring occasionally, until the butter starts to turn golden.
2. Add the garlic and heat for another 2 to 3 minutes, until the butter is dark golden brown and smells nutty. Watch the pan closely, because the butter can go from browned to burned quickly.
3. Add the mushrooms. Sprinkle with sea salt and black pepper. Cover and cook for 7 to 10 minutes, lifting the lid to stir occasionally, until the mushrooms are soft and most of the moisture evaporates. Uncover and stir-fry for another 3 minutes to evaporate any remaining excess moisture. Remove the mushrooms from the pan and cover to keep warm.
4. Melt the remaining 1 tablespoon butter in the pan. Add the fresh sage leaves in a single layer. Fry for just a few seconds, until crispy.
5. Use the crispy sage leaves for topping the mushrooms—whole for garnish or crumbled for flavor.

**Per Serving**

calories: 154 | fat: 14g | protein: 2g
carbs: 4g | net carbs: 3g | fiber: 1g

## Spicy Onion Rings

**Prep time: 15 minutes | Cook time: 20 minutes | Serves 4**

1 large onion, sliced into rings
½ cup almond flour
1 egg
½ teaspoon garlic

powder
1 teaspoon paprika
1 teaspoon cayenne pepper
1 teaspoon salt

1. Preheat the oven to 400ºF (205ºC), and line a baking sheet with parchment paper.
2. Add the egg to a mixing bowl and then add the almond flour and seasoning to another bowl. Stir the almond flour mixture well.
3. Dip the sliced onions into the egg mixture, followed by the almond flour mix, covering both sides of the sliced onions.
4. Add the onion rings to the baking sheet and bake for about 10 minutes on each side or until crispy.

**Per Serving**

calories: 51 | fat: 3g | protein: 3g
carbs: 4g | net carbs: 3g | fiber: 1g

## Avocado-Bacon Stuffed Eggs

**Prep time: 15 minutes | Cook time: 15 minutes | Serves 3**

1 ripe avocado
4 large hard-boiled eggs
4 slices bacon, cooked and crumbled
1 red chili pepper,

seeded and minced
1 garlic clove, minced
2 tablespoons lemon juice
Salt and black pepper, to taste

1. Peel the eggs, halve them lengthwise and transfer the yolks to a mixing bowl.
2. Add the avocado, chili pepper, garlic and lemon juice to the bowl.
3. Mash with a fork until well combined. Season with salt and black pepper.
4. Scoop the mixture into the egg whites and top with the crumbled bacon.
5. Refrigerate until cold or serve right away.

**Per Serving**

calories: 455 | fat: 37g | protein: 25g
carbs: 8g | net carbs: 3g | fiber: 5g

## Baked Broccoli Bites

**Prep time: 10 minutes | Cook time: 20 minutes | Serves 4**

1½ pounds (680 g) broccoli, cut into bite-sized florets
¼ cup extra-virgin olive oil
Juice of ½ lemon

2 cloves garlic, minced
Salt and pepper, to taste
Red pepper flakes (optional)

1. Preheat the oven to 400ºF (205ºC).
2. In a large mixing bowl, combine the broccoli, oil, lemon juice, and garlic and toss until well coated. Season lightly with salt, black pepper, and red pepper flakes, if using.
3. Pour onto a rimmed baking sheet and spread out in a single layer.
4. Bake for 18 to 20 minutes, until lightly golden brown.

**Per Serving**

calories: 133 | fat: 14g | protein: 1g
carbs: 4g | net carbs: 3g | fiber: 1g

## Parmesan Creamed Spinach

**Prep time: 5 minutes | Cook time: 5 minutes | Serves 4**

1 tablespoon unsalted butter
1 clove garlic, minced
9 ounces (255 g) fresh spinach, chopped
2 ounces (57 g) cream cheese

½ cup grated Parmesan cheese
2 tablespoons heavy whipping cream
Salt and pepper, to taste

1. In a large pot over medium heat, combine the butter and garlic. Sauté, stirring frequently, for 3 to 4 minutes, until fragrant.
2. Add the spinach and cream cheese and use a spatula to combine.
3. Stir in the Parmesan cheese and cream. Bring to a simmer and cook, stirring, for about 1 minute to reduce a bit.
4. Remove from the heat and season with salt and pepper to taste before serving.

**Per Serving**

calories: 172 | fat: 14g | protein: 7g
carbs: 4g | net carbs: 3g | fiber: 1g

## Zoodles with Almond-Basil Pesto

**Prep time: 10 minutes | Cook time: 10 to 13 minutes | Serves 4**

4 medium zucchini (1¼ pounds / 567 g total), spiralized
¾ teaspoon sea salt, divided
⅓ cup raw almonds
2 packed cups fresh basil
⅓ cup grated

Parmesan cheese
⅔ cup extra-virgin olive oil
2 cloves garlic, cut into a few pieces
⅛ teaspoon black pepper
1 tablespoon avocado oil

1. In a colander set in the sink, toss the zucchini noodles with ¼ teaspoon of the sea salt. Let sit for 30 minutes to drain, then squeeze to release more water. You don't have to get every last drop out, just most of it. Pat dry.
2. Meanwhile, preheat the oven to 400ºF (205ºC).
3. Arrange the almonds in a single layer on a baking sheet. Toast in the oven for 6 to 8 minutes, until golden and fragrant. Watch them carefully so they don't burn.
4. Transfer the almonds to a food processor. Pulse a few times until the almonds are broken up into coarse pieces—don't overmix.
5. Add the basil, Parmesan, olive oil, garlic, pepper, and remaining ½ teaspoon sea salt. Pulse on and off, scraping the sides occasionally, until you get a pesto consistency. Adjust sea salt and black pepper to taste—it should be on the salty side, as this will be diluted when you add the zucchini noodles.
6. In a large sauté pan, heat the avocado oil over medium-high heat. Add the zucchini noodles and stir-fry for 3 to 4 minutes, until al dente.
7. Add the pesto and toss to coat. Stir-fry for just 1 more minute, until hot. Serve immediately.

**Per Serving**

calories: 492 | fat: 48g | protein: 8g
carbs: 10g | net carbs: 7g | fiber: 3g

## Fried Cauliflower Rice with Peppers

**Prep time: 10 minutes | Cook time: 14 minutes | Serves 6**

1 head cauliflower
2 tablespoons butter, divided
½ medium orange bell pepper, finely diced
½ medium green bell pepper, finely diced
3 cloves garlic, minced
2 large eggs
1¼ teaspoons sea

salt, divided
¼ teaspoon black pepper
2 tablespoons coconut aminos
1 teaspoon toasted sesame oil
3 green onions, chopped

1. Remove the cauliflower leaves and stems. (Cut off as much of the stems as you can.) Push the cauliflower florets into a running food processor with a grating attachment, to make cauliflower rice. Alternatively, rice the cauliflower using a box grater.
2. In a large sauté pan, heat 1 tablespoon of the butter over medium heat. Add the bell peppers and sauté for about 5 minutes, until the peppers are soft. Add the garlic and sauté for about 1 minute, until fragrant.
3. Meanwhile, whisk the eggs with ¼ teaspoon sea salt and a pinch of black pepper.
4. Push the veggies to one side of the skillet. (If the pan is dry, you can melt in more butter.) Add the whisked eggs to the other side and cook for 3 minutes, until barely scrambled.
5. Push everything to the side again and add the remaining 1 tablespoon butter to the pan. Once it melts, increase the heat to medium-high, immediately add the cauliflower rice, and stir everything together. Season with 1 teaspoon sea salt and ¼ teaspoon black pepper, or to taste. Stir-fry for about 5 minutes, until the cauliflower is soft but not mushy.
6. Remove from the heat. Stir in the coconut aminos, sesame oil, and green onions.

**Per Serving**

calories: 106 | fat: 6g | protein: 4g
carbs: 8g | net carbs: 6g | fiber: 2g

## Smoked Mackerel and Turnip Patties

**Prep time: 5 minutes | Cook time: 14 minutes | Serves 6**

1 turnip, diced
1½ cup water
Salt and chili pepper, to taste
3 tablespoons olive oil, plus more for rubbing
4 smoked mackerel steaks, bones removed,
flaked
3 eggs, beaten
2 tablespoons mayonnaise
1 tablespoon pork rinds, crushed

1. Bring the turnip to boil in salted water in a saucepan over medium heat for 8 minutes or until tender. Drain the turnip through a colander, transfer to a mixing bowl, and mash the lumps.
2. Add the mackerel, eggs, mayonnaise, pork rinds, salt, and chili pepper; mix and make 6 compact patties. Heat olive oil in a skillet over medium heat and fry the patties for 3 minutes on each side until golden brown. Remove onto a wire rack to cool. Serve with sesame lime dipping sauce.

**Per Serving**

calories: 348 | fat: 22g | protein: 33g | carbs: 3g | net carbs: 2g | fiber: 1g

## Herbed Roasted Radishes

**Prep time: 5 minutes | Cook time: 16 to 26 minutes | Serves 6**

3 tablespoons avocado oil
3 cloves garlic, minced
1 tablespoon fresh thyme, chopped
1 tablespoon fresh rosemary, chopped
1½ teaspoons sea salt
¼ teaspoon black pepper
2 pounds (907 g) radishes, trimmed and halved

1. Preheat the oven to 425ºF (220ºC). Line a baking sheet with foil and grease it.
2. In a large bowl, whisk together the oil, garlic, thyme, rosemary, sea salt, and black pepper. Add the radishes and toss to coat.
3. Arrange the radishes in a single layer on the pan, making sure each one touches the pan. Spread them out as much as possible. Roast for 8 to 13 minutes, until golden on the bottom. Flip and roast for 8 to 13 more minutes.

**Per Serving**

calories: 98 | fat: 7g | protein: 1g | carbs: 6g | net carbs: 4g | fiber: 2g

## Baked Keto Granola

**Prep time: 10 minutes | Cook time: 27 minutes | Serves 10**

$1/_3$ cup sunflower seeds
$1/_3$ cup flaxseed meal
1 cup coconut, shredded, unsweetened
½ cup pecans, chopped
½ cup walnuts, chopped
½ stick butter
¼ cup water
½ teaspoon cinnamon ground
½ teaspoon grated nutmeg
A pinch of coarse sea salt
1 teaspoon vanilla paste

1. Thoroughly combine all ingredients until well combined.
2. Place the mixture on a parchment-lined roasting pan. Bake in the preheated oven at 300ºF (150ºC) for about 27 minutes.
3. Let it cool completely before storing. Bon appétit!

**Per Serving**

calories: 162 | fat: 16g | protein: 3g | carbs: 5g | net carbs: 2g | fiber: 3g

## Scrambled Eggs with Swiss Chard Pesto

**Prep time: 10 minutes | Cook time: 3 minutes | Serves 4**

3 tablespoons butter
8 eggs, beaten
**Swiss Chard Pesto:**
2 cups Swiss chard
1 cup Parmesan cheese, grated
2 garlic cloves, minced

¼ cup almond milk
Salt and black pepper, to taste

½ cup olive oil
2 tablespoons lime juice
½ cup walnuts, chopped

1. Set a pan over medium heat and warm butter. Mix eggs, black pepper, salt, and almond milk. Cook the egg mixture while stirring gently, until eggs are set but still tender and moist, for 3 minutes.
2. In your blender, place all the ingredients for the pesto, excluding the olive oil. Pulse until roughly blended. While the machine is still running, slowly add in the olive oil until the desired consistency is attained. Serve alongside warm scrambled eggs.

**Per Serving**

calories: 626 | fat: 58g | protein: 20g | carbs: 8g | net carbs: 7g | fiber: 1g

## Zucchini Noodles with Mushroom Sauce

**Prep time: 10 minutes | Cook time: 10 minutes | Serves 3**

1½ tablespoons olive oil
3 cups button mushrooms, chopped
2 cloves garlic, smashed
1 cup tomato purée

1 pound (454 g) zucchini, spiralized
Salt and ground black pepper, to taste
$^1/_3$ cup Pecorino Romano cheese, preferably freshly grated

1. Heat the olive oil in a saucepan over a moderate flame. Then, cook the mushrooms until tender and fragrant or about 4 minutes.
2. Stir in the garlic and continue to sauté an additional 30 seconds or until just tender and aromatic. Fold in the tomato purée and zucchini.
3. Reduce the heat to medium-low, partially cover and let it cook for about 6 minutes or until heated through. Season with salt and black pepper to taste.
4. Divide your zoodles and sauce between serving plates. Top with Pecorino Romano cheese and serve warm. Bon appétit!

**Per Serving**

calories: 161 | fat: 10.5g | protein: 10.0g | carbs: 7.4g | net carbs: 4.0g | fiber: 3.4g

## Ricotta Spinach Gnocchi

**Prep time: 5 minutes | Cook time: 7 minutes | Serves 4**

1 cup ricotta cheese
1 cup Parmesan cheese, grated
¼ teaspoon nutmeg powder
1 egg, cracked into a bowl
Salt and black pepper, to taste

3 cups chopped spinach
1½ cups almond flour
2½ cups water
2 tablespoons butter

1. To a bowl, add the ricotta cheese, half of the Parmesan cheese, egg, nutmeg powder, salt, spinach, almond flour, and black pepper. Mix well. Make gnocchi of the mixture using 2 tablespoons and set aside.

2. Bring the water to a boil over high heat on a stovetop, about 5 minutes. Place one gnocchi onto the water, if it breaks apart; add some more flour to the other gnocchi to firm it up.
3. Put the remaining gnocchi in the water to poach and rise to the top, about 2 minutes. Remove the gnocchi with a perforated spoon to a serving plate. Melt the butter in a microwave and pour over the gnocchi. Sprinkle with the remaining Parmesan cheese and serve with green salad.

**Per Serving**

calories: 238 | fat: 16g | protein: 18g | carbs: 9g | net carbs: 4g | fiber: 5g

## Cauli Rice with Cheddar and Bacon

**Prep time: 10 minutes | Cook time: 8 to 10 minutes | Serves 8**

1 head cauliflower, cut into florets
2 tablespoons butter
¼ cup sour cream
2 tablespoons heavy cream
3 cloves garlic, minced

1 teaspoon sea salt
1½ cups shredded Cheddar cheese
$1/_3$ cup cooked bacon bits
¼ cup chopped green onions

1. Bring a large pot of water to a boil on the stove top. Add the cauliflower florets and cook for 8 to 10 minutes, until very soft. Drain well and pat dry.
2. Meanwhile, in a microwave-safe bowl or in a saucepan, combine the butter, sour cream, heavy cream, garlic, and sea salt, and heat in the microwave or on the stove until hot and melted.
3. Transfer the cauliflower florets to a food processor. Add the butter-cream mixture and purée until smooth.
4. Transfer the cauliflower to a serving dish. Immediately stir in most of the Cheddar, bacon bits, and green onions, reserving a little of each for the topping. To serve, garnish with the reserved Cheddar, bacon, and green onions.

**Per Serving**

calories: 180 | fat: 13g | protein: 9g | carbs: 5g | net carbs: 3g | fiber: 2g

## Garlicky Roasted Broccoli

**Prep time: 5 minutes | Cook time: 20 to 30 minutes | Serves 6**

¼ cup olive oil
1 teaspoon lemon zest
1 tablespoon lemon juice
6 cloves garlic, minced

½ teaspoon sea salt
¼ teaspoon black pepper
1 pound (454 g) broccoli florets

1. Preheat the oven to 400ºF (205ºC). Grease a 20 × 14-inch baking sheet or two 10 × 14-inch pans.
2. In a large bowl, whisk together the oil, lemon zest, lemon juice, garlic, sea salt, and black pepper. (You can tilt the bowl to the side to help when whisking this small amount in a large bowl.)
3. Add the broccoli florets and toss to coat.
4. Arrange the broccoli florets in a single layer on the baking sheet so that each piece is touching the baking sheet.
5. Roast for 20 to 30 minutes, until the edges of the florets are browned.

**Per Serving**

calories: 109 | fat: 9g | protein: 2g | carbs: 5g | net carbs: 3g | fiber: 2g

# Chapter 8 Poultry

## Dijon Chicken Thighs

**Prep time: 10 minutes | Cook time: 16 minutes | Serves 4**

½ cup chicken stock
1 tablespoon olive oil
½ cup chopped onion
4 chicken thighs
¼ cup heavy cream

1 tablespoon Dijon mustard
1 teaspoon thyme
1 teaspoon garlic powder

1. Heat the olive oil in a pan. Cook the chicken for about 4 minutes per side. Set aside.
2. Sauté the onion in the same pan for 3 minutes, add the stock, and simmer for 5 minutes.
3. Stir in mustard and heavy cream, along with thyme and garlic powder.
4. Pour the sauce over the chicken and serve.

**Per Serving**

calories: 504 | fat: 39g | protein: 33g
carbs: 4g | net carbs: 3g | fiber: 1g

## Garlicky Drumsticks

**Prep time: 10 minutes | Cook time: 1 hour 10 minutes | Serves 5**

2 tablespoons olive oil
2 pounds (907 g) chicken drumsticks, boneless, skinless
Sea salt and ground black pepper, to taste

2 garlic cloves, minced
½ cup tomato paste
½ cup chicken broth
4 tablespoons rice vinegar
2 scallions, chopped

1. Start by preheating the oven to 330ºF (166ºC). Brush the sides and bottom of a baking pan with olive oil.
2. Arrange the chicken drumsticks in the baking pan. Add the salt, black pepper, garlic, tomato paste, chicken broth, and rice vinegar to the pan.
3. Bake for 1 hour 10 minutes or until everything is heated through.
4. Garnish with scallions and serve. Bon appétit!

**Per Serving**

calories: 353 | fat: 22.2g | protein: 33.2g
carbs: 2.6g | net carbs: 2.0g | fiber: 0.6g

## Hearty Stuffed Chicken

**Prep time: 20 minutes | Cook time: 35 minutes | Serves 4**

**For the Chicken:**

4 chicken breasts
⅓ cup baby spinach
¼ cup goat cheese
¼ cup shredded

cheddar cheese
1 tablespoon butter
Salt and black pepper, to taste

**For the Tomato Purée:**

1 tablespoon butter
1 shallot, chopped
2 garlic cloves, chopped
½ tablespoon red wine vinegar
1 tablespoon tomato purée

14 ounces (397 g) canned crushed tomatoes
½ teaspoon salt
1 teaspoon dried basil
1 teaspoon dried oregano
Black pepper, to taste

**For the Salad:**

2 cucumbers, spiralized
1 tablespoon olive oil

1 tablespoon rice vinegar

1. Set oven to 400ºF (205ºC) and grease a baking dish. Set aside.
2. Place a pan over medium heat. Melt 1 tablespoon of butter and sauté spinach until it shrinks; season with salt and pepper. Transfer to a bowl containing goat cheese, stir and set aside. Cut the chicken breasts lengthwise and stuff with the cheese mixture and set into the baking dish. On top, spread the grated cheddar cheese, add 1 tablespoon of butter then set into the oven. Bake until cooked through for 20 to 30 minutes.
3. Set a pan over medium-high heat and warm 1 tablespoon of butter. Add in garlic and shallot and cook until soft. Place in herbs, tomato purée, vinegar, tomatoes, salt, and pepper. Bring the mixture to a boil. Set heat to low and simmer for 15 minutes. Arrange the cucumbers on a serving platter, season with salt, pepper, olive oil, and vinegar, Top with the chicken and pour over the sauce.

**Per Serving**

calories: 453 | fat: 31g | protein: 43g
carbs: 9g | net carbs: 6g | fiber: 3g

## Rice Wine Duck with White Onion

**Prep time: 5 minutes | Cook time: 25 minutes | Serves 6**

1½ pounds (680 g) duck breast 1 tablespoon sesame oil 1 white onion, chopped ¼ cup rice wine 3 teaspoons soy sauce

1. Gently score the duck breast skin in a tight crosshatch pattern using a sharp knife.
2. Heat the sesame oil in a skillet over moderate heat. Now, sauté the onion until tender and translucent.
3. Add in the duck breasts; sear the duck breasts for 10 to 13 minutes or until the skin looks crispy with golden brown color; drain off the duck fat from the skillet.
4. Flip the breasts over and sear the other side for 3 minutes. Deglaze the skillet with rice wine, scraping up any brown bits stuck to the bottom. Transfer to a baking pan; add the rice wine and soy sauce to the baking pan.
5. Roast in the preheated oven at 400°F (205°C) for 4 minutes for medium-rare (145°F / 63°C), or 6 minutes for medium (165°F / 74°C).
6. Serve garnished with sesame seeds if desired. Enjoy!

**Per Serving**

calories: 264 | fat: 11.4g | protein: 34.2g carbs: 3.6g | net carbs: 3.0g | fiber: 0.6g

## Mexican Chicken Mole

**Prep time: 15 minutes | Cook time: 7 to 8 hours | Serves 6**

3 tablespoons extra-virgin olive oil or butter (here), divided 2 pounds (907 g) boneless chicken thighs and breasts Salt, for seasoning Freshly ground black pepper, for seasoning 1 sweet onion, chopped 1 tablespoon minced garlic 1 (28-ounce / 794-g) can diced tomatoes 4 dried chile peppers, soaked in water for 2 hours and chopped 3 ounces (1.4kg) dark chocolate, chopped ¼ cup natural peanut butter 1½ teaspoons ground cumin ¾ teaspoon ground cinnamon ½ teaspoon chili powder ½ cup coconut cream 2 tablespoons chopped cilantro, for garnish

1. Lightly grease the insert of the slow cooker with 1 tablespoon of the olive oil.
2. In a large skillet over medium-high heat, heat the remaining 2 tablespoons of the olive oil.
3. Lightly season the chicken with salt and pepper, add to the skillet, and brown for about 5 minutes, turning once.
4. Add the onion and garlic and sauté for an additional 3 minutes.
5. Transfer the chicken, onion, and garlic to the slow cooker, and stir in the tomatoes, chiles, chocolate, peanut butter, cumin, cinnamon, and chili powder.
6. Cover and cook on low for 7 to 8 hours.
7. Stir in the coconut cream, and serve hot, topped with the cilantro.

**Per Serving**

calories: 386 | fat: 30g | protein: 19g carbs: 11g | net carbs: 6g | fiber: 5g

## Salsa Turkey Cutlet and Zucchini Stir-Fry

**Prep time: 10 minutes | Cook time: 15 minutes | Serves 4**

2 tablespoons olive oil 1 pound (454 g) turkey cutlets 1 red onion, sliced 2 garlic cloves, minced 1 chili pepper, chopped Sea salt and ground black pepper, to taste ½ teaspoon cayenne pepper ½ teaspoon dried basil 1 teaspoon dried rosemary ½ teaspoon cumin seeds ½ teaspoon mustard seeds 1 zucchini, spiralized ½ cup salsa

1. Heat 1 tablespoon of the olive oil in a frying pan over a moderate flame. Cook the turkey cutlets until they are golden brown or about 10 minutes; shred the meat with two forks and reserve.
2. Heat the remaining tablespoon of olive oil in the same frying pan. Now, sauté the onion, garlic, and chili pepper until they have softened.
3. Add the spices and stir in the reserved turkey. Fold in the zucchini and cook for 3 minutes or until it is tender and everything is cooked through. Serve with salsa on the side. Enjoy!

**Per Serving**

calories: 211 | fat: 9.1g | protein: 26.1g carbs: 5.5g | net carbs: 4.4g | fiber: 1.1g

## Turkey and leek Goulash

**Prep time: 10 minutes | Cook time: 40 minutes | Serves 6**

2 tablespoons olive oil
1 large-sized leek, chopped
2 cloves garlic, minced
2 pounds (907 g)

turkey thighs, skinless, boneless and chopped
2 celery stalks, chopped

1. Heat the olive oil in a soup pot over a moderate flame. Then, sweat the leeks until just tender and fragrant.
2. Then, cook the garlic until aromatic.
3. Add in the turkey thighs and celery; add 4 cups of water and bring to a boil. Immediately reduce the heat and allow it to simmer for 35 to 40 minutes.
4. Ladle into individual bowls and serve hot. Bon appétit!

**Per Serving**

calories: 221 | fat: 7.3g | protein: 35.4g
carbs: 2.6g | net carbs: 2.2g | fiber: 0.4g

## Mediterranean Chicken with Peppers and Olives

**Prep time: 15 minutes | Cook time: 15 minutes | Serves 2**

2 chicken drumsticks, boneless and skinless
1 tablespoon extra-virgin olive oil
Sea salt and ground black pepper, to season
2 bell peppers,

deveined and halved
1 small chili pepper, finely chopped
2 tablespoons Greek aioli
6 Kalamata olives, pitted

1. Brush the chicken drumsticks with the olive oil. Season the chicken drumsticks with salt and black pepper.
2. Preheat your grill to moderate heat. Grill the chicken drumsticks for 8 minutes; turn them over and add the bell peppers.
3. Grill them for a further 5 minutes. Transfer to a serving platter; top with chopped chili pepper and Greek aioli.
4. Garnish with Kalamata olives and serve warm. Enjoy!

**Per Serving**

calories: 400 | fat: 31.3g | protein: 24.5g
carbs: 5.0g | net carbs: 3.9g | fiber: 1.1g

## Chicken Thighs with Caesar Salad

**Prep time: 15 minutes | Cook time: 15 minutes | Serves 4**

**Chicken:**
4 chicken thighs
¼ cup lemon juice
**Salad:**
½ cup caesar salad dressing
2 tablespoons olive oil
12 bok choy leaves

2 garlic cloves, minced
2 tablespoons olive oil

3 Parmesan cheese crisps
Parmesan cheese, grated

1. Combine the chicken ingredients in a Ziploc bag. Seal the bag, shake to combine, and refrigerate for 1 hour. Preheat the grill to medium heat, and grill the chicken about 4 minutes per side.
2. Cut bok choy leaves lengthwise, and brush it with oil. Grill for about 3 minutes. Place on a serving platter. Top with the chicken, and drizzle the dressing over. Sprinkle with Parmesan cheese and finish with Parmesan crisps to serve.

**Per Serving**

calories: 530 | fat: 39.0g | protein: 33.0g
carbs: 6.7g | net carbs: 5.0g | fiber: 1.7g

## Asian Spicy Chicken Skewers

**Prep time: 10 minutes | Cook time: 6 minutes | Serves 6**

2 pounds (907 g) chicken breasts, cubed
1 teaspoon sesame oil
1 tablespoon olive oil
1 cup red bell pepper pieces

1 tablespoon five spice powder
1 tablespoon granulated sweetener
1 tablespoon fish sauce

1. Combine the sesame and olive oils, fish sauce, and seasonings in a bowl. Add the chicken, and let marinate for 1 hour in the fridge.
2. Preheat the grill. Take 12 skewers and thread the chicken and bell peppers. Grill for 3 minutes per side.

**Per Serving**

calories: 297 | fat: 17g | protein: 32g
carbs: 2g | net carbs: 1g | fiber: 1g

## Mozzarella Spinach Stuffed Chicken

**Prep time: 10 minutes | Cook time: 30 minutes | Serves 6**

4 ounces (113 g) cream cheese
3 ounces (85 g) mozzarella slices
10 ounces (283 g) spinach
1/3 cup shredded

mozzarella cheese
1 tablespoon olive oil
1 cup tomato basil sauce
3 whole chicken breasts

1. Preheat your oven to 400ºF (205ºC). Combine the cream cheese, shredded mozzarella cheese, and spinach in the microwave. Cut the chicken a couple of times horizontally and stuff with the spinach mixture. Brush with olive oil. place on a lined baking dish and bake in the oven for 25 minutes.
2. Pour the tomato basil sauce over and top with mozzarella slices. Return to the oven and cook for an additional 5 minutes.

**Per Serving**

calories: 338 | fat: 28g | protein: 37g
carbs: 7g | net carbs: 3g | fiber: 4g

## Cooked Chicken in Creamy Spinach Sauce

**Prep time: 10 minutes | Cook time: 21 minutes | Serves 4**

1 pound (454 g) chicken thighs
1 tablespoon coconut oil
1 tablespoon coconut flour

2 cups spinach, chopped
1 teaspoon oregano
1 cup heavy cream
1 cup chicken broth
1 tablespoon butter

1. Warm the coconut oil in a skillet and brown the chicken on all sides, about 6-8 minutes. Set aside.
2. Add and melt the butter and whisk in the flour over medium heat. Whisk in the heavy cream and chicken broth and bring to a boil. Stir in oregano. Add the spinach to the skillet and cook until wilted. Add the thighs in the skillet and cook for an additional 15 minutes.

**Per Serving**

calories: 446 | fat: 38g | protein: 18g
carbs: 3g | net carbs: 2g | fiber: 1g

## Pesto Turkey with Zucchini Spaghetti

**Prep time: 10 minutes | Cook time: 32 minutes | Serves 6**

2 cups sliced mushrooms
1 teaspoon olive oil
1 pound (454 g) ground turkey
1 tablespoon pesto

sauce
1 cup diced onion
2 cups broccoli florets
6 cups zucchini, spiralized

1. Heat the oil in a skillet. Add zucchini and cook for 2-3 minutes, stirring continuously; set aside.
2. Add turkey to the skillet and cook until browned, about 7-8 minutes. Transfer to a plate. Add onion and cook until translucent, about 3 minutes. Add broccoli and mushrooms, and cook for 7 more minutes. Return the turkey to the skillet. Stir in the pesto sauce. Cover the pan, lower the heat, and simmer for 15 minutes. Stir in zucchini pasta and serve immediately.

**Per Serving**

calories: 273 | fat: 16g | protein: 19g
carbs: 7g | net carbs: 4g | fiber: 3g

## Roast Herbs Stuffed Chicken

**Prep time: 10 minutes | Cook time: 1½ hours | Serves 8**

5 pounds (2.3 kg) whole chicken
1 bunch oregano
1 bunch thyme
1 tablespoon marjoram

1 tablespoon parsley
1 tablespoon olive oil
2 pounds (907 g) Brussels sprouts
1 lemon
1 tablespoon butter

1. Preheat your oven to 450ºF (235ºC).
2. Stuff the chicken with oregano, thyme, and lemon. Roast for 15 minutes. Reduce the heat to 325ºF (163ºC) and cook for 40 minutes. Spread the butter over the chicken, and sprinkle parsley and marjoram. Add the brussels sprouts. Return to the oven and bake for 40 more minutes.
3. Let sit for 10 minutes before carving.

**Per Serving**

calories: 432 | fat: 32g | protein: 30g
carbs: 10g | net carbs: 5g | fiber: 5g

## Fried Turkey and Pork Meatballs

**Prep time: 20 minutes | Cook time: 15 minutes | Serves 4**

4 spring onions, finely chopped
2 spring garlic stalks, chopped
2 tablespoons cilantro, chopped
½ pound (227 g) ground pork
½ pound (227 g) ground turkey
1 egg, whisked
½ cup Parmesan cheese, grated
1 teaspoon dried rosemary
½ teaspoon mustard powder
Sea salt and freshly ground black pepper, to season
2 tablespoons olive oil

1. In a mixing bowl, thoroughly combine all ingredients, except for the olive oil. Shape the mixture into small balls.
2. Refrigerate your meatballs for 1 hour.
3. Then, heat the olive oil in a frying pan over medium-high heat. Once hot, fry the meatballs for 6 minutes until nicely browned.
4. Turn them and cook 6 minutes on the other side. Bon appétit!

**Per Serving**

calories: 367 | fat: 27.6g | protein: 25.9g
carbs: 3.0g | net carbs: 2.5g | fiber: 0.5g

## Ranch Turkey with Greek Aioli Sauce

**Prep time: 10 minutes | Cook time: 15 minutes | Serves 4**

2 eggs
Kosher salt and ground black pepper, to taste
1 teaspoon paprika
2 tablespoons pork rinds
2 tablespoons flaxseed
meal
½ cup almond meal
1 pound (454 g) turkey tenders, ½-inch thick
2 tablespoons sesame seeds
2 tablespoons olive oil

**Sauce:**

2 tablespoons Greek aioli
½ cup Greek yogurt
Flaky sea salt and freshly ground black pepper, to season

1. In a mixing bowl, whisk the eggs with salt and black pepper until well combined.
2. In a separate bowl, make the keto breading. Thoroughly combine the paprika, pork rinds, flaxseed meal, and almond meal. Dip the turkey tenders into the egg mixture.
3. Then, press the turkey tenders into the keto breading. Dip them into the egg mixture again and roll them over the sesame seeds to coat well.
4. Heat the olive oil in a large frying pan over medium-high heat. Once hot, add the turkey tenders and let them brown, about 4 minutes per side.
5. Meanwhile, whisk the sauce ingredients until everything is well incorporated. Serve the turkey tenders with the sauce on the side. Enjoy!

**Per Serving**

calories: 397 | fat: 27.4g | protein: 32.9g
carbs: 3.8g | net carbs: 2.0g | fiber: 1.8g

## Chicken Wing and Italian Pepper Soup

**Prep time: 15 minutes | Cook time: 50 minutes | Serves 6**

1 tablespoon olive oil
6 chicken wings
1 Italian pepper, deveined and sliced
½ cup celery, chopped
½ cup onions, finely chopped
2 sprigs rosemary,
leaves picked
2 sprigs thyme, leaves picked
Sea salt and ground black pepper, to taste
6 cups vegetable stock
1 whole egg

1. Heat the olive oil in a soup pot over a moderate flame. Brown the chicken wings for 4 to 5 minutes per side or until no longer pink; reserve.
2. Then, cook the Italian pepper, celery and onions in the same pot until they have softened.
3. Stir in the rosemary, thyme, salt, black pepper, and vegetable stock; return the chicken to the pot.
4. Stir with a spoon and bring to a boil. Reduce the heat to medium-low and let it simmer an additional 45 minutes, stirring once or twice.
5. Transfer the chicken to a cutting board and shred the chicken, discarding the bones.
6. Add the egg to the pot and whisk until well combined. Add the chicken back to the pot, stir, and serve warm. Enjoy!

**Per Serving**

calories: 284 | fat: 18.8g | protein: 25.3g
carbs: 2.5g | net carbs: 2.1g | fiber: 0.4g

## Basil Turkey Meatballs

**Prep time: 10 minutes | Cook time: 5 minutes | Serves 4**

1 pound (454 g) ground turkey
1 tablespoon chopped sun-dried tomatoes
1 tablespoon chopped basil
½ teaspoon garlic powder

1 egg
½ teaspoon salt
¼ cup almond flour
1 tablespoon olive oil
½ cup shredded mozzarella cheese
¼ teaspoon pepper

1. Place everything, except the oil in a bowl. Mix with your hands until combined. Form into 16 balls. Heat the olive oil in a skillet over medium heat. Cook the meatballs for 4-5 minutes per each side.
2. Serve immediately.

**Per Serving**

calories: 310 | fat: 26g | protein: 22g
carbs: 3g | net carbs: 2g | fiber: 1g

## Lemony Chicken Wings

**Prep time: 10 minutes | Cook time: 15 minutes | Serves 4**

A pinch of garlic powder
1 teaspoon lemon zest
1 tablespoon lemon juice
½ teaspoon ground cilantro
1 tablespoon fish sauce

1 tablespoon butter
¼ teaspoon xanthan gum
1 tablespoon Swerve sweetener
20 chicken wings
Salt and black pepper, to taste

1. Combine lemon juice and zest, fish sauce, cilantro, sweetener, and garlic powder in a saucepan. Bring to a boil, cover, lower the heat, and let simmer for 10 minutes. Stir in the butter and xanthan gum. Set aside. Season the wings with some salt and pepper.
2. Preheat the grill and cook for 5 minutes per side.
3. Serve topped with the sauce.

**Per Serving**

calories: 365 | fat: 25g | protein: 21g
carbs: 4g | net carbs: 4g | fiber: 0g

## Chicken Thigh Green Chowder

**Prep time: 10 minutes | Cook time: 35 minutes | Serves 5**

5 chicken thighs
½ cup Italian peppers, deseeded and chopped
½ cup green cabbage, shredded
½ cup celery, chopped
1 shallot, chopped

5 cups roasted vegetable broth
Freshly ground black pepper, to taste
7 ounces (198 g) full-fat cream cheese

1. Add the chicken thighs, Italian peppers, cabbage, celery, shallot, broth, and black pepper to a soup pot.
2. Cook, partially covered, over a moderate heat for 25 minutes. Shred the chicken, discarding the bones.
3. Fold in the cream cheese, stir and cover. Let it sit in the residual heat for 10 minutes. Ladle into individual bowls and serve warm.

**Per Serving**

calories: 512 | fat: 37.9g | protein: 35.2g
carbs: 5.3g | net carbs: 4.9g | fiber: 0.4g

## Chicken and Broccoli Marsala

**Prep time: 10 minutes | Cook time: 15 minutes | Serves 2**

1 tablespoon olive oil
2 chicken fillets
¼ cup marsala wine
1 cup broccoli florets
1 teaspoon fresh garlic, chopped

¼ tomato paste
½ cup double cream
½ teaspoon paprika
Sea salt and ground black pepper, to taste

1. Heat the olive oil in a frying pan over a moderate flame. Once hot, brown the chicken fillets for 7 minutes on each side.
2. Add a splash of wine to deglaze the pot. Add in the broccoli, garlic, and tomato paste and gently stir to combine. Turn the heat to simmer.
3. Continue to cook an additional 5 minutes. After that, stir in the double cream, paprika, salt, and black pepper.
4. Continue to simmer for 5 minutes more or until heated through. Bon appétit!

**Per Serving**

calories: 350 | fat: 20.5g | protein: 35.2g
carbs: 4.6g | net carbs: 3.4g | fiber: 1.2g

## Coconut-Chicken Breasts

**Prep time: 15 minutes | Cook time: 7 to 8 hours | Serves 6**

| | |
|---|---|
| 3 tablespoons extra-virgin olive oil, divided | butter |
| 1½ pounds (680 g) boneless chicken breasts | 1 tablespoon red thai curry paste |
| ½ sweet onion, chopped | 1 tablespoon coconut aminos |
| 1 cup quartered baby bok choy | 2 teaspoons grated fresh ginger |
| 1 red bell pepper, diced | Pinch red pepper flakes |
| 2 cups coconut milk | ¼ cup chopped peanuts, for garnish |
| 2 tablespoons almond | 2 tablespoons chopped cilantro, for garnish |

1. Lightly grease the insert of the slow cooker with 1 tablespoon of the olive oil.
2. In a large skillet over medium-high heat, heat the remaining 2 tablespoons of the olive oil. Add the chicken and brown for about 7 minutes.
3. Transfer the chicken to the slow cooker and add the onion, baby bok choy, and bell pepper.
4. In a medium bowl, whisk together the coconut milk, almond butter, curry paste, coconut aminos, ginger, and red pepper flakes, until well blended.
5. Pour the sauce over the chicken and vegetables, and mix to coat.
6. Cover and cook on low for 7 to 8 hours.
7. Serve topped with the peanuts and cilantro.

**Per Serving**

calories: 543 | fat: 42g | protein: 35g
carbs: 10g | net carbs: 5g | fiber: 5g

## Roasted Whole Chicken

**Prep time: 15 minutes | Cook time: 7 to 8 hours | Serves 8**

| | |
|---|---|
| ¼ cup extra-virgin olive oil, divided | 1 lemon, quartered |
| 1 (3-pound / 1.4-kg) whole chicken, washed and patted dry | 6 thyme sprigs |
| | 4 garlic cloves, crushed |
| Salt, for seasoning | 3 bay leaves |
| Freshly ground black pepper, for seasoning | 1 sweet onion, quartered |

1. Lightly grease the insert of the slow cooker with 1 tablespoon of the olive oil.
2. Rub the remaining olive oil all over the chicken and season with the salt and pepper. Stuff the lemon quarters, thyme, garlic, and bay leaves into the cavity of the chicken.
3. Place the onion quarters on the bottom of the slow cooker and place the chicken on top so it does not touch the bottom of the insert.
4. Cover and cook on low for 7 to 8 hours, or until the internal temperature reaches 165ºF (74ºC) on an instant-read thermometer.
5. Serve warm.

**Per Serving**

calories: 427 | fat: 34g | protein: 29g
carbs: 2g | net carbs: 2g | fiber: 0g

## Garlicky Chicken Thighs

**Prep time: 15 minutes | Cook time: 7 to 8 hours | Serves 4**

| | |
|---|---|
| ¼ cup extra-virgin olive oil, divided | 1 sweet onion, chopped |
| 1½ pounds (680 g) boneless chicken thighs | 4 garlic cloves, thinly sliced |
| 1 teaspoon paprika | ½ cup chicken broth |
| Salt, for seasoning | 2 tablespoons freshly squeezed lemon juice |
| Freshly ground black pepper, for seasoning | ½ cup greek yogurt |

1. Lightly grease the insert of the slow cooker with 1 tablespoon of the olive oil.
2. Season the thighs with paprika, salt, and pepper.
3. In a large skillet over medium-high heat, heat the remaining olive oil. Add the chicken and brown for 5 minutes, turning once.
4. Transfer the chicken to the insert and add the onion, garlic, broth, and lemon juice.
5. Cover and cook on low for 7 to 8 hours.
6. Stir in the yogurt and serve.

**Per Serving**

calories: 434 | fat: 36g | protein: 22g
carbs: 5g | net carbs: 4g | fiber: 1g

## Chicken Garam Masala

**Prep time: 15 minutes | Cook time: 26 minutes | Serves 4**

1 pound (454 g) chicken breasts, sliced lengthwise
1 tablespoon butter
1 tablespoon olive oil
1 yellow bell pepper, finely chopped

1¼ cups heavy whipping cream
1 tablespoon fresh cilantro, finely chopped
Salt and pepper, to taste

**For the Garam Masala:**

1 teaspoon ground cumin
1 teaspoon ground coriander
1 teaspoon ground cardamom
1 teaspoon turmeric

1 teaspoon ginger
1 teaspoon paprika
1 teaspoon cayenne, ground
1 pinch ground nutmeg

1. Set your oven to 400°F (205°C). In a bowl, mix the garam masala spices. Coat the chicken with half of the masala mixture. Heat the olive oil and butter in a frying pan over medium-high heat, and brown the chicken for 3 to 5 minutes per side. Transfer to a baking dish.
2. To the remaining masala, add heavy cream and bell pepper. Season with salt and pepper and pour over chicken. Bake for 20 minutes until the mixture starts to bubble. Garnish with chopped cilantro to serve.

**Per Serving**

calories: 564 | fat: 50g | protein: 33g
carbs: 6g | net carbs: 5g | fiber: 1g

## Pepper, Cheese, and Sauerkraut Stuffed Chicken

**Prep time: 15 minutes | Cook time: 30 minutes | Serves 5**

2 tablespoons olive oil
5 chicken cutlets
½ teaspoon cayenne pepper
½ teaspoon oregano
Sea salt and ground black pepper, to taste
1 tablespoon Dijon mustard

2 garlic cloves, minced
5 Italian peppers, deveined and chopped
1 chili pepper, chopped
1 cup Romano cheese, shredded
5 tablespoons sauerkraut, for serving

1. Brush a baking pan with 1 tablespoon of the olive oil. Bruch the chicken cutlets with the remaining tablespoon of olive oil.
2. Season the chicken cutlets with the cayenne pepper, oregano, salt, and black pepper. Spread mustard on one side of each chicken cutlet.
3. Divide the garlic, peppers, and Romano cheese on the mustard side. Roll up tightly and use toothpicks to secure your rolls. Transfer to the prepared baking pan.
4. Bake in the preheated oven at 370°F (188°C) for about 30 minutes until golden brown on all sides (an instant-read thermometer should register 165°F (74°C)).
5. Spoon the sauerkraut over the chicken and serve. Bon appétit!

**Per Serving**

calories: 378 | fat: 16.6g | protein: 47.0g
carbs: 5.7g | net carbs: 4.7g | fiber: 1.0g

## Chimichurri Chicken Tender

**Prep time: 10 minutes | Cook time: 35 minutes | Serves 5**

½ cup fresh parsley, chopped
¼ cup olive oil
4 tablespoons white wine vinegar
2 garlic cloves, minced

1½ pounds (680 g) chicken tenders
Sea salt and ground black pepper, to taste
1 cup sour cream

1. In a food processor or blender, process the parsley, olive oil, vinegar, and garlic until chunky sauce forms. Now, pierce the chicken randomly with a small knife.
2. Pour half of the chimichurri sauce on top, cover, and refrigerate for 1 hour; discard the chimichurri sauce.
3. Brush the sides and bottom of a baking pan with nonstick cooking spray. Arrange the chicken tenders in the baking pan.
4. Then, season your chicken with salt and black pepper to taste. Pour in the sour cream and bake in the preheated oven at 370°F (188°C) for 35 minutes or until cooked through.
5. Serve with the remaining chimichurri sauce. Bon appétit!

**Per Serving**

calories: 316 | fat: 29.8g | protein: 29.4g
carbs: 4.0g | net carbs: 3.8g | fiber: 0.2g

## Chicken Puttanesca

**Prep time: 15 minutes | Cook time: 20 minutes | Serves 5**

2 tablespoons olive oil
1 bell pepper, chopped
1 red onion, chopped
1 teaspoon garlic, minced
1½ pounds (680 g) chicken wings, boneless

2 cups tomato sauce
1 tablespoon capers
¼ teaspoon red pepper, crushed
¼ cup Parmesan cheese, preferably freshly grated
2 basil sprigs, chopped

1. Heat the olive oil in a non-stick skillet over a moderate flame. Once hot, sauté the bell peppers and onions until tender and fragrant.
2. Stir in the garlic and continue to cook an additional 30 seconds.
3. Stir in the chicken wings, tomato sauce, capers, and red pepper; continue to cook for a further 20 minutes or until everything is heated through.
4. Serve garnished with freshly grated Parmesan and basil. Bon appétit!

**Per Serving**

calories: 266 | fat: 11.3g | protein: 32.6g
carbs: 6.4g | net carbs: 5.1g | fiber: 1.3g

## Sri Lankan Curry

**Prep time: 15 minutes | Cook time: 25 minutes | Serves 6**

2 tablespoons coconut oil
½ teaspoon cumin seeds
½ cup shallot, chopped
1 chili pepper, chopped
2 tablespoons curry paste
1 teaspoon ginger-garlic paste

Kosher salt and freshly ground black pepper, to taste
1½ pounds (680 g) chicken tenders, cut into chunks
½ cup coconut milk
½ cup chicken broth
2 tablespoons fresh cilantro, chopped

1. Warm the coconut oil in a large frying pan over a moderate flame. Then, sauté the cumin seeds for 30 seconds or until aromatic.
2. Add in the shallot and chili pepper and continue to sauté for a further 3 minutes or until tender and fragrant.
3. Add in the curry paste, ginger-garlic paste, salt, black pepper, and chicken tenders. Cook for 3 minutes, stirring periodically. Then, pour in the coconut milk and chicken broth; bring to a boil.
4. Immediately turn the heat to simmer and continue cooking for a further for 22 minutes. Serve warm garnished with fresh cilantro. Enjoy!

**Per Serving**

calories: 371 | fat: 16.0g | protein: 51.0g
carbs: 0.8g | net carbs: 0.6g | fiber: 0.2g

## Bacon and Chicken Frittata

**Prep time: 15 minutes | Cook time: 25 minutes | Serves 4**

4 slices of bacon
1 pound (454 g) chicken breasts, cut into small strips
1 red bell pepper, chopped
1 onion, chopped
2 garlic cloves, minced
6 eggs

½ cup yogurt
½ teaspoon hot paprika
Sea salt and freshly ground black pepper
½ teaspoon oregano
½ teaspoon rosemary
1 cup Asiago cheese, shredded

1. In an oven-safe pan, cook the bacon until crisp, crumbling with a fork; reserve. Then, in the same pan, cook the chicken breasts for 5 to 6 minutes or until no longer pink; reserve.
2. Then, sauté the pepper, onion, and garlic in the bacon grease. Cook until they have softened.
3. In a mixing bowl, whisk the eggs with the yogurt, paprika, salt, black pepper, oregano, and rosemary. Add the bacon and chicken back to the pan.
4. Pour the egg mixture over the chicken mixture. Top with Asiago cheese. Bake in the preheated oven at 390ºF (199ºC) for 20 minutes until the eggs are puffed and opaque.
5. You can cut a slit in the center of the frittata to check the doneness. Bon appétit!

**Per Serving**

calories: 485 | fat: 31.7g | protein: 41.8g
carbs: 5.7g | net carbs: 4.9g | fiber: 0.8g

## Buffalo Chicken Bake

**Prep time: 10 minutes | Cook time: 55 minutes | Serves 6**

1 tablespoon olive oil
2 pounds (907 g) chicken drumettes
**Sauce:**

| | |
|---|---|
| ½ cup melted butter | ¼ teaspoon granulated garlic |
| ½ cup hot sauce | |
| 2 tablespoons white vinegar | Sea salt and ground black, to season |

1. Start by preheating your oven to 320ºF (160ºC). Brush a baking pan with olive oil. Arrange the chicken drumettes in the greased pan.
2. Prepare the sauce by whisking the melted butter, hot sauce, white vinegar, garlic, salt and black pepper until well combined.
3. Pour the sauce over the chicken drumettes. Bake for 55 minutes, flipping the chicken drumettes once or twice.
4. Taste, adjust the seasonings and serve warm.

**Per Serving**

calories: 289 | fat: 20.5g | protein: 23.4g
carbs: 1.3g | net carbs: 1.0g | fiber: 0.3g

## Italian Parmesan Turkey Fillets

**Prep time: 10 minutes | Cook time: 15 minutes | Serves 5**

| | |
|---|---|
| 2 eggs | to taste |
| 1 cup sour cream | ½ cup grated Parmesan cheese |
| 1 teaspoon Italian seasoning blend | |
| Kosher salt and ground black pepper, | 2 pounds (907 g) turkey fillets |

1. In a mixing bowl, whisk the eggs until frothy and light. Stir in the sour cream and continue whisking until well combined.
2. In another bowl, mix the Italian seasoning blend with the salt, black pepper, and Parmesan cheese; mix to combine well.
3. Dip the turkey fillets into the egg mixture; then, press them into the Parmesan mixture.
4. Cook in the greased frying pan until browned on all sides. Bon appétit!

**Per Serving**

calories: 336 | fat: 12.7g | protein: 47.5g
carbs: 5.2g | net carbs: 5.0g | fiber: 0.2g

## Tarragon Chicken and Mushrooms

**Prep time: 10 minutes | Cook time: 20 minutes | Serves 6**

| | |
|---|---|
| 2 cups sliced mushrooms | mustard |
| ½ teaspoon onion powder | 1 tablespoon tarragon, chopped |
| ½ teaspoon garlic powder | 2 pounds (907 g) chicken thighs |
| ¼ cup butter | Salt and black pepper, to taste |
| 1 teaspoon Dijon | |

1. Season the thighs with salt, pepper, garlic, and onion powder. Melt the butter in a skillet, and cook the chicken until browned; set aside. Add mushrooms to the same fat and cook for about 5 minutes.
2. Stir in Dijon mustard and ½ cup of water. Return the chicken to the skillet. Season to taste with salt and pepper, reduce the heat and cover, and let simmer for 15 minutes. Stir in tarragon. Serve warm.

**Per Serving**

calories: 405 | fat: 33g | protein: 25g
carbs: 1g | net carbs: 1g | fiber: 0g

## Chicken Breast with Steamed Broccoli

**Prep time: 10 minutes | Cook time: 15 minutes | Serves 6**

| | |
|---|---|
| 1 tablespoon smoked paprika | powder |
| Salt and black pepper to taste | 1 tablespoon olive oil |
| | 6 chicken breasts |
| 1 teaspoon garlic | 1 head broccoli, cut into florets |

1. Place broccoli florets onto the steamer basket over the boiling water; steam approximately 8 minutes or until crisp-tender. Set aside. Grease grill grate with cooking spray and preheat to 400ºF (205ºC).
2. Combine paprika, salt, black pepper, and garlic powder in a bowl. Brush chicken with olive oil and sprinkle spice mixture over and massage with hands.
3. Grill chicken for 7 minutes per side until well-cooked, and plate. Serve warm with steamed broccoli.

**Per Serving**

calories: 42 | fat: 18g | protein: 50g
carbs: 2g | net carbs: 2g | fiber: 0g

## Whole Chicken with Leek and Mushrooms

**Prep time: 15 minutes | Cook time: 45 minutes | Serves 4**

1 tablespoon olive oil
1½ pounds (680 g) whole chicken, skinless and boneless
2 cups button mushrooms, sliced
1 serrano pepper, sliced
1 medium-sized leek, chopped
1 teaspoon ginger-garlic paste
¼ cup dry red wine
Sea salt and ground black pepper, to season
2 tablespoons capers
1 cup tomato paste

1. Heat the olive oil in a frying pan over a moderate flame. Fry the chicken until golden brown on all sides or about 10 minutes; set aside.
2. Then, cook the mushrooms, serrano pepper, and leek in the pan drippings. Cook until they have softened or about 6 minutes.
3. After that, stir in the ginger-garlic paste and fry for a further 30 seconds. Add a splash of red wine to deglaze the pan.
4. Add the chicken back to the frying pan. Add in salt, black pepper, capers, and tomato paste; stir to combine well and bring to a rapid boil.
5. Turn the heat to medium-low and let it cook for 30 minutes more or until everything is heated through. Serve immediately.

**Per Serving**

calories: 425 | fat: 29.1g | protein: 33.4g
carbs: 5.6g | net carbs: 4.4g | fiber: 1.2g

## Mexican Cotija Chicken Breasts

**Prep time: 15 minutes | Cook time: 20 minutes | Serves 6**

2 tablespoons olive oil
1½ pounds (680 g) chicken breasts, cut into bite-sized cubes
1 teaspoon garlic, finely chopped
1 Mexican chili pepper, finely chopped
2 ripe tomatoes, puréed
Sea salt and black pepper, to taste
½ teaspoon paprika
½ teaspoon Mexican oregano
4 ounces (113 g) sour cream
6 ounces (170 g) Cotija cheese, crumbled
2 tablespoons fresh chives, chopped

1. Heat the olive oil in a frying pan over a medium-high flame. Now, brown the chicken breasts for 4 to 5 minutes per side.
2. Then, sauté the garlic and pepper until they are tender and aromatic.
3. Fold in the puréed tomatoes and cook for a further 4 minutes. Season with salt, black pepper, paprika, and Mexican oregano. Transfer the chicken with the sauce to a lightly greased casserole dish.
4. Top with the sour cream and Cotija cheese. Bake in the preheated oven for 12 to 13 minutes or until thoroughly cooked.
5. Garnish with fresh chives and serve warm.

**Per Serving**

calories: 355 | fat: 23.1g | protein: 29.2g
carbs: 5.9g | net carbs: 5.4g | fiber: 0.5g

## Chili Chicken Breast

**Prep time: 10 minutes | Cook time: 25 minutes | Serves 4**

4 chicken breasts, skinless, boneless, cubed
1 tablespoon butter
½ onion, chopped
2 cups chicken broth
8 ounces (227 g) diced tomatoes
2 ounces (57 g) tomato puree
1 tablespoon chili powder
1 tablespoon cumin
½ tablespoon garlic powder
1 Serrano pepper, minced
½ cup shredded cheddar cheese
Salt and black pepper, to taste

1. Set a large pan over medium-high heat and add the chicken. Cover with water and bring to a boil. Cook until no longer pink, for 10 minutes. Transfer the chicken to a flat surface to shred with forks.
2. In a large pot, pour in the butter and set over medium heat. Sauté onion until transparent for 5 minutes. Stir in the chicken, tomatoes, cumin, serrano pepper, garlic powder, tomato puree, broth, and chili powder. Adjust the seasoning and let the mixture boil. Reduce heat to simmer for about 10 minutes. Divide chili among bowls and top with shredded cheese to serve.

**Per Serving**

calories: 421 | fat: 21g | protein: 45g
carbs: 7g | net carbs: 5g | fiber: 2g

## Herbed Chicken Legs

**Prep time: 10 minutes | Cook time: 15 minutes | Serves 5**

2 tablespoons butter, softened at room temperature
5 chicken legs, skinless
2 scallions, chopped
1 teaspoon fresh basil, chopped
1 teaspoon fresh

thyme, chopped
1 garlic clove, minced
½ teaspoon black peppercorns, freshly cracked
1 cup vegetable broth
½ teaspoon paprika
Sea salt, to taste

1. Melt 1 tablespoon of butter in a frying pan over a medium-high flame. Once hot, brown the chicken legs for 4 to 5 minutes per side.
2. Add in the scallions, basil, thyme, and garlic; continue to sauté about a minute or so.
3. Add the remaining tablespoon of butter, black peppercorns, broth, and paprika. Bring to a boil and immediately reduce the heat to simmer.
4. Let it simmer for 10 minutes or until everything is cooked through. Season with salt to taste and serve. Bon appétit!

**Per Serving**

calories: 371 | fat: 15.9g | protein: 51.0g
carbs: 0.8g | net carbs: 0.5g | fiber: 0.3g

## Hungarian Chicken Paprikash

**Prep time: 15 minutes | Cook time: 30 minutes | Serves 5**

2 tablespoons olive oil
2 pounds (907 g) chicken drumsticks
½ cup leeks, sliced
1 bell pepper, deseeded and chopped
1 Hungarian wax pepper, chopped
3 garlic cloves,

chopped
1 cup tomato purée
4 cups vegetable broth
Sea salt and freshly ground black pepper, to taste
1 tablespoon Hungarian paprika
1 bay laurel

1. Heat the olive oil in a soup pot over a moderate flame. Once hot, brown the chicken drumsticks for about 7 minutes or until no longer pink; shred the meat and reserve.
2. Then, cook the leeks and peppers in the pan drippings for about 5 minutes or until they have softened.

3. Now, add in the garlic and cook for a minute or so. Add in the tomato purée, vegetable broth, salt, black pepper, Hungarian paprika, and bay laurel.
4. Stir in the reserved chicken and bring to a boil; turn the heat to medium-low, cover, and let it simmer for 22 minutes.
5. Ladle into individual bowls and serve. Enjoy!

**Per Serving**

calories: 359 | fat: 22.1g | protein: 33.2g
carbs: 4.5g | net carbs: 3.9g | fiber: 0.6g

## Veg Stuffed Chicken with Spiralized Cucumber

**Prep time: 20 minutes | Cook time: 55 minutes | Serves 4**

**Chicken:**
2 tablespoons butter
4 chicken breasts
1 cup baby spinach
1 carrot, shredded
1 tomato, chopped
**Salad:**
2 cucumbers, spiralized
2 tablespoons olive oil

¼ cup goat cheese
Salt and black pepper, to taste
1 teaspoon dried oregano

1 tablespoon rice vinegar

1. Preheat oven to 390ºF (199ºC) and grease a baking dish with cooking spray.
2. Place a pan over medium heat. Melt half of the butter and sauté spinach, carrot, and tomato until tender, for about 5 minutes. Season with salt and pepper. Transfer to a medium bowl and let cool for 10 minutes.
3. Add in the goat cheese and oregano, stir and set to one side. Cut the chicken breasts lengthwise and stuff with the cheese mixture and set into the baking dish.
4. On top, put the remaining butter and bake until cooked through for 20-30 minutes.
5. Arrange the cucumbers on a serving platter, season with salt, black pepper, olive oil, and vinegar. Top with the chicken and pour over the sauce.

**Per Serving**

calories: 618 | fat: 46.4g | protein: 40.6g
carbs: 9.4g | net carbs: 7.6g | fiber: 1.8g

## Roasted Whole Chicken with Black Olives

**Prep time: 10 minutes | Cook time: 1 hour 15 minutes | Serves 5**

2 pounds (907 g) whole chicken
1 teaspoon paprika
1 teaspoon lemon zest, slivered
Kosher salt and freshly ground black pepper,

to taste
1 cup oil-cured black olives, pitted
4 cloves garlic
1 bunch fresh thyme, leaves picked

1. Begin by preheating your oven to 360°F (182°C). Then, spritz the sides and bottom of a baking dish with nonstick cooking oil.
2. Sprinkle the chicken with paprika, lemon zest, salt, and black pepper. Bake for 60 minutes.
3. Scatter black olives, garlic, and thyme around the chicken and bake an additional 10 to 13 minutes; a meat thermometer should read 180°F (82°C). Bon appétit!

**Per Serving**

calories: 236 | fat: 7.4g | protein: 37.1g
carbs: 2.6g | net carbs: 1.6g | fiber: 1.0g

## Bacon Fat Browned Chicken

**Prep time: 15 minutes | Cook time: 7 to 8 hours | Serves 8**

3 tablespoons coconut oil, divided
¼ pound (113 g) bacon, diced
2 pounds (907 g) chicken (breasts, thighs, drumsticks)
2 cups quartered

button mushrooms
1 sweet onion, diced
1 tablespoon minced garlic
½ cup chicken broth
2 teaspoons chopped thyme
1 cup coconut cream

1. Lightly grease the insert of the slow cooker with 1 tablespoon of the coconut oil.
2. In a large skillet over medium-high heat, heat the remaining 2 tablespoons of the coconut oil.
3. Add the bacon and cook until it is crispy, about 5 minutes. Using a slotted spoon, transfer the bacon to a plate and set aside.
4. Add the chicken to the skillet and brown for 5 minutes, turning once.
5. Transfer the chicken and bacon to the insert and add the mushrooms, onion, garlic, broth, and thyme.

6. Cover and cook on low for 7 to 8 hours.
7. Stir in the coconut cream and serve.

**Per Serving**

calories: 406 | fat: 34g | protein: 22g
carbs: 5g | net carbs: 3g | fiber: 2g

## Chicken Thighs and Chorizo Sausages

**Prep time: 20 minutes | Cook time: 45 minutes | Serves 4**

½ cup mushrooms, chopped
1 pound (454 g) chorizo sausages, chopped
1 tablespoon avocado oil
4 cherry peppers, chopped
1 red bell pepper, seeded, chopped
1 onion, peeled and sliced
1 tablespoon garlic,

minced
2 cups tomatoes, chopped
4 chicken thighs
Salt and black pepper, to taste
½ cup chicken stock
1 teaspoon turmeric
1 tablespoon vinegar
1 teaspoon dried oregano
Fresh parsley, chopped, for serving

1. Set a pan over medium heat and warm half of the avocado oil, stir in the chorizo sausages, and cook for 5 to 6 minutes until browned; remove to a bowl.
2. Heat the rest of the oil, place in the chicken thighs, and apply pepper and salt for seasoning. Cook each side for 3 minutes and set aside on a bowl.
3. In the same pan, add the onion, bell pepper, cherry peppers, and mushrooms, and cook for 4 minutes. Stir in the garlic and cook for 2 minutes.
4. Pour in the stock, turmeric, salt, tomatoes, pepper, vinegar, and oregano. Stir in the chorizo sausages and chicken, place everything to the oven at 400°F (205°C), and bake for 30 minutes. Ladle into serving bowls and garnish with chopped parsley to serve.

**Per Serving**

calories: 415 | fat: 33g | protein: 25g
carbs: 11g | net carbs: 4g | fiber: 7g

## Cream Cheese Chicken and Zucchini

**Prep time: 15 minutes | Cook time: 35 minutes | Serves 6**

| | |
|---|---|
| 2 pound (907 g) chicken breasts, cubed | ½ teaspoon black pepper |
| 1 tablespoon butter | 8 ounces (227 g) cream cheese, softened |
| 1 cup green bell peppers, sliced | ½ cup mayonnaise |
| 1 cup yellow onions, sliced | 1 tablespoon Worcestershire sauce (sugar-free) |
| 1 zucchini, cubed | 2 cups cheddar cheese, shredded |
| 2 garlic cloves, divided | |
| 1 teaspoon Italian seasoning | |
| ½ teaspoon salt | |

1. Set oven to 370ºF (188ºC) and grease and line a baking dish.
2. Set a pan over medium heat. Place in the butter and let melt, then add in the chicken. Cook until lightly browned, about 5 minutes. Place in onions, zucchini, black pepper, garlic, bell peppers, salt, and 1 teaspoon of Italian seasoning. Cook until tender and set aside.
3. In a bowl, mix cream cheese, garlic, remaining seasoning, mayonnaise, and Worcestershire sauce. Stir in meat and sauteed vegetables. Place the mixture into the prepared baking dish, sprinkle with the shredded cheddar cheese and insert into the oven. Cook until browned for 30 minutes.
4. Serve immediately.

**Per Serving**

calories: 489 | fat: 37g | protein: 21g
carbs: 6g | net carbs: 5g | fiber: 1g

## Chicken Breast with Anchovy Tapenade

**Prep time: 10 minutes | Cook time: 10 minutes | Serves 2**

| | |
|---|---|
| 1 chicken breast, cut into 4 pieces | anchovy fillets, rinsed |
| 1 tablespoon coconut oil | 1 garlic clove, crushed |
| 3 garlic cloves, crushed | Salt and ground black pepper, to taste |
| For the tapenade: | 1 tablespoon olive oil |
| 1 cup black olives, pitted | ¼ cup fresh basil, chopped |
| 1 ounce (28 g) | 1 tablespoon lemon juice |

1. Using a food processor, combine the olives, salt, olive oil, basil, lemon juice, anchovy, and black pepper, blend well. Set a pan over medium heat and warm coconut oil, stir in the garlic, and sauté for 2 minutes.
2. Place in the chicken pieces and cook each side for 4 minutes. Split the chicken among plates and apply a topping of the anchovy tapenade.
3. Serve immediately.

**Per Serving**

calories: 155 | fat: 13g | protein: 25g
carbs: 3g | net carbs: 3g | fiber: 0g

## Chicken Fingers

**Prep time: 15 minutes | Cook time: 30 minutes | Serves 8**

| | |
|---|---|
| 1½ pounds (680 g) chicken breasts, skinless, boneless, cubed | parsley |
| | ½ teaspoon dried basil |
| | 1 tablespoon avocado oil |
| Salt and ground black pepper, to taste | 4 cups spaghetti squash, cooked |
| 1 egg | 6 ounces (170 g) gruyere cheese, shredded |
| 1 cup almond flour | |
| ¼ cup Parmesan cheese, grated | 1½ cups tomato purée |
| ½ teaspoon garlic powder | Fresh basil, chopped, for serving |
| 1½ teaspoon dried | |

1. In a bowl, combine the almond flour with 1 teaspoon parsley, Parmesan cheese, black pepper, garlic powder, and salt. In a separate bowl, combine the egg with black pepper and salt. Dip the chicken in the egg, and then in almond flour mixture.
2. Set a pan over medium heat and warm 3 tablespoons avocado oil, add in the chicken, cook until golden, and remove to paper towels. In a bowl, combine the spaghetti squash with salt, dried basil, rest of the parsley, 1 tablespoon avocado oil, and black pepper.
3. Sprinkle this into a baking dish, top with the chicken pieces, followed by the tomato purée. Scatter shredded gruyere cheese on top, and bake for 30 minutes at 360ºF (182ºC). Remove, and sprinkle with fresh basil before serving.

**Per Serving**

calories: 415 | fat: 36g | protein: 28g
carbs: 7g | net carbs: 5g | fiber: 2g

## Chicken and Shallot Mull

**Prep time: 10 minutes | Cook time: 30 minutes | Serves 4**

2 tablespoons butter
1 pound (454 g) chicken thighs, boneless and skinless
½ cup shallots, chopped
1 celery stalk, chopped
4 cups chicken broth
Sea salt and ground black pepper, to your liking
½ teaspoon cayenne pepper
½ teaspoon mustard seeds
½ teaspoon celery seeds
1 cup milk
1 tablespoon fresh cilantro, chopped

1. Melt the butter in a heavy-bottomed pot over a moderate flame. Now, brown the chicken until no longer pink or about 6 minutes.
2. Add in the shallots, celery, broth, salt, black pepper, cayenne pepper, mustard seeds, and celery seeds; stir to combine.
3. Turn the heat to simmer and let it cook for 25 minutes longer or until heated through.
4. Pour in the milk, stir and ladle into soup bowls. Garnish with fresh cilantro and serve warm. Bon appétit!

**Per Serving**

calories: 342 | fat: 26.6g | protein: 20.8g
carbs: 3.7g | net carbs: 3.4g | fiber: 0.3g

## Turkey Chili

**Prep time: 15 minutes | Cook time: 35 minutes | Serves 5**

1 pound (454 g) ground turkey
½ pound (227 g) ground pork
4 tablespoons red wine
1 chili pepper, deveined and minced
2 medium Italian peppers, deveined and sliced
1 onion, diced
2 cloves garlic, minced
3 cups vegetable broth
1 vine-ripe tomato, crushed
½ teaspoon cayenne pepper
Sea salt and ground black pepper, to your liking
5 ounces (142 g) Monterey Jack cheese, shredded

1. Preheat a saucepan over medium-high heat. Then, brown the ground meat for 5 minutes, crumbling with a wide spatula.
2. Add in a splash of red wine to scrape up the browned bits that stick to the bottom of the saucepan.

3. Add in the remaining ingredients, except for the Monterey Jack cheese; stir to combine well. When the mixture starts to boil, turn the heat to a medium-low. Let it cook, partially covered, for 30 minutes.
4. Serve with the shredded Monterey Jack cheese. Bon appétit!

**Per Serving**

calories: 391 | fat: 25.1g | protein: 33.6g
carbs: 4.6g | net carbs: 3.4g | fiber: 1.2g

## Bacon on Cheesy Chicken Breast

**Prep time: 10 minutes | Cook time: 20 minutes | Serves 4**

4 bacon strips
4 chicken breasts
3 green onions, chopped
4 ounces (113 g) ranch dressing
1 ounce coconut
aminos
1 tablespoon coconut oil
4 ounces (113 g) Monterey Jack cheese, grated

1. Set a pan over high heat and warm the oil. Place in the chicken breasts, cook for 7 minutes, then flip to the other side; cook for an additional 7 minutes. Set another pan over medium heat, place in the bacon, cook until crispy, remove to paper towels, drain the grease, and crumble.
2. Add the chicken breast to a baking dish. Place the green onions, coconut aminos, cheese, and crumbled bacon on top, set in an oven, turn on the broiler, and cook for 5 minutes at high temperature. Split among serving plates and serve.

**Per Serving**

calories: 423 | fat: 21g | protein: 34g
carbs: 4g | net carbs: 3g | fiber: 1g

## Chicken and Mushroom Ramen

**Prep time: 15 minutes | Cook time: 30 minutes | Serves 6**

| | |
|---|---|
| 1 tablespoon peanut oil | enokitake or enoki mushrooms |
| 1 pound (454 g) chicken thigs | 4 garlic cloves, chopped |
| 6 cups water | 2 tablespoons sake |
| 1 dashi pack | 1 tablespoon fresh chives, minced |
| 4 ounces (113 g) | |

1. Heat the peanut oil in a stockpot over medium-high heat. Then, brown the chicken thighs for 4 to 5 minutes per side.
2. Then, add the water, dashi, enoki mushrooms, and garlic to the pot. When the soup reaches boiling, turn the heat to a simmer. Let it cook, partially covered, for 28 minutes.
3. Shred the chicken, discarding the bones and add it back to the pot. Add in the sake and stir to combine.
4. Ladle into soup bowls and garnish with minced chives. Enjoy!

**Per Serving**

calories: 200 | fat: 13.6g | protein: 14.6g
carbs: 2.3g | net carbs: 1.8g | fiber: 0.5g

## Traditional Chicken Stroganoff

**Prep time: 10 minutes | Cook time: 4 hours | Serves 4**

| | |
|---|---|
| 2 garlic cloves, minced | chicken breasts |
| 8 ounces (227 g) mushrooms, chopped | 1½ teaspoon dried thyme |
| ¼ teaspoon celery seeds, ground | 1 tablespoon fresh parsley, chopped |
| 1 cup chicken stock | Salt and black pepper, to taste |
| 1 cup sour cream | 4 zucchinis, spiralized |
| 1 cup leeks, chopped | |
| 1 pound (454 g) | |

1. Place the chicken in a slow cooker. Place in the salt, leeks, sour cream, half of the parsley, celery seeds, garlic, black pepper, mushrooms, stock, and thyme. Cook on high for 4 hours while covered.
2. Uncover the pot and add the rest of the parsley. Heat a pan with water over medium heat, place in some salt, bring to a boil, stir in the zucchini pasta, cook for 1 minute, and drain.

3. Place in serving bowls, top with the chicken mixture, and serve.

**Per Serving**

calories: 365 | fat: 22g | protein: 26g
carbs: 11g | net carbs: 4g | fiber: 7g

## Chicken Skewers and Celery Fries

**Prep time: 10 minutes | Cook time: 40 minutes | Serves 4**

| | |
|---|---|
| 2 chicken breasts | black pepper |
| ½ teaspoon salt | 1 tablespoon olive oil |
| ¼ teaspoon ground | ¼ cup chicken broth |

**For the Fries:**

| | |
|---|---|
| 1 pound (454 g) celery root | ½ teaspoon salt |
| 1 tablespoon olive oil | ¼ teaspoon ground black pepper |

1. Set oven to 400°F (205°C). Grease and line a baking sheet. In a bowl, mix oil, spices and the chicken; set in the fridge for 10 minutes while covered. Peel and chop celery root to form fry shapes and place into a separate bowl. Apply oil to coat and add pepper and salt for seasoning. Arrange to the baking tray in an even layer and bake for 10 minutes.
2. Take the chicken from the refrigerator and thread onto the skewers. Place over the celery, pour in the chicken broth, then set in the oven for 30 minutes. Serve with lemon wedges.

**Per Serving**

calories: 579 | fat: 43g | protein: 39g
carbs: 8g | net carbs: 6g | fiber: 2g

# Chapter 9 Beef and Lamb

## Double Cheese Stuffed Venison

**Prep time: 10 minutes | Cook time: 25 minutes | Serves 8**

2 pounds (907 g) venison tenderloin
2 garlic cloves, minced
2 tablespoons chopped almonds
½ cup Gorgonzola cheese
½ cup Feta cheese
1 teaspoon chopped onion
½ teaspoon salt

1. Preheat your grill to medium. Slice the tenderloin lengthwise to make a pocket for the filling.Combine the rest of the ingredients in a bowl. Stuff the tenderloin with the filling.
2. Shut the meat with skewers and grill for as long as it takes to reach your desired density.

**Per Serving**

calories: 196 | fat: 11.9g | protein: 25.1g carbs: 2.1g | net carbs: 1.6g | fiber: 0.5g

## Veal with Ham and Sauerkraut

**Prep time: 15 minutes | Cook time: 55 minutes | Serves 4**

1 pound (454 g) veal, cut into cubes
18 ounces (510 g) sauerkraut, rinsed and drained
Salt and black pepper, to taste
½ cup ham, chopped
1 onion, chopped
2 garlic cloves, minced
1 tablespoon butter
½ cup Parmesan cheese, grated
½ cup sour cream

1. Heat a pot with the butter over medium heat, add in the onion, and cook for 3 minutes. Stir in garlic, and cook for 1 minute. Place in the veal and ham, and cook until slightly browned. Place in the sauerkraut, and cook until the meat becomes tender, about 30 minutes. Stir in sour cream, pepper, and salt. Top with Parmesan cheese and bake for 20 minutes at 350ºF (180ºC).

**Per Serving**

calories: 431 | fat: 26.9g | protein: 28.6g carbs: 10.1g | net carbs: 5.9g | fiber: 4.2g

## Simple Pesto Beef Chuck Roast

**Prep time: 5 minutes | Cook time: 9 to 10 hours | Serves 8**

1 tablespoon extra-virgin olive oil
2 pounds (907 g) beef chuck roast
¾ cup prepared pesto
½ cup beef broth

1. Lightly grease the insert of the slow cooker with the olive oil.
2. Slather the pesto all over the beef. Place the beef in the insert and pour in the broth.
3. Cover and cook on low for 9 to 10 hours.
4. Serve warm.

**Per Serving**

calories: 529 | fat: 42.9g | protein: 31.9g carbs: 1.9g | net carbs: 1.9g | fiber: 0g

## Sour Cream Beef Carne Asada

**Prep time: 15 minutes | Cook time: 9 to 10 hours | Serves 8**

½ cup extra-virgin olive oil, divided
¼ cup lime juice
2 tablespoons apple cider vinegar
2 teaspoons minced garlic
1½ teaspoons paprika
1 teaspoon ground cumin
1 teaspoon chili powder
¼ teaspoon cayenne pepper
1 sweet onion, cut into eighths
2 pounds (907 g) beef rump roast
1 cup sour cream, for garnish

1. Lightly grease the insert of the slow cooker with 1 tablespoon of the olive oil.
2. In a small bowl, whisk together the remaining olive oil, lime juice, apple cider vinegar, garlic, paprika, cumin, chili powder, and cayenne until well blended.
3. Place the onion in the bottom of the insert and the beef on top of the vegetable. Pour the sauce over the beef.
4. Cover and cook on low for 9 to 10 hours.
5. Shred the beef with a fork.
6. Serve topped with the sour cream.

**Per Serving**

calories: 540 | fat: 43.9g | protein: 30.9g carbs: 2.9g | net carbs: 1.9g | fiber: 1.0g

## Chimichurri Skirt Steak

**Prep time: 10 minutes | Cook time: 10 minutes | Serves 2**

¼ cup soy sauce
½ cup olive oil
Juice of 1 lime
2 tablespoons apple cider vinegar
1 pound (454 g) skirt steak

Pink Himalayan salt
Freshly ground black pepper
2 tablespoons butter
¼ cup chimichurri sauce

1. In a small bowl, mix together the soy sauce, olive oil, lime juice, and apple cider vinegar. Pour into a large zip-top bag, and add the skirt steak. Marinate for as long as possible: at least all day or, ideally, overnight.
2. Dry the steak with a paper towel. Season both sides of the steak with pink Himalayan salt and pepper.
3. In a large skillet over high heat, melt the butter. Add the steak and sear for about 4 minutes on each side, until well browned. Transfer the steak to a chopping board to rest for at least 5 minutes.
4. Slice the skirt steak against the grain. Divide the slices between two plates, top with the chimichurri sauce, and serve.

**Per Serving**

calories: 715 | fat: 45.8g | protein: 69.8g
carbs: 5.9g | net carbs: 4.1g | fiber: 1.8g

## Beef Chuck and Pumpkin Stew

**Prep time: 15 minutes | Cook time: 8 hours | Serves 6**

3 tablespoons extra-virgin olive oil, divided
1 (2-pound / 907-g) beef chuck roast, cut into 1-inch chunks
½ teaspoon salt
¼ teaspoon freshly ground black pepper
2 cups beef broth
1 cup diced tomatoes
¼ cup apple cider vinegar

1½ cups cubed pumpkin, cut into 1-inch chunks
½ sweet onion, chopped
2 teaspoons minced garlic
1 teaspoon dried thyme
1 tablespoon chopped fresh parsley, for garnish

1. Lightly grease the insert of the slow cooker with 1 tablespoon of the olive oil.
2. Lightly season the beef chucks with salt and pepper.
3. In a large skillet over medium-high heat, heat the remaining 2 tablespoons of the olive oil. Add the beef and brown on all sides, about 7 minutes.
4. Transfer the beef to the insert and stir in the broth, tomatoes, apple cider vinegar, pumpkin, onion, garlic, and thyme.
5. Cover and cook on low heat for about 8 hours, until the beef is very tender.
6. Serve topped with the parsley.

**Per Serving**

calories: 460 | fat: 33.9g | protein: 32.0g
carbs: 10.2g | net carbs: 7.3g | fiber: 2.9g

## Coffee Rib-Eye Steaks

**Prep time: 5 minutes | Cook time: 15 minutes | Serves 2**

**Rub:**

1 tablespoon ground coffee
1 tablespoon unsweetened cocoa powder
2 teaspoons kosher

salt
¼ teaspoon cayenne pepper
2 (8-ounce / 227-g) bone-in rib-eye steaks, room temperature

**Balsamic Butter:**

3 tablespoons butter, softened
2 tablespoons balsamic vinegar (no sugar added)

1 teaspoon granulated erythritol
For Garnish (optional): Chopped fresh parsley

1. Preheat a grill to medium heat. Combine the coffee, cocoa powder, salt, and cayenne in a small bowl. Rub the steaks generously with the coffee mixture.
2. Grill the steaks on direct heat for 6 minutes (for medium) to 8 minutes (for medium-well) per side, or until your desired doneness is reached.
3. Remove the steaks from the grill and let rest for 5 minutes. Meanwhile, place the butter, balsamic vinegar, and sweetener in a small bowl and mix with a fork until blended. Serve the steaks with a generous dollop of balsamic butter. Garnish with chopped parsley, if desired.

**Per Serving**

calories: 584 | fat: 44.9g | protein: 52.8g
carbs: 3.9g | net carbs: 2.9g | fiber: 1.0g

## Broccoli and Beef Roast

**Prep time: 10 minutes | Cook time: 4 hours 30 minutes | Serves 2**

1 pound (454 g) beef chuck roast
Pink Himalayan salt
Freshly ground black pepper
½ cup beef broth, plus more if needed
¼ cup soy sauce (or coconut aminos)
1 teaspoon toasted sesame oil
1 (16-ounce / 454-g) bag frozen broccoli

1. With the crock insert in place, preheat the slow cooker to low.
2. On a cutting board, season the chuck roast with pink Himalayan salt and pepper, and slice the roast thin. Put the sliced beef in the slow cooker.
3. In a small bowl, mix together the beef broth, soy sauce, and sesame oil. Pour over the beef.
4. Cover and cook on low for 4 hours.
5. Add the frozen broccoli, and cook for 30 minutes more. If you need more liquid, add additional beef broth.
6. Serve hot.

**Per Serving**

calories: 805 | fat: 48.9g | protein: 73.8g
carbs: 18.1g | net carbs: 11.9g | fiber: 6.2g

## Beef Stuffed Pepper with Avocado Crema

**Prep time: 10 minutes | Cook time: 20 minutes | Serves 2**

1 tablespoon butter
½ pound (227 g) ground beef
Pink Himalayan salt
Freshly ground black
pepper
3 large bell peppers, in different colors
½ cup shredded cheese

**Avocado Crema:**

1 avocado
¼ cup sour cream

1. Preheat the oven to 400ºF (205ºC). Line a baking sheet with aluminum foil or a silicone baking mat.
2. In a large skillet over medium-high heat, melt the butter. When the butter is hot, add the ground beef and season with pink Himalayan salt and pepper. Stir occasionally with a wooden spoon, breaking up the beef chunks. Continue cooking until the beef is done, 7 to 10 minutes.
3. Meanwhile, cut off the top of each pepper, slice it in half, and pull out the seeds and ribs.
4. Place the bell peppers on the prepared baking sheet.
5. Spoon the ground beef into the peppers, sprinkle the cheese on top of each, and bake for 10 minutes.
6. Meanwhile, in a medium bowl, mix the avocado and sour cream to create an avocado crema. Mix until smooth.
7. When the peppers and beef are done baking, divide them between two plates, top each with the avocado crema, and serve.

**Per Serving**

calories: 705 | fat: 51.9g | protein: 40.1g
carbs: 21.9g | net carbs: 12.8g | fiber: 9.1g

## Barbacoa Beef with Green Jalapeño

**Prep time: 10 minutes | Cook time: 8 hours | Serves 2**

1 pound (454 g) beef chuck roast
Pink Himalayan salt
Freshly ground black pepper
4 chipotle peppers in adobo sauce
1 (6-ounce / 170-g) can green jalapeño chiles
2 tablespoons apple cider vinegar
½ cup beef broth

1. With the crock insert in place, preheat the slow cooker to low.
2. Season the beef chuck roast on both sides with pink Himalayan salt and pepper. Put the roast in the slow cooker.
3. In a food processor (or blender), combine the chipotle peppers and their adobo sauce, jalapeños, and apple cider vinegar, and pulse until smooth. Add the beef broth, and pulse a few more times. Pour the chile mixture over the top of the roast.
4. Cover and cook on low for 8 hours.
5. Transfer the beef to a cutting board, and use two forks to shred the meat.
6. Serve hot.

**Per Serving**

calories: 720 | fat: 45.8g | protein: 65.9g
carbs: 6.9g | net carbs: 2.1g | fiber: 4.8g

## Lamb Shanks with Wild Mushrooms

**Prep time: 15 minutes | Cook time: 7 to 8 hours | Serves 6**

3 tablespoons extra-virgin olive oil, divided
2 pounds (907 g) lamb shanks
½ pound (227 g) wild mushrooms, sliced
1 leek, thoroughly cleaned and chopped
2 celery stalks, chopped
1 carrot, diced
1 tablespoon minced garlic
1 (15-ounce / 425-g) can crushed tomatoes
½ cup beef broth
2 tablespoons apple cider vinegar
1 teaspoon dried rosemary
½ cup sour cream, for garnish

1. Lightly grease the insert of the slow cooker with 1 tablespoon of the olive oil.
2. In a large skillet over medium-high heat, heat the remaining 2 tablespoons of the olive oil. Add the lamb; brown for 6 minutes, turning once; and transfer to the insert.
3. In the skillet, sauté the mushrooms, leek, celery, carrot, and garlic for 5 minutes.
4. Transfer the vegetables to the insert along with the tomatoes, broth, apple cider vinegar, and rosemary.
5. Cover and cook on low for 7 to 8 hours.
6. Serve topped with the sour cream.

**Per Serving**

calories: 474 | fat: 35.9g | protein: 30.9g
carbs: 11.1g | net carbs: 5.0g | fiber: 6.1g

## Tunisian Lamb and Pumpkin Ragout

**Prep time: 15 minutes | Cook time: 8 hours | Serves 6**

¼ cup extra-virgin olive oil
1½ pounds (680 g) lamb shoulder, cut into 1-inch chunks
1 sweet onion, chopped
1 tablespoon minced garlic
4 cups pumpkin, cut into 1-inch pieces
2 carrots, diced
1 (14.5-ounce / 411-g) can diced tomatoes
3 cups beef broth
2 tablespoons ras el hanout
1 teaspoon hot chili powder
1 teaspoon salt
1 cup Greek yogurt

1. Lightly grease the slow cooker insert with 1 tablespoon olive oil.
2. Place a large skillet over medium–high heat and add the remaining oil.
3. Brown the lamb for 6 minutes, then add the onion and garlic.
4. Sauté 3 minutes more, then transfer the lamb and vegetables to the insert.
5. Add the pumpkin, carrots, tomatoes, broth, ras el hanout, chili powder, and salt to the insert and stir to combine.
6. Cover and cook on low for 8 hours
7. Serve topped with yogurt.

**Per Serving**

calories: 450 | fat: 34.9g | protein: 22.1g
carbs: 11.9g | net carbs: 8.8g | fiber: 3.1g

## Sauerbraten

**Prep time: 15 minutes | Cook time: 9 to 10 hours | Serves 6**

3 tablespoons extra-virgin olive oil, divided
2 pounds (907 g) beef brisket
Salt, for seasoning
Freshly ground black pepper, for seasoning
1 sweet onion, cut into eighths
1 carrot, cut into chunks
2 celery stalks, cut into chunks
¾ cup beef broth
½ cup german-style mustard
¼ cup apple cider vinegar
½ teaspoon ground cloves
2 bay leaves

1. Lightly grease the insert of the slow cooker with 1 tablespoon of the olive oil.
2. In a large skillet over medium-high heat, heat the remaining 2 tablespoons of the olive oil.
3. Season the beef with salt and pepper. Add the beef to the skillet and brown on all sides for 6 minutes.
4. Place the onion, carrot, and celery in the bottom of the insert and the beef on top of the vegetables.
5. In a small bowl, whisk together the broth, mustard, apple cider vinegar, and cloves, and add to the beef along with the bay leaves
6. Cover and cook on low for 9 to 10 hours.
7. Remove the bay leaves before serving.

**Per Serving**

calories: 505 | fat: 42.1g | protein: 28.9g
carbs: 3.2g | net carbs: 2.1g | fiber: 1.0g

## Braised Beef Chuck Roast with Tomatoes

**Prep time: 15 minutes | Cook time: 7 to 8 hours | Serves 4**

3 tablespoons extra-virgin olive oil, divided
1 pound (454 g) beef chuck roast, cut into 1-inch cubes
Salt, for seasoning
Freshly ground black pepper, for seasoning
1 (15-ounce / 425-g) can diced tomatoes
2 tablespoons tomato paste
2 teaspoons minced garlic
2 teaspoons dried basil
1 teaspoon dried oregano
½ teaspoon whole black peppercorns
1 cup shredded Mozzarella cheese, for garnish
2 tablespoons chopped parsley, for garnish

1. Lightly grease the insert of the slow cooker with 1 tablespoon of the olive oil.
2. In a large skillet over medium-high heat, heat the remaining 2 tablespoons of the olive oil.
3. Season the beef with salt and pepper. Add the beef to the skillet and brown for 7 minutes. Transfer the beef to the insert.
4. In a medium bowl, stir together the tomatoes, tomato paste, garlic, basil, oregano, and peppercorns, and add the tomato mixture to the beef in the insert.
5. Cover and cook on low for 7 to 8 hours.
6. Serve topped with the cheese and parsley.

**Per Serving**

calories: 540 | fat: 42.9g | protein: 29.8g
carbs: 6.9g | net carbs: 4.8g | fiber: 2.1g

## Lamb Roast with Tomatoes

**Prep time: 10 minutes | Cook time: 7 to 8 hours | Serves 6**

1 tablespoon extra-virgin olive oil
2 pounds (907 g) lamb shoulder roast
Salt, for seasoning
Freshly ground black pepper, for seasoning
1 (14.5-ounce / 411-g) can diced tomatoes
1 tablespoon cumin
2 teaspoons minced garlic
1 teaspoon paprika
1 teaspoon chili powder
1 cup sour cream
2 teaspoons chopped fresh parsley, for garnish

1. Lightly grease the insert of the slow cooker with the olive oil.
2. Lightly season the lamb with salt and pepper.
3. Place the lamb in the insert and add the tomatoes, cumin, garlic, paprika, and chili powder.
4. Cover and cook on low for 7 to 8 hours.
5. Stir in the sour cream.
6. Serve topped with the parsley.

**Per Serving**

calories: 524 | fat: 43.1g | protein: 27.9g
carbs: 5.9g | net carbs: 4.9g | fiber: 1.0g

## Hot Beef Tenderloin with Bell Peppers

**Prep time: 15 minutes | Cook time: 9 to 10 hours | Serves 6**

3 tablespoons extra-virgin olive oil, divided
1 pound (454 g) beef tenderloin, cut into 1-inch chunks
½ sweet onion, chopped
2 teaspoons minced garlic
1 red bell pepper, diced
1 yellow bell pepper, diced
2 cups coconut cream
1 cup beef broth
3 tablespoons coconut aminos
1 tablespoon hot sauce
1 scallion, white and green parts, chopped, for garnish
1 tablespoon sesame seeds, for garnish

1. Lightly grease the insert of the slow cooker with 1 tablespoon of the olive oil.
2. In a large skillet over medium-high heat, heat the remaining 2 tablespoons of the olive oil. Add the beef and brown for 6 minutes. Transfer to the insert.
3. In the skillet, sauté the onion and garlic for 3 minutes.
4. Transfer the onion and garlic to the insert along with the red pepper, yellow pepper, coconut cream, broth, coconut aminos, and hot sauce.
5. Cover and cook on low for 9 to 10 hours.
6. Serve topped with the scallion and sesame seeds.

**Per Serving**

calories: 442 | fat: 33.9g | protein: 24.8g
carbs: 10.9g | net carbs: 6.9g | fiber: 4.0g

## Hungarian Beef and Carrot Goulash

**Prep time: 15 minutes | Cook time: 9 to 10 hours | Serves 6**

1 tablespoon extra-virgin olive oil
1½ pounds (680 g) beef, cut into 1-inch pieces
½ sweet onion, chopped
1 carrot, cut into ½-inch-thick slices
1 red bell pepper, diced
2 teaspoons minced garlic
1 cup beef broth
¼ cup tomato paste
1 tablespoon Hungarian paprika
1 bay leaf
1 cup sour cream
2 tablespoons chopped fresh parsley, for garnish

1. Lightly grease the insert of the slow cooker with the olive oil.
2. Add the beef, onion, carrot, red bell pepper, garlic, broth, tomato paste, paprika, and bay leaf to the insert.
3. Cover and cook on low for 9 to 10 hours.
4. Remove the bay leaf and stir in the sour cream.
5. Serve topped with the parsley.

**Per Serving**

calories: 550 | fat: 41.9g | protein: 31.8g
carbs: 7.9g | net carbs: 5.8g | fiber: 2.1g

## Braised Beef Short Ribs with Sweet Onion

**Prep time: 10 minutes | Cook time: 7 to 8 hours | Serves 8**

1 tablespoon extra-virgin olive oil
2 pounds (907 g) beef short ribs
1 sweet onion, sliced
2 cups beef broth
2 tablespoons
granulated erythritol
2 tablespoons balsamic vinegar
2 teaspoons dried thyme
1 teaspoon hot sauce

1. Lightly grease the insert of the slow cooker with the olive oil.
2. Place the ribs, onion, broth, erythritol, balsamic vinegar, thyme, and hot sauce in the insert.
3. Cover and cook on low for 7 to 8 hours.
4. Serve warm.

**Per Serving**

calories: 475 | fat: 42.8g | protein: 17.9g
carbs: 2.0g | net carbs: 2.0g | fiber: 0g

## Paprika Roast Beef Brisket

**Prep time: 10 minutes | Cook time: 1 hour | Serves 4**

2 pounds (907 g) beef brisket
½ teaspoon celery salt
1 teaspoon chili powder
2 tablespoons olive oil
1 tablespoon sweet paprika
Pinch of cayenne
pepper
½ teaspoon garlic powder
½ cup beef stock
3 onions, cut into quarters
¼ teaspoon dry mustard

1. Grease a baking dish with cooking spray and preheat oven to 360ºF (182ºC). In a bowl, combine the paprika with dry mustard, chili powder, salt, garlic powder, cayenne pepper, and celery salt. Rub the meat with this mixture.
2. Set a pan over medium heat and warm olive oil, place in the beef, and sear until brown.
3. Remove to the baking dish. Pour in the stock, add onions and bake for 60 minutes.
4. Set the beef to a cutting board, and leave to cool before slicing. Take the juices from the baking dish and strain, sprinkle over the meat to serve.

**Per Serving**

calories: 601 | fat: 41g | protein: 36g
carbs: 19g | net carbs: 16g | fiber: 3g

## Grilled Lamb Kebabs

**Prep time: 5 minutes | Cook time: 10 minutes | Serves 4**

1 pound (454 g) ground lamb
¼ teaspoon cinnamon
1 egg
1 onion, grated
Salt and ground black pepper, to taste

1. Place all ingredients in a bowl. Mix with your hands to combine well. Divide the meat into 4 pieces. Shape all meat portions around previously-soaked skewers.
2. Preheat grill to medium and grill the kebabs for about 5 minutes per side.

**Per Serving**

calories: 246 | fat: 15g | protein: 25g
carbs: 3g | net carbs: 2g | fiber: 1g

## Hearty Beef and Pork Meatloaf

**Prep time: 15 minutes | Cook time: 7 to 8 hours | Serves 8**

3 tablespoons extra-virgin olive oil, divided
½ sweet onion, chopped
2 teaspoons minced garlic
1 pound (454 g) ground beef
1 pound (454 g) ground pork
½ cup almond flour
½ cup heavy whipping cream
2 eggs
2 teaspoons dried oregano
1 teaspoon dried basil
¼ teaspoon salt
¼ teaspoon freshly ground black pepper
¾ cup tomato purée
1 cup goat cheese

1. Lightly grease the insert of the slow cooker with 1 tablespoon of the olive oil.
2. In a medium skillet over medium-high heat, heat the remaining 2 tablespoons of the olive oil. Add the onion and garlic and sauté until the onion is softened, about 3 minutes.
3. In a large bowl mix the onion mixture, beef, pork, almond flour, heavy cream, eggs, oregano, basil, salt, and pepper until well combined.
4. Transfer the meat mixture to the insert and form into a loaf with about ½-inch gap on the sides. Spread the tomato purée on top of the meatloaf and sprinkle with goat cheese.
5. Cover and cook on low for 7 to 8 hours.
6. Serve warm.

**Per Serving**

calories: 411 | fat: 28.9g | protein: 32.1g
carbs: 4.2g | net carbs: 1.1g | fiber: 3.1g

## Beef and Cauliflower Stuffed Peppers

**Prep time: 25 minutes | Cook time: 6 hours | Serves 4**

3 tablespoons extra-virgin olive oil, divided
1 pound (454 g) ground beef
½ cup finely chopped cauliflower
1 tomato, diced
½ sweet onion, chopped
2 teaspoons minced garlic
2 teaspoons dried oregano
1 teaspoon dried basil
4 bell peppers, tops cut off and seeded
1 cup shredded Cheddar cheese
½ cup chicken broth
1 tablespoon basil, sliced into thin strips, for garnish

1. Lightly grease the insert of the slow cooker with 1 tablespoon of the olive oil.
2. In a large skillet over medium-high heat, heat the remaining 2 tablespoons of the olive oil. Add the beef and sauté until it is cooked through, about 10 minutes.
3. Add the cauliflower, tomato, onion, garlic, oregano, and basil. Sauté for an additional 5 minutes.
4. Spoon the meat mixture into the bell peppers and top with the cheese.
5. Place the peppers in the slow cooker and add the broth to the bottom.
6. Cover and cook on low for 6 hours.
7. Serve warm, topped with the basil.

**Per Serving**

calories: 572 | fat: 41.1g | protein: 38.2g
carbs: 11.9g | net carbs: 8.8g | fiber: 3.1g

## Hot Beef Curry with Bok Choy

**Prep time: 10 minutes | Cook time: 7 to 8 hours | Serves 6**

1 tablespoon extra-virgin olive oil
1 pound (454 g) beef chuck roast, cut into 2-inch pieces
1 sweet onion, chopped
1 red bell pepper, diced
2 cups coconut milk
2 tablespoons hot curry powder
1 tablespoon coconut aminos
2 teaspoons grated fresh ginger
2 teaspoons minced garlic
1 cup shredded baby bok choy

1. Lightly grease the insert of the slow cooker with the olive oil.
2. Add the beef, onion, and bell pepper to the insert.
3. In a medium bowl, whisk together the coconut milk, curry, coconut aminos, ginger, and garlic. Pour the sauce into the insert and stir to combine.
4. Cover and cook on low for 7 to 8 hours.
5. Stir in the bok choy and let stand 15 minutes.
6. Serve warm.

**Per Serving**

calories: 505 | fat: 41.8g | protein: 22.9g
carbs: 9.8g | net carbs: 6.8g | fiber: 3.0g

## Garlicky Lamb Chops with Sage

**Prep time: 10 minutes | Cook time: 1 hour 10 minutes | Serves 6**

6 lamb chops
1 tablespoon sage
1 teaspoon thyme
1 onion, sliced
1 cup water

3 garlic cloves, minced
2 tablespoons olive oil
½ cup white wine
Salt and black pepper, to taste

1. Heat the olive oil in a pan. Add onions and garlic, and cook for 4 minutes, until soft. Rub the sage and thyme over the lamb chops. Cook the lamb for about 3 minutes per side. Set aside. Pour the white wine and water into the pan, bring the mixture to a boil. Cook until the liquid is reduced by half. Add the chops in the pan, reduce the heat, and let simmer for 1 hour.

**Per Serving**

calories: 215 | fat: 13g | protein: 23g
carbs: 3g | net carbs: 2g | fiber: 1g

## Beef and Mushrooms in Red Wine

**Prep time: 15 minutes | Cook time: 10 minutes | Serves 4**

3 tablespoons olive oil
1 tablespoon parsley, chopped
1 cup red wine
1 teaspoon dried thyme
Salt and black pepper, to taste
1 bay leaf
1 cup beef stock

1 pound (454 g) stewed beef, cubed
12 pearl onions, halved
1 tomato, chopped
2 ounces (57 g) pancetta, chopped
2 garlic cloves, minced
½ pound (227 g) mushrooms, chopped

1. Heat a pan over high heat, stir in the pancetta and beef and cook until lightly browned; set aside.
2. Place in the onions, mushrooms, and garlic, and cook for 5 minutes. Pour in the wine to deglaze the bottom of the pan and add beef stock, bay leaf, and tomato. Season with salt, black pepper and thyme. Return the meat and pancetta, cover and cook for 50 minutes.
3. Serve sprinkled with parsley.

**Per Serving**

calories: 468 | fat: 22g | protein: 46g
carbs: 23g | net carbs: 18g | fiber: 5g

## Garlicky Lamb Chops in White Wine

**Prep time: 5 minutes | Cook time: 1 hour 9 minutes | Serves 6**

6 lamb chops
1 tablespoon sage
1 teaspoon thyme
1 onion, sliced
3 garlic cloves, minced

2 tablespoons olive oil
½ cup white wine
Salt and black pepper, to taste

1. Heat the olive oil in a pan. Add onion and garlic and cook for 3 minutes, until soft. Rub the sage and thyme over the lamb chops. Cook the lamb for about 3 minutes per side. Set aside.
2. Pour the white wine and 1 cup of water into the pan, bring the mixture to a boil. Cook until the liquid is reduced by half. Add the chops in the pan, reduce the heat, and let simmer for 1 hour.

**Per Serving**

calories: 392 | fat: 35g | protein: 18g
carbs: 2g | net carbs: 1g | fiber: 1g

## Basil Lamb Shoulder with Pine Nuts

**Prep time: 10 minutes | Cook time: 50 minutes | Serves 4**

1 pound (454 g) rolled lamb shoulder, boneless
1½ cups basil leaves, chopped
5 tablespoons pine

nuts, chopped
½ cup green olives, pitted and chopped
3 cloves garlic, minced
Salt and black pepper, to taste

1. Preheat the oven to 450ºF.
2. In a bowl, combine the basil, pine nuts, olives, and garlic. Season with salt and pepper. Untie the lamb flat onto a chopping board, spread the basil mixture all over, and rub the spices onto the meat.
3. Roll the lamb over the spice mixture and tie it together using 3 to 4 strings of butcher's twine. Place the lamb onto a baking dish and cook in the oven for 10 minutes. Reduce the heat to 350ºF and continue cooking for 40 minutes. When ready, transfer the meat to a cleaned chopping board; let it rest for 10 minutes before slicing. Serve with roasted root vegetables.

**Per Serving**

calories: 391 | fat: 33g | protein: 21g
carbs: 3g | net carbs: 2g | fiber: 1g

## Balsamic Glazed Meatloaf

**Prep time: 20 minutes | Cook time: 1 hour 10 minutes | Serves 6**

1 cup white mushrooms, chopped
2 pounds (907 g) ground beef
2 tablespoons fresh parsley, chopped
2 garlic cloves, minced
1 onion, chopped
1 red bell pepper, seeded and chopped
½ cup almond flour
⅓ cup Parmesan cheese, grated

2 eggs
Salt and black pepper, to taste
1 teaspoon plus 2 cups balsamic vinegar, divided
1 tablespoon Swerve natural sweetener
1 tablespoon coconut aminos
2 tablespoons tomato purée

1. In a bowl, combine the beef with salt, mushrooms, bell pepper, Parmesan cheese, 1 teaspoon vinegar, parsley, garlic, black pepper, onion, almond flour, salt, and eggs. Set this into a loaf pan, and bake for 30 minutes in the oven at 370ºF (188ºC).
2. Meanwhile, heat a small pan over medium heat, add in the 2 cups vinegar, Swerve, coconut aminos, and tomato purée, and cook for 20 minutes. Remove the meatloaf from the oven, spread the glaze over the meatloaf, and bake in the oven for 20 more minutes. Allow the meatloaf to cool, slice, and enjoy.

**Per Serving**

calories: 469 | fat: 22g | protein: 35g
carbs: 14g | net carbs: 12g | fiber: 2g

## Sirloin Steak with Sauce Diane

**Prep time: 15 minutes | Cook time: 18 minutes | Serves 6**

**Sirloin Steak:**

1½ pounds (680 g) sirloin steak
Salt and black pepper,

to taste
1 teaspoon olive oil

**Sauce Diane:**

1 tablespoon olive oil
1 clove garlic, minced
1 cup sliced porcini mushrooms
1 small onion, finely diced
2 tablespoons butter
1 tablespoon Dijon

mustard
2 tablespoons Worcestershire sauce
¼ cup whiskey
2 cups heavy whipping cream
Salt and black pepper, to taste

1. Put a grill pan over high heat and as it heats, brush the steak with oil, sprinkle with salt and pepper, and rub the seasoning into the meat with your hands. Cook the steak in the pan for 4 minutes on each side for medium rare and transfer to a chopping board to rest for 4 minutes before slicing. Reserve the juice.
2. Heat the oil in a frying pan over medium heat and sauté the onion for 3 minutes. Add the butter, garlic, and mushrooms, and cook for 2 minutes.
3. Add the Worcestershire sauce, the reserved juice, and mustard. Stir and cook for 1 minute. Pour in the whiskey and cook further 1 minute until the sauce reduces by half. Swirl the pan and add the cream. Let it simmer to thicken for about 3 minutes. Adjust the taste with salt and pepper. Spoon the sauce over the steaks slices and serve with celeriac mash.

**Per Serving**

calories: 436 | fat: 34g | protein: 25g
carbs: 6g | net carbs: 5g | fiber: 1g

## Italian Beef Roast with Jalapeño

**Prep time: 5 minutes | Cook time: 1 hour 15 minutes | Serves 4**

3½ pounds (1.5 kg) beef roast
4 ounces (113 g) mushrooms, sliced
12 ounces (340 g) beef stock

1 ounce (28 g) onion soup mix
½ cup Italian dressing
2 jalapeño peppers, shredded

1. In a bowl, combine the stock with the Italian dressing and onion soup mixture. Place the beef roast in a pan, stir in the stock mixture, mushrooms, and jalapeños; cover with aluminum foil.
2. Set in the oven at 300ºF, and bake for 1 hour. Take out the foil and continue baking for 15 minutes. Allow the roast to cool, slice, and serve alongside a topping of the gravy.

**Per Serving**

calories: 616 | fat: 26g | protein: 88g
carbs: 9g | net carbs: 8g | fiber: 1g

## Lemon-Mint Grilled Lamb Chops

**Prep time: 10 minutes | Cook time: 6 minutes | Serves 4**

8 lamb chops
2 tablespoons favorite spice mix
2 tablespoons olive oil

**Sauce:**
¼ cup olive oil
1 teaspoon red pepper flakes
2 tablespoons lemon juice
2 tablespoons fresh mint
3 garlic cloves, pressed
2 tablespoons lemon zest
¼ cup parsley
½ teaspoon smoked paprika

1. Rub lamb with olive oil and sprinkle with the seasoning. Preheat the grill to medium. Grill the lamb chops for about 3 minutes per side. Whisk together the sauce ingredients. Serve the lamb with sauce.

**Per Serving**

calories: 488 | fat: 31g | protein: 49g
carbs: 5g | net carbs: 3g | fiber: 2g

## Rack of Lamb with Pepper Butter Sauce

**Prep time: 15 minutes | Cook time: 21 minutes | Serves 4**

1 pound (454 g) rack of lamb
Salt, to taste
3 cloves garlic, minced
$\frac{1}{3}$ cup olive oil
$\frac{1}{3}$ cup white wine
6 sprigs fresh rosemary

**Sauce:**
2 tablespoons olive oil
1 large red bell pepper, seeded and diced
2 cloves garlic, minced
1 cup chicken broth
2 ounces (57 g) butter
Salt and white pepper, to taste

1. Fill a large bowl with water and soak in the lamb for 30 minutes. Drain the meat after and season with salt. Let the lamb sit on a rack to drain completely and then rinse it afterward. Put in a bowl.
2. Mix the olive oil with wine and garlic, and brush the mixture all over the lamb. Drop the rosemary sprigs on it, cover the bowl with plastic wrap, and place in the refrigerator to marinate the meat.
3. The next day, preheat the grill to 450°F and cook the lamb for 6 minutes on both sides. Remove after and let rest for 4 minutes.
4. Heat the olive oil in a frying pan and sauté the garlic and bell pepper for 5 minutes. Pour in the chicken broth and continue cooking the ingredients until the liquid reduces by half, about 10 minutes. Add the butter, salt, and white pepper. Stir to melt the butter and turn the heat off.
5. Use the stick blender to purée the ingredients until very smooth and strain the sauce through a fine mesh into a bowl. Slice the lamb, serve with the sauce, and your favorite red wine.

**Per Serving**

calories: 601 | fat: 56g | protein: 22g
carbs: 5g | net carbs: 4g | fiber: 1g

## Smoked Paprika Beef Ragout

**Prep time: 15 minutes | Cook time: 1 hour 48 minutes | Serves 4**

1 pound (454 g) chuck steak, trimmed and cubed
2 tablespoons olive oil
Salt and black pepper, to taste
2 tablespoons almond flour
1 medium onion, diced
½ cup dry white wine
1 red bell pepper, seeded and diced
2 teaspoons Worcestershire sauce
4 ounces (113 g) tomato purée
3 teaspoons smoked paprika
1 cup beef broth
Thyme leaves, for garnish

1. First, lightly dredge the meat in the almond flour and set aside. Place a large skillet over medium heat, add 1 tablespoon of oil to heat and then sauté the onion, and bell pepper for 3 minutes. Stir in the paprika, and add the remaining olive oil.
2. Add the beef and cook for 10 minutes in total while turning them halfway. Stir in white wine, let it reduce by half, about 3 minutes, and add Worcestershire sauce, tomato purée, and beef broth.
3. Let the mixture boil for 2 minutes, then reduce the heat to lowest and let simmer for 1½ hours; stirring now and then. Adjust the taste and dish the ragout. Serve garnished with thyme leaves.

**Per Serving**

calories: 299 | fat: 17g | protein: 27g
carbs: 11g | net carbs: 9g | fiber: 2g

## Beef Meatball Salad with Dilled Yogurt

**Prep time: 15 minutes | Cook time: 8 minutes | Serves 6**

¼ cup almond milk
2 pounds (907 g) ground beef
1 onion, grated
5 zero carb bread slices, torn
1 egg, whisked
¼ cup fresh parsley, chopped
Salt and black pepper, to taste
2 garlic cloves, minced
¼ cup fresh mint, chopped
2½ teaspoons dried oregano
¼ cup olive oil
1 cup cherry tomatoes, halved
1 cucumber, sliced
1 cup baby spinach
1½ tablespoons lemon juice
1 cup dilled Greek yogurt

1.  Place the torn bread in a bowl, add in the milk, and set aside for 3 minutes. Squeeze the bread, chop, and place into a bowl. Stir in the beef, salt, mint, onion, parsley, pepper, egg, oregano, and garlic.
2.  Form balls out of this mixture and place on a working surface. Set a pan over medium heat and warm half of the oil; fry the meatballs for 8 minutes. Flip occasionally, and set aside in a tray.
3.  In a salad plate, combine the spinach with the cherry tomatoes and cucumber. Mix in the remaining oil, lemon juice, black pepper, and salt. Spread dilled yogurt over, and top with meatballs to serve.

**Per Serving**

calories: 568 | fat: 41g | protein: 32g
carbs: 17g | net carbs: 12g | fiber: 5g

## Rump Steak Salad

**Prep time: 15 minutes | Cook time: 29 minutes | Serves 4**

½ pound (227 g) rump steak, excess fat trimmed
3 green onions, sliced
3 tomatoes, sliced
1 cup green beans, steamed and sliced
2 kohlrabi, peeled and chopped
½ cup water
2 cups mixed salad greens
Salt and black pepper, to season
Salad Dressing:
2 teaspoons Dijon mustard
1 teaspoon erythritol
Salt and black pepper, to taste
3 tablespoons olive oil, plus more for drizzling
1 tablespoon red wine vinegar

1.  Preheat the oven to 400ºF (205ºC). Place the kohlrabi on a baking sheet, drizzle with olive oil and bake in the oven for 25 minutes. After cooking, remove, and set aside to cool.
2.  In a bowl, mix the Dijon mustard, erythritol, salt, black pepper, vinegar, and olive oil. Set aside.
3.  Then, preheat a grill pan over high heat while you season the meat with salt and black pepper. Place the steak in the pan and brown on both sides for 4 minutes each. Remove to rest on a chopping board for 4 more minutes before slicing thinly.
4.  In a salad bowl, add green onions, tomatoes, green beans, kohlrabi, salad greens, and steak slices. Drizzle the dressing over and toss with two spoons. Serve the steak salad warm with chunks of low carb bread.

**Per Serving**

calories: 232 | fat: 14g | protein: 15g
carbs: 13g | net carbs: 7g | fiber: 6g

## Sirloin Steak Skewers with Ranch Dressing

**Prep time: 5 minutes | Cook time: 13 minutes | Serves 4**

1 pound (454 g) sirloin steak, boneless, cubed
¼ cup ranch dressing, divided
Chopped scallions, for garnish

1.  Preheat the grill on medium heat to 400ºF (205ºC) and thread the beef cubes on the skewers, about 4 to 5 cubes per skewer. Brush half of the ranch dressing on the skewers (all around) and place them on the grill grate to cook for 6 minutes. Turn the skewers once and cook further for 6 minutes.
2.  Brush the remaining ranch dressing on the meat and cook them for 1 more minute on each side. Plate, garnish with the scallions, and serve with a mixed veggie salad, and extra ranch dressing.

**Per Serving**

calories: 278 | fat: 19g | protein: 24g
carbs: 1g | net carbs: 1g | fiber: 0g

## Beef-Stuffed Zucchini Boats

**Prep time: 20 minutes | Cook time: 33 minutes | Serves 4**

2 garlic cloves, minced
1 teaspoon cumin
1 tablespoon olive oil
1 pound (454 g) ground beef
½ cup onions, chopped
1 teaspoon smoked paprika
Salt and black pepper, to taste
4 zucchinis

¼ cup fresh cilantro, chopped
½ cup Monterey Jack cheese, shredded
1½ cups enchilada sauce
1 avocado, chopped, for serving
Green onions, chopped, for serving
Tomatoes, chopped, for serving

1. Set a pan over high heat and warm the oil. Add the onions, and cook for 2 minutes. Stir in the beef, and brown for 4-5 minutes. Stir in the paprika, pepper, garlic, cumin, and salt; cook for 2 minutes.
2. Slice the zucchini in half lengthwise and scoop out the seeds. Set the zucchini in a greased baking pan, stuff each with the beef, scatter enchilada sauce on top, and spread with the Monterey cheese.
3. Bake in the oven at 350°F for 20 minutes while covered. Uncover, spread with cilantro, and bake for 5 minutes. Top with tomatoes, green onions and avocado, place on serving plates and enjoy.

**Per Serving**

calories: 520 | fat: 36g | protein: 34g
carbs: 20g | net carbs: 13g | fiber: 7g

## Beef and Egg Cauliflower Rice Bowls

**Prep time: 5 minutes | Cook time: 14 minutes | Serves 4**

2 cups cauliflower rice
3 cups frozen mixed vegetables
3 tablespoons butter
1 pound (454 g) skirt steak

Salt and black pepper, to taste
4 eggs
Hot sauce, for topping (optional)

1. Mix the cauliflower rice and mixed vegetables in a bowl, sprinkle with a little water, and steam in the microwave for 1 minute until tender. Share into 4 serving bowls.

2. Melt the butter in a skillet, season the beef with salt and black pepper, and brown for 5 minutes on each side. Use a perforated spoon to ladle the meat onto the vegetables.
3. Wipe out the skillet and return to medium heat, crack in an egg, season with salt and pepper and cook until the egg white has set, but the yolk is still runny 3 minutes. Remove egg onto the vegetable bowl and fry the remaining 3 eggs. Add to the other bowls. Drizzle the beef bowls with hot sauce (if desired) and serve.

**Per Serving**

calories: 470 | fat: 25g | protein: 42g
carbs: 21g | net carbs: 14g | fiber: 7g

## Lemon-Mustard Beef Rump Steak

**Prep time: 20 minutes | Cook time: 17 minutes | Serves 4**

2 tablespoons olive oil
1 tablespoon fresh rosemary, chopped
2 garlic cloves, minced
1½ pounds (680 g) beef rump steak, thinly sliced
Salt and black pepper, to taste
1 shallot, chopped
½ cup heavy cream

½ cup beef stock
1 tablespoon mustard
2 teaspoons Worcestershire sauce
2 teaspoons lemon juice
1 teaspoon erythritol
2 tablespoons butter
A sprig of rosemary
A sprig of thyme

1. In a bowl, combine 1 tablespoon of oil with black pepper, garlic, rosemary, and salt. Toss in the beef to coat, and set aside for some minutes. Heat a pan with the rest of the oil over medium heat, place in the beef steak, cook for 6 minutes, flipping halfway through; set aside and keep warm.
2. Set the pan to medium heat, stir in the shallot, and cook for 3 minutes; stir in the stock, Worcestershire sauce, erythritol, thyme, cream, mustard, and rosemary, and cook for 8 minutes.
3. Stir in the butter, lemon juice, black pepper, and salt. Get rid of the rosemary and thyme, and remove from heat. Arrange the beef slices on serving plates, sprinkle over the sauce, and enjoy.

**Per Serving**

calories: 600 | fat: 49g | protein: 35g
carbs: 4g | net carbs: 3g | fiber: 1g

## Seared Ribeye Steak with Shitake Mushrooms

**Prep time: 5 minutes | Cook time: 12 minutes | Serves 1**

6 ounces (170 g) ribeye steak
2 tablespoons butter
1 teaspoon olive oil
½ cup shitake mushrooms, sliced
Salt and black pepper, to taste

1. Heat the olive oil in a pan over medium heat. Rub the steak with salt and black pepper and cook about 4 minutes per side; set aside. Melt the butter in the pan and cook the shitakes for 4 minutes. Pour the butter and mushrooms over the steak to serve.

**Per Serving**

calories: 569 | fat: 47g | protein: 34g
carbs: 4g | net carbs: 3g | fiber: 1g

## Buttery Habanero and Beef Balls

**Prep time: 20 minutes | Cook time: 34 minutes | Serves 6**

3 garlic cloves, minced
1 pound (454 g) ground beef
1 small onion, chopped
2 habanero peppers, chopped
1 teaspoon dried thyme
2 teaspoons cilantro
½ teaspoon allspice
2 teaspoons cumin
Pinch of ground cloves
Salt and black pepper,
to taste
2 tablespoons butter
3 tablespoons butter, melted
6 ounces (170 g) cream cheese
1 teaspoon turmeric
¼ teaspoon stevia
½ teaspoon baking powder
1½ cups flax meal
½ cup coconut flour

1. In a blender, mix onion with garlic, habaneros, and ½ cup water. Set a pan over medium heat, add in 2 tablespoons butter and cook the beef for 3 minutes. Stir in the onion mixture, and cook for 2 minutes.
2. Stir in cilantro, cloves, salt, cumin, ½ teaspoon turmeric, thyme, allspice, and black pepper, and cook for 3 minutes. In a bowl, combine the remaining turmeric, with coconut flour, stevia, flax meal, and baking powder. In a separate bowl, combine the melted butter with the cream cheese.
3. Combine the 2 mixtures to obtain a dough. Form 12 balls from this mixture, set them on a parchment paper, and roll each into a circle. Split the beef mix on one-half of the dough circles, cover with the other half, seal edges, and lay on a lined sheet. Bake for 25 minutes in the oven at 350ºF.

**Per Serving**

calories: 570 | fat: 41g | protein: 25g
carbs: 18g | net carbs: 13g | fiber: 5g

## Balsamic Skirt Steak

**Prep time: 2 minutes | Cook time: 6 minutes | Serves 6**

¼ cup balsamic vinegar (no sugar added)
2 tablespoons extra-virgin olive oil
1 tablespoon fresh chopped parsley
1 teaspoon minced garlic
1 teaspoon kosher salt
¼ teaspoon ground black pepper
2 pounds (907 g) skirt steak, trimmed of fat

1. In a medium-sized bowl, whisk together the vinegar, olive oil, parsley, garlic, salt, and pepper. Add the skirt steak and flip to ensure that the entire surface is covered in marinade. Cover with plastic wrap and marinate in the refrigerator for at least 2 hours, or up to 24 hours.
2. Take the bowl out of the refrigerator and let the steak and marinade come to room temperature. Meanwhile, preheat a grill to high heat.
3. Remove the steak from the marinade (reserve the marinade) and place on the grill over direct high heat. Grill for 3 minutes per side for medium (recommended) or 5 minutes per side for well-done.
4. Remove the steak from the grill when the desired doneness is reached and let rest for 10 minutes before slicing. Meanwhile, place the reserved marinade in the microwave and cook on high for 3 minutes, or until boiling. Stir and set aside; you will use the boiled marinade as a sauce for the steak.
5. Slice the steak, being sure to cut against the grain for best results. Serve with the sauce.

**Per Serving**

calories: 355 | fat: 25.1g | protein: 30.9g
carbs: 0g | net carbs: 0g | fiber: 0g

## Traditional Italian Bolognese Sauce

**Prep time: 5 minutes | Cook time: 22 minutes | Serves 5**

1 pound (454 g) ground beef
2 garlic cloves
1 onion, chopped
1 teaspoon oregano
1 teaspoon sage
1 teaspoon rosemary
7 ounces (198 g) canned chopped tomatoes
1 tablespoon olive oil

1. Heat olive oil in a saucepan. Add onion and garlic and cook for 3 minutes. Add beef and cook until browned, about 4-5 minutes. Stir in the herbs and tomatoes. Cook for 15 minutes. Serve with zoodles.

**Per Serving**

calories: 216 | fat: 14g | protein: 18g
carbs: 4g | net carbs: 3g | fiber: 1g

## Beef-Cabbage Casserole

**Prep time: 5 minutes | Cook time: 26 minutes | Serves 6**

2 pounds (907 g) ground beef
Salt and black pepper, to taste
1 cup cauliflower rice
2 cups chopped
cabbage
1 (14-ounce / 397-g) can diced tomatoes
1 cup shredded Colby jack cheese

1. Preheat oven to 370ºF and grease a baking dish with cooking spray. Put beef in a pot and season with salt and black pepper and cook over medium heat for 6 minutes until no longer pink. Drain the grease. Add cauliflower rice, cabbage, tomatoes, and ¼ cup water. Stir and bring to boil covered for 5 minutes to thicken the sauce. Adjust taste with salt and black pepper.
2. Spoon the beef mixture into the baking dish and spread evenly. Sprinkle with cheese and bake in the oven for 15 minutes until cheese has melted and it's golden brown. Remove and cool for 4 minutes and serve with low carb crusted bread.

**Per Serving**

calories: 402 | fat: 27g | protein: 36g
carbs: 6g | net carbs: 4g | fiber: 2g

## Pepperoni and Beef Pizza Meatloaf

**Prep time: 10 minutes | Cook time: 60 minutes | Serves 8**

2 pounds (907 g) ground beef (80/20)
1/3 cup superfine blanched almond flour
¼ cup grated Parmesan cheese
1 tablespoon dried parsley
1 tablespoon dried onion flakes
1 teaspoon kosher salt
½ teaspoon dried oregano leaves
½ teaspoon garlic powder
½ teaspoon ground black pepper
2 large eggs
1 cup marinara sauce, store-bought or homemade, plus more for serving if desired
2 cups shredded whole-milk Mozzarella cheese
4 ounces (113 g) thinly sliced pepperoni
Chopped fresh parsley, for garnish (optional)

1. Preheat the oven to 375ºF (190ºC). Line a 9 by 5-inch loaf pan with foil, leaving 2 inches of foil folded over the outside edges of the pan. The extra foil will make it easier to lift the cooked meatloaf out of the pan.
2. Place the ground beef, almond flour, Parmesan cheese, parsley, onion flakes, salt, oregano, garlic powder, pepper, and eggs in a large bowl and mix well by hand until the texture is uniform.
3. Press the meatloaf mixture into the prepared loaf pan and flatten it out. Spoon the marinara evenly over the top and then sprinkle with the Mozzarella cheese. Layer the pepperoni slices on top. Bake, uncovered, for 1 hour, or until a meat thermometer inserted in the center reads 165ºF (74ºC).
4. Remove the meatloaf from the oven and let cool for at least 10 minutes in the pan to allow it to firm up before slicing.
5. Carefully remove the meatloaf from the pan using the foil as handles. Place on a cutting board and remove the foil. You can then cut it into slices and serve on individual plates, or, to dress it up a bit, spread some warm marinara sauce on the bottom of a serving platter, then place the loaf on top of the sauce and garnish with fresh parsley, as shown.

**Per Serving**

calories: 440 | fat: 30.9g | protein: 32.8g
carbs: 3.4g | net carbs: 2.4g | fiber: 1.0g

## Beef Chuck Chili con Carne

**Prep time: 8 minutes | Cook time: 2 hours 15 minutes | Serves 6**

2 pounds (907 g) boneless beef chuck, trimmed and cut into 1-inch cubes
1 teaspoon kosher salt
½ teaspoon ground black pepper
2 tablespoons avocado oil or other light-tasting oil
½ cup chopped yellow onions
1 tablespoon minced garlic
3 cups beef broth, store-bought or homemade
1 tablespoon chili powder
2 teaspoons ground cumin
1 teaspoon cayenne pepper
1 teaspoon dried oregano leaves
1 teaspoon ground coriander
¼ teaspoon ground cinnamon
¼ cup canned chipotles in adobo sauce
1 tablespoon apple cider vinegar
1 tablespoon coconut flour

1. Season the beef with the salt and pepper. Heat the oil in a large heavy-bottomed saucepan (make sure it has a lid) or a 4- or 6-quart Dutch oven over medium-high heat.
2. Add the beef and brown on all sides, about 4 minutes. Remove the meat and set aside.
3. Add the onions and garlic to the pan and cook for 5 minutes, or until browned and translucent. Add the meat back to the pan along with the broth, spices, and chipotles. Simmer, covered, until the meat is tender, about 2 hours.
4. Stir in the vinegar. Remove about ¼ cup of the sauce to a small bowl. Whisk the coconut flour into the bowl of sauce, then add the sauce back to the pot and stir well. Simmer, uncovered, for 5 more minutes, until the sauce has thickened. Taste and season with more salt and pepper, if desired.

**Per Serving**
calories: 364 | fat: 26.9g | protein: 28.9g
carbs: 3.6g | net carbs: 2.0g | fiber: 1.6g

## Parmesan Beef Meatball alla Parmigiana

**Prep time: 10 minutes | Cook time: 40 minutes | Serves 4**

**For the Meatballs:**
1 pound (454 g) ground beef (80/20)
2 tablespoons chopped fresh parsley, plus more for garnish if desired
$1/_3$ cup grated Parmesan cheese
¼ cup superfine blanched almond flour
1 large egg, beaten
1 teaspoon kosher salt
¼ teaspoon ground black pepper
¼ teaspoon garlic powder
¼ teaspoon onion powder
¼ teaspoon dried oregano leaves
¼ cup warm filtered water
1 cup marinara sauce, store-bought or homemade
1 cup shredded whole-milk Mozzarella cheese

1. Preheat the oven to 350°F (180°C). Line a 15 by 10-inch sheet pan with foil or parchment paper.
2. Put the ground beef, parsley, Parmesan, almond flour, egg, salt, pepper, garlic powder, onion powder, oregano, and water in a medium-sized bowl. Mix thoroughly by hand until fully combined.
3. Form the meat mixture into 12 meatballs about 2 inches in diameter and place them 2 inches apart on the sheet pan. Bake for 20 minutes.
4. Place the meatballs in a casserole dish large enough to fit all of the meatballs. Spoon the marinara evenly over the meatballs, then sprinkle the cheese over the meatballs. Bake for 20 minutes, or until the meatballs are cooked through, the sauce is bubbling, and the cheese is golden. Garnish with chopped fresh parsley, if desired.

**Per Serving**
calories: 431 | fat: 30.9g | protein: 32.9g
carbs: 4.8g | net carbs: 2.8g | fiber: 2.0g

# Chapter 10 Pork

## Cumin Pork Chops

**Prep time: 10 minutes | Cook time: 20 minutes | Serves 4**

4 pork chops
Salt and black pepper, to taste
3 tablespoons paprika
¾ cup cumin powder
1 teaspoon chili powder

1. In a bowl, combine the paprika with black pepper, cumin, salt, and chili. Place in the pork chops and rub them well. Heat a grill over medium temperature, add in the pork chops, cook for 5 minutes, flip, and cook for 5 minutes. Serve with steamed veggies.

**Per Serving**

calories: 350 | fat: 18.6g | protein: 41.9g
carbs: 10.4g | net carbs: 3.9g | fiber: 6.5g

## Roasted Pork Loin with Collard

**Prep time: 10 minutes | Cook time: 60 minutes | Serves 4**

2 tablespoons olive oil
Salt and black pepper, to taste
1½ pounds (680 g) pork loin
A pinch of dry mustard
1 teaspoon hot red pepper flakes
½ teaspoon ginger, minced
1 cup collard greens, chopped
2 garlic cloves, minced
½ lemon, sliced
¼ cup water

1. In a bowl, combine the ginger with salt, mustard, and black pepper. Add in the meat, toss to coat. Heat the oil in a saucepan over medium heat, brown the pork on all sides, for 10 minutes.
2. Transfer to the oven and roast for 40 minutes at 390ºF (199ºC). To the saucepan, add collard greens, lemon slices, garlic, and water; cook for 10 minutes. Serve on a platter and sprinkle pan juices on top.

**Per Serving**

calories: 431 | fat: 23.0g | protein: 45.0g
carbs: 3.6g | net carbs: 3.0g | fiber: 0.6g

## Pork, Squash, and Mushroom Casserole

**Prep time: 15 minutes | Cook time: 30 minutes | Serves 4**

1 pound (454 g) ground pork
1 large yellow squash, thinly sliced
Salt and black pepper to taste
1 clove garlic, minced
4 green onions, chopped
1 cup chopped cremini mushrooms
1 (15-ounce / 425-g) can diced tomatoes
½ cup pork rinds, crushed
¼ cup chopped parsley
1 cup cottage cheese
1 cup Mexican cheese blend
3 tablespoons olive oil
¹/₃ cup water

1. Preheat the oven to 370ºF (188ºC).
2. Heat the olive oil in a skillet over medium heat, add the pork, season it with salt and black pepper, and cook for 3 minutes or until no longer pink. Stir occasionally while breaking any lumps apart.
3. Add the garlic, half of the green onions, mushrooms, and 2 tablespoons of pork rinds. Cook for 3 minutes. Stir in the tomatoes, half of the parsley, and water. Cook further for 3 minutes, and then turn the heat off.
4. Mix the remaining parsley, cottage cheese, and Mexican cheese blend. Set aside. Sprinkle the bottom of a baking dish with 3 tablespoons of pork rinds; top with half of the squash and a season of salt, ²/₃ of the pork mixture, and the cheese mixture. Repeat the layering process a second time to exhaust the ingredients.
5. Cover the baking dish with foil and bake for 20 minutes. After, remove the foil and brown the top of the casserole with the broiler side of the oven for 2 minutes. Remove the dish when ready and serve warm.

**Per Serving**

calories: 496 | fat: 29.1g | protein: 36.6g
carbs: 7.1g | net carbs: 2.6g | fiber: 4.5g

## Double Cheese BBQ Pork Pizza

**Prep time: 10 minutes | Cook time: 25 minutes | Serves 4**

1 low carb pizza bread
Olive oil for brushing
1 cup grated
Manchego cheese
2 cups leftover pulled

pork
½ cup sugar-free BBQ
sauce
1 cup crumbled goat
cheese

1. Preheat oven to 400ºF (205ºC) and put pizza bread on a pizza pan. Brush with olive oil and sprinkle the Manchego cheese all over. Mix the pork with BBQ sauce and spread over the cheese. Drop goat cheese on top and bake for 25 minutes until the cheese has melted. Slice the pizza with a cutter and serve.

**Per Serving**

calories: 345 | fat: 24.1g | protein: 17.9g
carbs: 6.9g | net carbs: 6.6g | fiber: 0.3g

## Pork and Cucumber Lettuce Cups

**Prep time: 10 minutes | Cook time: 15 minutes | Serves 6**

2 pounds (907 g)
ground pork
1 tablespoon ginger-
garlic paste
Pink salt and chili
pepper to taste
1 teaspoon butter

1 head Iceberg lettuce
2 sprigs green onion,
chopped
1 red bell pepper,
seeded and chopped
½ cucumber, finely
chopped

1. Put the pork with ginger-garlic paste, salt, and chili pepper seasoning in a saucepan. Cook for 10 minutes over medium heat while breaking any lumps until the pork is no longer pink. Drain liquid and add the butter, melt and brown the meat for 4 minutes, continuously stirring. Turn the heat off.
2. Pat the lettuce dry with a paper towel and in each leaf, spoon two to three tablespoons of pork, top with green onions, bell pepper, and cucumber. Serve with soy drizzling sauce.

**Per Serving**

calories: 312 | fat: 24.2g | protein: 19.1g
carbs: 3.1g | net carbs: 1.0g | fiber: 2.1g

## Mushroom and Pork Bake

**Prep time: 10 minutes | Cook time: 45 minutes | Serves 6**

1 onion, chopped
2 (10.5 ounce / 298-
g) cans mushroom
soup
6 pork chops

½ cup sliced
mushrooms
Salt and ground
pepper, to taste

1. Preheat the oven to 370ºF (188ºC).
2. Season the pork chops with salt and black pepper, and place in a baking dish. Combine the mushroom soup, mushrooms, and onion, in a bowl. Pour this mixture over the pork chops. Bake for 45 minutes.

**Per Serving**

calories: 402 | fat: 32.5g | protein: 19.5g
carbs: 8.4g | net carbs: 7.9g | fiber: 0.5g

## Spiralized Zucchini, Bacon, and Spinach Gratin

**Prep time: 15 minutes | Cook time: 30 minutes | Serves 4**

2 large zucchinis,
spiralized
4 slices bacon,
chopped
2 cups baby spinach
4 ounces (113 g)
halloumi cheese, cut
into cubes
2 cloves garlic, minced

1 cup heavy cream
½ cup sugar-free
tomato sauce
1 cup grated
Mozzarella cheese
½ teaspoon dried
Italian mixed herbs
Salt and black pepper
to taste

1. Preheat the oven to 350ºF (180ºC). Place the cast iron pan over medium heat and fry the bacon for 4 minutes, then add garlic and cook for 1 minute.
2. In a bowl, mix the heavy cream, tomato sauce, and ⅙ cup water and add it to the pan. Stir in the zucchini, spinach, halloumi, Italian herbs, salt, and pepper. Sprinkle the Mozzarella cheese on top, and transfer the pan to the oven. Bake for 20 minutes or until the cheese is golden. Serve the gratin warm.

**Per Serving**

calories: 351 | fat: 27.2g | protein: 15.9g
carbs: 6.6g | net carbs: 5.2g | fiber: 1.4g

## Rosemary Pork Chops with Kalamata Olives

**Prep time: 10 minutes | Cook time: 40 minutes | Serves 4**

4 pork chops, bone-in
Salt and ground black pepper, to taste
1 teaspoon dried rosemary
3 garlic cloves, peeled and minced
½ cup kalamata olives, pitted and sliced
2 tablespoons olive oil
¼ cup vegetable broth

1. Season pork chops with black pepper and salt, and add in a roasting pan. Stir in the garlic, olives, olive oil, broth, and rosemary, set in the oven at 425ºF (220ºC), and bake for 10 minutes. Reduce heat to 350ºF (180ºC) and roast for 25 minutes. Slice the pork and sprinkle with pan juices all over to serve.

**Per Serving**

calories: 416 | fat: 25.1g | protein: 36.1g
carbs: 2.9g | net carbs: 2.1g | fiber: 0.8g

## Pork and Cauliflower Goulash

**Prep time: 15 minutes | Cook time: 10 minutes | Serves 4**

1 red bell pepper, seeded and chopped
2 tablespoons olive oil
1½ pounds (680 g) ground pork
Salt and black pepper, to taste
2 cups cauliflower florets
1 onion, chopped
14 ounces (397 g) canned diced tomatoes
¼ teaspoon garlic powder
1 tablespoon tomato purée
1½ cups water

1. Heat olive oil in a pan over medium heat, stir in the pork, and brown for 5 minutes. Place in the bell pepper and onion, and cook for 4 minutes. Stir in the water, tomatoes, and cauliflower, bring to a simmer and cook for 5 minutes while covered. Place in the black pepper, tomato paste, salt, and garlic powder. Stir well, remove from the heat, split into bowls, and enjoy.

**Per Serving**

calories: 476 | fat: 36.9g | protein: 43.9g
carbs: 8.3g | net carbs: 4.4g | fiber: 3.9g

## Pork Chops with Mushrooms

**Prep time: 10 minutes | Cook time: 45 minutes | Serves 3**

8 ounces (227 g) mushrooms, sliced
1 teaspoon garlic powder
1 onion, peeled and chopped
1 cup heavy cream
3 pork chops, boneless
1 teaspoon ground nutmeg
¼ cup coconut oil

1. Set a pan over medium heat and warm the oil, add in the onion and mushrooms, and cook for 4 minutes. Stir in the pork chops, season with garlic powder, and nutmeg, and sear until browned.
2. Put the pan in the oven at 350ºF (180ºC), and bake for 30 minutes. Remove pork chops to plates and maintain warm. Place the pan over medium heat, pour in the heavy cream over the mushroom mixture, and cook for 5 minutes; remove from heat. Sprinkle sauce over pork chops and enjoy.

**Per Serving**

calories: 610 | fat: 40.1g | protein: 41.9g
carbs: 16.6g | net carbs: 6.7g | fiber: 9.9g

## Pork Medallions with Onions and Bacon

**Prep time: 10 minutes | Cook time: 25 minutes | Serves 4**

2 onions, chopped
6 bacon slices, chopped
½ cup vegetable stock
Salt and black pepper,
to taste
1 pound (454 g) pork tenderloin, cut into medallions

1. Set a pan over medium heat, stir in the bacon, cook until crispy, and remove to a plate. Add onions, black pepper, and salt, and cook for 5 minutes; set to the same plate with bacon.
2. Add the pork medallions to the pan, season with black pepper and salt, brown for 3 minutes on each side, turn, reduce heat to medium, and cook for 7 minutes. Stir in the stock, and cook for 2 minutes. Return the bacon and onions to the pan and cook for 1 minute.

**Per Serving**

calories: 326 | fat: 17.9g | protein: 35.9g
carbs: 7.2g | net carbs: 5.9g | fiber: 1.3g

## Dijon Pork Loin Chops

**Prep time: 15 minutes | Cook time: 10 minutes | Serves 4**

4 pork loin chops
1 teaspoon Dijon mustard
1 tablespoon soy sauce
1 teaspoon lemon juice
1 tablespoon water
Salt and black pepper, to taste
1 tablespoon butter
A bunch of scallions, chopped

1. In a bowl, combine the water with lemon juice, mustard and soy sauce. Set aside.
2. Set a pan over medium heat and melt butter, add in the pork chops, season with salt, and black pepper. Cook for 4 minutes, turn, and cook for an additional 4 minutes. Remove to a plate and keep warm.
3. In the same pan, pour mustard sauce, and simmer for 5 minutes. Drizzle the sauce over the pork, top with scallions, and serve.

**Per Serving**

calories: 383 | fat: 21.6g | protein: 38.1g
carbs: 1.5g | net carbs: 1.1g | fiber: 0.4g

## Pesto Pork Chops with Pistachios

**Prep time: 10 minutes | Cook time: 2 hours | Serves 4**

1 cup parsley
1 cup mint
1½ onions, chopped
⅓ cup pistachios
1 teaspoon lemon zest
5 tablespoons avocado
oil
Salt, to taste
4 pork chops
5 garlic cloves, minced
Juice from 1 lemon

1. In a food processor, combine the parsley with avocado oil, mint, pistachios, salt, lemon zest, and 1 onion. Rub the pork with this mixture, place in a bowl, and refrigerate for 1 hour while covered.
2. Remove the chops and set to a baking dish, place in ½ onion, and garlic; sprinkle with lemon juice, and bake for 2 hours in the oven at 250ºF (121ºC). Split amongst plates and enjoy.

**Per Serving**

calories: 565 | fat: 40.1g | protein: 37.1g
carbs: 8.3g | net carbs: 5.4g | fiber: 2.9g

## Pork and Ricotta Bacon Wraps

**Prep time: 15 minutes | Cook time: 35 minutes | Serves 6**

6 bacon slices
2 tablespoons fresh parsley, chopped
1 pound (454 g) pork cutlets, sliced
⅓ cup ricotta cheese
1 tablespoon coconut oil
¼ cup onions, chopped
3 garlic cloves, peeled and minced
2 tablespoons Parmesan cheese, grated
15 ounces (425 g) canned diced tomatoes
⅓ cup vegetable stock
Salt and black pepper, to taste
½ teaspoon Italian seasoning

1. Use a meat pounder to flatten the pork pieces. Set the bacon slices on top of each piece, then divide the parsley, ricotta cheese, and Parmesan cheese. Roll each pork piece and secure with a toothpick. Set a pan over medium heat and warm oil, cook the pork rolls until browned, and remove to a plate.
2. Add in onions and garlic, and cook for 5 minutes. Place in the stock and cook for 3 minutes. Get rid of the toothpicks from the rolls and return to the pan. Stir in the pepper, salt, tomatoes, and Italian seasoning, bring to a boil, set heat to medium-low, and cook for 20 minutes covered. Split among bowls to serve.

**Per Serving**

calories: 436 | fat: 37.1g | protein: 33.9g
carbs: 3.8g | net carbs: 2.1g | fiber: 1.7g

## Easy Jamaican Pork Roast

**Prep time: 10 minutes | Cook time: 4 hours | Serves 12**

4 pounds (1.8 kg) pork roast
1 tablespoon olive oil
¼ cup jerk spice blend
½ cup vegetable stock
Salt and black pepper, to taste

1. Rub the pork with olive oil and the spice blend. Heat a dutch oven over medium heat and sear the meat well on all sides; add in the stock. Cover the pot, reduce the heat, and let cook for 4 hours.

**Per Serving**

calories: 283 | fat: 24.1g | protein: 23.1g
carbs: 0.4g | net carbs: 0g | fiber: 0.4g

## Spicy Tomato Pork Chops

**Prep time: 15 minutes | Cook time: 36 minutes | Serves 4**

4 pork chops
1 tablespoon fresh oregano, chopped
2 garlic cloves, minced
1 tablespoon canola oil
15 ounces (425 g) canned diced

tomatoes
1 tablespoon tomato paste
Salt and black pepper, to taste
¼ cup tomato juice
1 red chili, finely chopped

1. Set a pan over medium heat and warm oil, place in the pork, season with pepper and salt, cook for 6 minutes on both sides; remove to a bowl. Add in the garlic, and cook for 30 seconds. Stir in the tomato paste, tomatoes, tomato juice, and chili; bring to a boil, and reduce heat to medium-low.
2. Place in the pork chops, cover the pan and simmer everything for 30 minutes. Remove the pork to plates and sprinkle with fresh oregano to serve.

**Per Serving**

calories: 412 | fat: 21.0g | protein: 39.1g
carbs: 6.3g | net carbs: 3.5g | fiber: 2.8g


## Avocado Pulled Pork Shoulder

**Prep time: 10 minutes | Cook time: 2 hours 5 minutes | Serves 12**

4 pounds (1.8 kg) pork shoulder
1 tablespoon avocado oil

½ cup vegetable stock
¼ cup jerk seasoning
6 avocado, sliced

1. Rub the pork shoulder with jerk seasoning, and set in a greased baking dish. Pour in the stock, and cook for 1 hour 45 minutes in your oven at 350ºF (180ºC) covered with aluminium foil.
2. Discard the foil and cook for another 20 minutes. Leave to rest for 30 minutes, and shred it with 2 forks. Serve topped with avocado slices.

**Per Serving**

calories: 566 | fat: 42.5g | protein: 41.9g
carbs: 11.4g | net carbs: 4.2g | fiber: 7.2g


## Pork and Mixed Vegetable Stir-Fry

**Prep time: 10 minutes | Cook time: 20 minutes | Serves 4**

1½ tablespoons butter
2 pounds (907 g) pork loin, cut into strips
Pink salt and chili pepper to taste
2 teaspoons ginger-

garlic paste
¼ cup chicken broth
5 tablespoons peanut butter
2 cups mixed stir-fry vegetables

1. Melt the butter in a wok and mix the pork with salt, chili pepper, and ginger-garlic paste. Pour the pork into the wok and cook for 6 minutes until no longer pink.
2. Mix the peanut butter with some broth until smooth, add to the pork and stir; cook for 2 minutes. Pour in the remaining broth, cook for 4 minutes, and add the mixed veggies. Simmer for 5 minutes. Adjust the taste with salt and black pepper, and spoon the stir-fry to a side of cilantro cauli rice.

**Per Serving**

calories: 572 | fat: 49.1g | protein: 22.6g
carbs:5.3 g | net carbs: 1.1g | fiber: 4.2g


## Pork Sausage with Spinach and Chili

**Prep time: 10 minutes | Cook time: 30 minutes | Serves 6**

1 onion, chopped
2 tablespoons olive oil
2 pounds (907 g) Italian pork sausage, sliced
1 red bell pepper, seeded and chopped
Salt and black pepper,

to taste
4 pounds (1.8 kg) spinach, chopped
1 garlic, minced
¼ cup green chili peppers, chopped
1 cup water

1. Set pan over medium heat, warm oil and cook sausage for 10 minutes. Stir in onion, garlic and bell pepper and fry for 4 minutes. Place in spinach, salt, water, pepper, chili pepper, and cook for 10 minutes.

**Per Serving**

calories: 351 | fat: 27.9g | protein: 28.9g
carbs: 13.8g | net carbs: 6.3g | fiber: 7.5g

## Lime Pork Chops with Dill Pickles

**Prep time: 15 minutes | Cook time: 15 minutes | Serves 4**

¼ cup lime juice
4 pork chops
1 tablespoon coconut oil, melted
2 garlic cloves, minced
1 tablespoon chili powder
1 teaspoon ground

cinnamon
2 teaspoons cumin
Salt and black pepper, to taste
½ teaspoon hot pepper sauce
4 dill pickles, cut into spears and squeezed

1. In a bowl, combine the lime juice with oil, cumin, salt, hot pepper sauce, black pepper, cinnamon, garlic, and chili powder. Place in the pork chops, toss to coat, and refrigerate for 4 hours.
2. Arrange the pork on a preheated grill over medium heat, cook for 7 minutes, turn, add in the dill pickles, and cook for another 7 minutes. Split among serving plates and enjoy.

**Per Serving**

calories: 316 | fat: 18.0g | protein: 36.0g
carbs: 3.9g | net carbs: 2.3g | fiber: 1.6g

## Bacon Smothered Pork with Thyme

**Prep time: 10 minutes | Cook time: 20 minutes | Serves 6**

7 strips bacon, chopped
6 pork chops
Pink salt and black pepper to taste

5 sprigs fresh thyme plus extra to garnish
¼ cup chicken broth
½ cup heavy cream

1. Cook bacon in a large skillet on medium heat for 5 minutes. Remove with a slotted spoon onto a paper towel-lined plate to soak up excess fat.
2. Season pork chops with salt and black pepper, and brown in the bacon fat for 4 minutes on each side. Remove to the bacon plate. Stir in the thyme, chicken broth, and heavy cream and simmer for 5 minutes.
3. Return the chops and bacon, and cook further for another 2 minutes. Serve chops and a generous ladle of sauce with cauli mash. Garnish with thyme leaves.

**Per Serving**

calories: 434 | fat: 37.1g | protein: 22.1g
carbs: 3.1g | net carbs: 2.9g | fiber: 0.2g

## Pesto Pork Sausage Links

**Prep time: 10 minutes | Cook time: 10 minutes | Serves 8**

8 pork sausage links, sliced
1 pound (454 g) mixed cherry tomatoes, cut in half
4 cups baby spinach
1 tablespoon olive oil
1 pound (454 g)

Monterrey Jack cheese, cubed
2 tablespoons lemon juice
1 cup basil pesto
Salt and black pepper, to taste

1. Warm oil in a pan and cook sausage links for 4 minutes per side. In a salad bowl, combine spinach, cheese, salt, pesto, pepper, cherry tomatoes, and lemon juice, and toss to coat. Mix in the sausage.

**Per Serving**

calories: 366 | fat: 26.1g | protein: 17.9g
carbs: 8.0g | net carbs: 6.7g | fiber: 1.3g

## Balsamic Pork Loin Chops

**Prep time: 5 minutes | Cook time: 15 minutes | Serves 4**

4 pork loin chops, boneless
1 tablespoon rosemary, chopped
1 tablespoon balsamic

vinegar
1 garlic clove, minced
1 tablespoon olive oil
Salt and black pepper to taste

1. Put the pork in a deep dish. Add in the balsamic vinegar, rosemary, garlic, olive oil, salt, and black pepper, and toss to coat. Cover the dish with plastic wrap and marinate the pork for 1 to 2 hours.
2. Preheat grill to medium heat. Remove the pork when ready, reserve the marinade and grill covered for 10 minutes per side. Remove the pork chops and let them sit for 4 minutes on a serving plate.
3. In a saucepan over medium heat, pour in the reserved marinade, add in 1 tablespoon water and bring to a boil for 2-3 minutes until the liquid becomes thickened. Top the chops with the sauce and serve.

**Per Serving**

calories: 363 | fat: 21g | protein: 40g
carbs: 1g | net carbs: 1g | fiber: 0g

## Smoked Sausages with Peppers and Mushrooms

**Prep time: 10 minutes | Cook time: 1 hour | Serves 6**

3 yellow bell peppers, seeded and chopped
2 pounds (907 g) smoked sausage, sliced
Salt and black pepper, to taste
2 pounds (907

g) portobello mushrooms, sliced
2 sweet onions, chopped
1 tablespoon Swerve
2 tablespoons olive oil
Arugula to garnish

1. In a baking dish, combine the sausages with Swerve, oil, black pepper, onion, bell peppers, salt, and mushrooms. Pour in 1 cup of water and toss well to ensure everything is coated, set in the oven at 320ºF (160ºC) to bake for 1 hour. To serve, divide the sausages between plates and scatter over the arugula.

**Per Serving**

calories: 524 | fat: 32.0g | protein: 28.9g
carbs: 14.4g | net carbs: 7.4g | fiber: 7.0g

## Buttered Pork Chops

**Prep time: 5 minutes | Cook time: 12 minutes | Serves 4**

½ tablespoon olive oil
1 tablespoon butter
1 tablespoon rosemary
4 pork chops
Salt and black pepper,

to taste
A pinch of paprika
½ teaspoon chili powder

1. Rub the pork chops with olive oil, salt, black pepper, paprika, and chili powder. Heat a grill over medium, add in the pork chops and cook for 10 minutes, flipping once halfway through.
2. Remove to a serving plate. In a pan over low heat, warm the butter until it turns nutty brown. Pour over the pork chops, sprinkle with rosemary and serve.
3. Serve immediately.

**Per Serving**

calories: 370 | fat: 22g | protein: 40g
carbs: 1g | net carbs: 1g | fiber: 0g

## Bacon and Cauliflower Stew

**Prep time: 10 minutes | Cook time: 35 minutes | Serves 6**

8 ounces (227 g) Mozzarella cheese, grated
2 cups chicken broth
½ teaspoon garlic powder
½ teaspoon onion powder

Salt and black pepper, to taste
4 garlic cloves, minced
¼ cup heavy cream
3 cups bacon, chopped
1 head cauliflower, cut into florets

1. In a pot, combine the bacon with broth, cauliflower, salt, heavy cream, black pepper, garlic powder, cheese, onion powder, and garlic, and cook for 35 minutes. Share into serving plates, and enjoy.

**Per Serving**

calories: 381 | fat: 25.1g | protein: 32.9g
carbs: 8.7g | net carbs: 6.0g | fiber: 2.7g

## Pork Loin Chops

**Prep time: 10 minutes | Cook time: 13 minutes | Serves 2**

½ tablespoon butter
½ tablespoon olive oil
4 pork loin chops
½ teaspoon Dijon mustard
½ tablespoon coconut aminos
½ teaspoon lemon

juice
1 teaspoon cumin seeds
½ tablespoon water
Salt and black pepper, to taste
½ cup chives, chopped

1. Set a pan over medium heat and warm butter and olive oil, add in the pork chops, season with salt, and pepper, cook for 4 minutes, turn and cook for additional 4 minutes. Remove to a plate.
2. In a bowl, mix the water with lemon juice, cumin seeds, mustard and coconut aminos. Pour the mustard sauce in the same pan and simmer for 5 minutes. Spread over pork, top with chives and serve.

**Per Serving**

calories: 382 | fat: 21g | protein: 38g
carbs: 1g | net carbs: 1g | fiber: 0g

## Lemony Pork Loin Roast

**Prep time: 15 minutes | Cook time: 7 to 8 hours | Serves 6**

3 tablespoons extra-virgin olive oil, divided
1 tablespoon butter
2 pounds pork loin roast
½ teaspoon salt
¼ teaspoon freshly ground black pepper
¼ cup chicken broth
Juice and zest of 1 lemon
1 tablespoon minced garlic
½ cup heavy (whipping) cream

1. Lightly grease the insert of the slow cooker with 1 tablespoon of the olive oil.
2. In a large skillet over medium-high heat, heat the remaining 2 tablespoons of the olive oil and the butter.
3. Lightly season the pork with salt and pepper. Add the pork to the skillet and brown the roast on all sides for about 10 minutes. Transfer it to the insert.
4. In a small bowl, stir together the broth, lemon juice and zest, and garlic.
5. Add the broth mixture to the roast.
6. Cover, and cook on low for 7 to 8 hours.
7. Stir in the heavy cream and serve.

**Per Serving**

calories: 448 | fat: 31g | protein: 39g
carbs: 1g | net carbs: 1g | fiber: 0g

## Pork with Cranberry Sauce

**Prep time: 20 minutes | Cook time: 2⅔ hours | Serves 4**

4 pork chops
1 teaspoon garlic powder
Salt and black pepper, to taste
1 teaspoon fresh basil, chopped
A drizzle of olive oil
1 shallot, chopped
1 cup white wine
1 bay leaf
2 cups vegetable stock
Fresh parsley, chopped, for serving
2 cups cranberries
½ teaspoon fresh rosemary, chopped
½ cup Swerve
Juice of 1 lemon
1 cup water
1 teaspoon harissa paste

1. In a bowl, combine the pork chops with 1 teaspoon of basil, salt, garlic powder and black pepper. Heat a pan with a drizzle of oil over medium heat, place in the pork and cook until browned; set aside.

2. Stir in the shallot, and cook for 2 minutes. Place in the bay leaf and wine, and cook for 4 minutes. Pour in juice from ½ lemon, and vegetable stock, and simmer for 5 minutes. Return the pork, and cook for 10 minutes. Cover the pan, and place in the oven to bake at 350°F (180°C) for 2 hours.
3. Set a pan over medium heat, add cranberries, rosemary, harissa paste, water, 1 teaspoon basil, Swerve, and juice from ½ lemon, simmer for 15 minutes. Remove the pork chops from the oven, remove and discard the bay leaf. Split among plates, spread over with the cranberry sauce, sprinkle with parsley to serve.

**Per Serving**

calories: 450 | fat: 34g | protein: 26g
carbs: 12g | net carbs: 6g | fiber: 6g

## Cranberry Pork Roast

**Prep time: 15 minutes | Cook time: 7 to 8 hours | Serves 6**

3 tablespoons extra-virgin olive oil, divided
2 tablespoons butter
2 pounds (907 g) pork shoulder roast
1 teaspoon ground cinnamon
¼ teaspoon allspice
¼ teaspoon salt
⅛ teaspoon freshly ground black pepper
½ cup cranberries
½ cup chicken broth
½ cup granulated erythritol
2 tablespoons dijon mustard
Juice and zest of ½ lemon
1 scallion, white and green parts, chopped, for garnish

1. Lightly grease the insert of the slow cooker with 1 tablespoon of the olive oil.
2. In a large skillet over medium-high heat, heat the remaining 2 tablespoons of the olive oil and the butter.
3. Lightly season the pork with cinnamon, allspice, salt, and pepper. Add the pork to the skillet and brown on all sides for about 10 minutes. Transfer to the insert.
4. In a small bowl, stir together the cranberries, broth, erythritol, mustard, and lemon juice and zest, and add the mixture to the pork.
5. Cover and cook on low for 7 to 8 hours.
6. Serve topped with the scallion.

**Per Serving**

calories: 492 | fat: 40g | protein: 26g
carbs: 4g | net carbs: 3g | fiber: 1g

## Italian Pork Sausage with Bell Peppers

**Prep time: 15 minutes | Cook time: 20 minutes | Serves 6**

¼ cup olive oil
2 pounds (907 g) Italian pork sausage, chopped
1 onion, sliced
4 sun-dried tomatoes, sliced thin
Salt and black pepper, to taste
½ pound (227 g)

Gruyere cheese, grated
3 yellow bell peppers, seeded and chopped
3 orange bell peppers, seeded and chopped
A pinch of red pepper flakes
½ cup fresh parsley, chopped

1. Set a pan over medium heat and warm oil, place in the sausage slices, cook each side for 3 minutes, remove to a bowl, and set aside. Stir in tomatoes, bell peppers, and onion, and cook for 5 minutes. Season with black pepper, pepper flakes, and salt and mix well. Cook for 1 minute, and remove from heat.
2. Lay sausage slices onto a baking dish, place the bell pepper mixture on top, scatter with the Gruyere cheese, set in the oven at 340ºF (171ºC). Bake for 10 minutes, until the cheese melts. Serve topped with parsley.

**Per Serving**

calories: 566 | fat: 45.0g | protein: 34.0g
carbs: 9.7g | net carbs: 7.6g | fiber: 2.1g

## Stewed Pork and Veggies

**Prep time: 15 minutes | Cook time: 30 minutes | Serves 4**

1 tablespoon olive oil
1 red bell pepper, chopped
1 pound (454 g) stewed pork, cubed
Salt and black pepper, to taste
2 cups cauliflower florets
2 cups broccoli florets
1 onion, chopped

14 ounces (397 g) canned diced tomatoes
¼ teaspoon garlic powder
1 tablespoon tomato puree
1½ cups water
1 tablespoon parsley, chopped

1. In a pan, heat olive oil and cook the pork over medium heat for 5 minutes, until browned.

2. Place in the bell pepper, and onion, and cook for 4 minutes. Stir in the water, tomatoes, broccoli, cauliflower, tomato purée, and garlic powder; bring to a simmer and cook for 20minutes while covered. Adjust the seasoning and serve sprinkled with parsley.

**Per Serving**

calories: 299 | fat: 13g | protein: 35g
carbs: 10g | net carbs: 6g | fiber: 4g

## Pork Tenderloin with Lemon Chimichurri

**Prep time: 10 minutes | Cook time: 50 minutes | Serves 6**

**Lemon Chimichurri:**

1 lemon, juiced
¼ cup chopped mint leaves
¼ cup chopped

oregano leaves
2 cloves garlic, minced
¼ cup olive oil
Salt to taste

**Pork:**

1 (4-pound / 1.8-kg) pork tenderloin
Salt and black pepper

to season
Olive oil for rubbing

1. Make the lemon chimichurri to have the flavors incorporate while the pork cooks.
2. In a bowl, mix the mint, oregano, and garlic. Then, add the lemon juice, olive oil, and salt, and combine well. Set the sauce aside at room temperature.
3. Preheat the charcoal grill to 450ºF (235ºC) in medium heat creating a direct heat area and indirect heat area. Rub the pork with olive oil, season with salt and pepper. Place the meat over direct heat and sear for 3 minutes on each side, after which, move to the indirect heat area. Close the lid and cook for 25 minutes on one side, then open, turn the meat, and grill for 20 minutes on the other side. Remove the pork from the grill and let it sit for 5 minutes before slicing. Spoon lemon chimichurri over the pork and serve with fresh salad.

**Per Serving**

calories: 400 | fat: 17g | protein: 28g
carbs: 2g | net carbs: 2g | fiber: 0g

## Pork Loin and Brussels Sprouts

**Prep time: 10 minutes | Cook time: 1¼ hours | Serves 4**

½ pound (227 g) Brussels sprouts, chopped
1 tablespoon olive oil
Salt and black pepper, to taste
1½ pounds (680 g) pork loin
A pinch of dry mustard
1 teaspoon hot red pepper flakes
½ teaspoon ginger, minced
2 garlic cloves, minced
½ lemon sliced
¼ cup water

1. Preheat oven to 380ºF (193ºC). In a bowl, combine the ginger with salt, mustard, and black pepper.
2. Add in meat, toss to coat. Heat the oil in a saucepan over medium heat, brown the pork on all sides, for 8 minutes. Transfer to the oven and roast for 1 hour.
3. To the saucepan, add Brussels sprouts, lemon slices, garlic, and water; cook for 10 minutes. Serve on a platter, sprinkled with pan juices on top.

**Per Serving**

calories: 418 | fat: 22g | protein: 45g
carbs: 7g | net carbs: 4g | fiber: 3g

## Pork Medallions with Rosemary

**Prep time: 10 minutes | Cook time: 20 minutes | Serves 4**

2 onions, chopped
4 ounces (113 g) bacon, chopped
½ cup vegetable stock
Salt and black pepper,
to taste
1 tablespoon fresh rosemary, chopped
1 pound (454 g) pork medallions

1. Fry the bacon in a pan over medium heat, until crispy, and remove to a plate. Add in onions, black pepper, and salt, and cook for 5 minutes; set to the same plate with bacon.
2. Add pork to the pan, brown for 3 minutes, turn, and cook for 7 minutes. Stir in stock and cook for 2 minutes. Return bacon and onions to the pan and cook for 1 minute. Garnish with rosemary.

**Per Serving**

calories: 258 | fat: 15g | protein: 23g
carbs: 8g | net carbs: 6g | fiber: 2g

## Cheesy Pork Nachos

**Prep time: 5 minutes | Cook time: 10 minutes | Serves 4**

1 bag low carb tortilla chips
2 cups leftover pulled pork
1 red bell pepper,
seeded and chopped
1 red onion, diced
2 cups shredded Monterey Jack cheese

1. Preheat oven to 350ºF (180ºC).
2. Arrange the chips in a medium cast iron pan, scatter pork over, followed by red bell pepper, and onion, and sprinkle with cheese.
3. Place the pan in the oven and cook for 10 minutes until the cheese has melted. Allow cooling for 3 minutes and serve.

**Per Serving**

calories: 473 | fat: 25g | protein: 37g
carbs: 11g | net carbs: 9g | fiber: 2g

## Herbed Pork Chops with Raspberry Sauce

**Prep time: 10 minutes | Cook time: 10 minutes | Serves 4**

1 tablespoon olive oil, extra for brushing
2 pound (907 g) pork chops
Pink salt and black pepper to taste
2 cups raspberries
¼ cup water
1½ tablespoon Italian Herb mix
1 tablespoon balsamic vinegar
1 teaspoon sugar-free Worcestershire sauce

1. Heat oil in a skillet over medium heat, season the pork with salt and black pepper and cook for 5 minutes on each side. Put on serving plates and reserve the pork drippings.
2. Mash the raspberries with a fork in a bowl until jam-like. Pour into a saucepan, add the water, and herb mix. Bring to boil on low heat for 4 minutes. Stir in pork drippings, vinegar, and Worcestershire sauce. Simmer for 1 minute. Spoon sauce over the pork chops and serve with braised rapini.

**Per Serving**

calories: 413 | fat: 32g | protein: 26g
carbs: 5g | net carbs: 1g | fiber: 4g

## Pork Pie

**Prep time: 15 minutes | Cook time: 1 hour | Serves 8**

### Crust:

| | |
|---|---|
| 1 egg | gum |
| ¼ cup butter | ¼ cup shredded |
| 2 cups almond flour | mozzarella |
| ¼ teaspoon xanthan | A pinch of salt |

### Filling:

| | |
|---|---|
| 2 pounds ground pork | mashed cauliflower |
| ½ cup water | 1 tablespoon ground |
| ⅓ cup pureed onion | sage |
| ¾ teaspoon allspice | 1 tablespoon butter |
| 1 cup cooked and | |

1. Preheat your oven to 350ºF (180ºC).
2. Whisk together all crust ingredients in a bowl. Make two balls out of the mixture and refrigerate for 10 minutes. Combine the water, meat, and salt, in a pot over medium heat. Cook for about 15 minutes, place the meat along with the other ingredients in a bowl. Mix with your hands to combine.
3. Roll out the pie crusts and place one at the bottom of a greased pie pan. Spread the filling over the crust. Top with the other coat. Bake in the oven for 50 minutes then serve.

**Per Serving**

calories: 435 | fat: 31g | protein: 31g
carbs: 5g | net carbs: 4g | fiber: 1g

## Homemade Pork Osso Bucco

**Prep time: 15 minutes | Cook time: 1¾ hours | Serves 6**

| | |
|---|---|
| 1 tablespoon butter, softened | ½ cup chopped onions |
| 6 (16-ounce / 454-g) pork shanks | ½ cup chopped celery |
| 1 tablespoon olive oil | 2 cups Cabernet Sauvignon |
| 3 cloves garlic, minced | 5 cups vegetable broth |
| 1 cup diced tomatoes | ½ cup chopped |
| Salt and black pepper to taste | parsley, extra to garnish |
| | 1 teaspoon lemon zest |

1. Melt the butter in a large saucepan over medium heat. Season the pork with salt and black pepper and brown it for 12 minutes; remove to a plate.
2. In the same pan, sauté 2 cloves of garlic and onions in the oil, for 3 minutes; return the pork shanks. Stir in the Cabernet, celery, tomatoes, and vegetable broth; season with salt and pepper. Cover the pan and let simmer on low heat for 1½ hours basting the pork every 15 minutes with the sauce.
3. In a bowl, mix the remaining garlic, parsley, and lemon zest to make a gremolata, and stir the mixture into the sauce when it is ready. Turn the heat off and dish the Osso Bucco.
4. Garnish with parsley and serve with creamy turnip mash.

**Per Serving**

calories: 533 | fat: 40g | protein: 34g
carbs: 4g | net carbs: 2g | fiber: 2g

## Classic Carnitas

**Prep time: 15 minutes | Cook time: 9 to 10 hours | Serves 8**

| | |
|---|---|
| 3 tablespoons extra-virgin olive oil, divided | 1 teaspoon ground coriander |
| 2 pounds pork shoulder, cut into 2-inch cubes | 1 teaspoon ground cumin |
| 2 cups diced tomatoes | ½ teaspoon salt |
| 2 cups chicken broth | 1 avocado, peeled, pitted, and diced, for garnish |
| ½ sweet onion, chopped | 1 cup sour cream, for garnish |
| 2 fresh chipotle peppers, chopped | 2 tablespoons chopped cilantro, for garnish |
| Juice of 1 lime | |

1. Lightly grease the insert of the slow cooker with 1 tablespoon of the olive oil.
2. In a large skillet over medium-high heat, heat the remaining 2 tablespoons of the olive oil.
3. Add the pork and brown on all sides for about 10 minutes.
4. Transfer to the insert and add the tomatoes, broth, onion, peppers, lime juice, coriander, cumin, and salt.
5. Cover and cook on low for 9 to 10 hours.
6. Shred the cooked pork with a fork and stir the meat into the sauce.
7. Serve topped with the avocado, sour cream, and cilantro.

**Per Serving**

calories: 508 | fat: 41g | protein: 29g
carbs: 7g | net carbs: 4g | fiber: 3g

## Pork Steaks with Broccoli

**Prep time: 10 minutes | Cook time: 25 minutes | Serves 4**

1 tablespoon olive oil
1 tablespoon butter
4 pork steaks, bone-in
½ cup water
Salt and black pepper, to taste
2 garlic cloves, minced
1 tablespoon fresh parsley, chopped
½ head broccoli, cut into florets
½ lemon, sliced

1. Heat oil and butter over high heat. Add in the pork steaks, season with pepper and salt, and cook until browned; set to a plate. In the same pan, add garlic and broccoli and cook for 4 minutes.
2. Pour the water, lemon slices, salt, and black pepper, and cook everything for 5 minutes.
3. Return the pork steaks to the pan and cook for 10 minutes. Serve the steaks sprinkled with sauce with parsley.

**Per Serving**

calories: 561 | fat: 39g | protein: 47g
carbs: 3g | net carbs: 2g | fiber: 1g

## Pork Chops with Broccoli

**Prep time: 10 minutes | Cook time: 51 minutes | Serves 4**

1 shallot, chopped
2 (10½-ounce / 298-g) cans mushroom soup
4 pork chops
½ cup sliced
mushrooms
Salt and black pepper to taste
1 tablespoon parsley
½ head broccoli, cut into florets

1. Steam the broccoli in salted water over medium heat for 6-8 minutes until tender. Set aside.
2. Preheat the oven to 370ºF (188ºC). Season the pork chops with salt and pepper, and place in a greased baking dish. Combine the mushroom soup, mushrooms and onion, in a bowl. Pour this mixture over the pork chops. Bake for 45 minutes. Sprinkle with parsley and serve with broccoli.

**Per Serving**

calories: 434 | fat: 20g | protein: 40g
carbs: 7g | net carbs: 5g | fiber: 2g

## Mediterranean Pork

**Prep time: 10 minutes | Cook time: 35 minutes | Serves 4**

1 garlic clove, minced
4 pork chops, bone-in
Salt and black pepper, to taste
1 teaspoon dried oregano
¼ cup kalamata
olives, pitted and sliced
1 tablespoon olive oil
1 tablespoon vegetable broth
¼ cup feta cheese, crumbled

1. Preheat the oven to 425ºF (220ºC).
2. Rub pork chops with pepper and salt, and add in a roasting pan. Stir in the garlic, olives, olive oil, broth, and oregano, set in the oven and bake for 10 minutes. Reduce heat to 350ºF (180ºC) and roast for 25 minutes.
3. Slice the pork, divide among plates, and sprinkle with pan juices and feta cheese all over.
4. Serve immediately.

**Per Serving**

calories: 394 | fat: 24g | protein: 41g
carbs: 1g | net carbs: 1g | fiber: 0g

## Lemony Peanuts Pork Chops

**Prep time: 10 minutes | Cook time: 30 minutes | Serves 4**

⅓ cup cilantro
⅓ cup mint
1 onion, chopped
¼ cup peanuts
1 tablespoon olive oil
Salt, to taste
4 pork chops
2 garlic cloves, minced
Juice and zest from 1 lemon

1. Preheat oven to 250ºF (121ºC).
2. In a food processor, combine the cilantro with olive oil, mint, peanuts, salt, lemon zest, garlic, and onion. Rub the pork with this mixture, place in a bowl, and refrigerate for 1 hour while covered.
3. Remove to a greased baking dish, sprinkle with lemon juice, and bake for 30 minutes in the oven.
4. Serve immediately.

**Per Serving**

calories: 428 | fat: 26g | protein: 42g
carbs: 6g | net carbs: 5g | fiber: 1g

## Creamy Pork Chops and Canadian Ham

**Prep time: 5 minutes | Cook time: 25 minutes | Serves 4**

4 ounces (113 g) Canadian ham, chopped
4 pork chops
Salt and black pepper to taste
2 sprigs fresh thyme
1 tablespoon heavy cream
½ teaspoon Dijon mustard

1. Cook ham in a skillet over medium heat for 5 minutes. Remove to a plate. Season pork chops with salt and pepper, and brown in the bacon fat for 4 minutes on each side.
2. Remove to the bacon plate. Stir in thyme, 1 tablespoon of water, mustard, and heavy cream and simmer for 5 minutes. Return the chops and bacon, and cook for another 10 minutes. Garnish with thyme leaves.
3. Serve immediately.

**Per Serving**

calories: 373 | fat: 19g | protein: 40g
carbs: 1g | net carbs: 1g | fiber: 0g

## Pork Shoulder and Sauerkraut Casserole

**Prep time: 15 minutes | Cook time: 9 to 10 hours | Serves 6**

3 tablespoons extra-virgin olive oil, divided
2 tablespoons butter
2 pounds (907 g) pork shoulder roast
1 (28-ounce / 794-g)
jar sauerkraut, drained
1 cup chicken broth
½ sweet onion, thinly sliced
¼ cup granulated erythritol

1. Lightly grease the insert of the slow cooker with 1 tablespoon of the olive oil.
2. In a large skillet over medium-high heat, heat the remaining 2 tablespoons of the olive oil and the butter. Add the pork to the skillet and brown on all sides for about 10 minutes.
3. Transfer to the insert and add the sauerkraut, broth, onion, and erythritol.
4. Cover and cook on low for 9 to 10 hours.
5. Serve warm.

**Per Serving**

calories: 516 | fat: 42g | protein: 28g
carbs: 7g | net carbs: 3g | fiber: 4g

## Balsamic Pork Loin Chops

**Prep time: 5 minutes | Cook time: 10 minutes | Serves 6**

6 pork loin chops, boneless
1 tablespoon erythritol
¼ cup balsamic vinegar
3 cloves garlic, minced
¼ cup olive oil
⅓ teaspoon salt
Black pepper, to taste

1. Put the pork in a plastic bag. In a bowl, mix the erythritol, balsamic vinegar, garlic, olive oil, salt, pepper, and pour the sauce over the pork. Seal the bag, shake it, and place in the refrigerator.
2. Marinate the pork for 2 hours. Preheat the grill to medium heat, remove the pork when ready, and grill covered for 10 minutes on each side. Remove and let sit for 4 minutes, and serve immediately.

**Per Serving**

calories: 419 | fat: 26g | protein: 40g
carbs: 2g | net carbs: 2g | fiber: 0g

## Pork Wraps with Veggies

**Prep time: 10 minutes | Cook time: 10 minutes | Serves 4**

1 tablespoon avocado oil
1 pound (454 g) ground pork
1 tablespoon ginger paste
Salt and black pepper to taste
1 teaspoon butter
1 head Iceberg lettuce
½ onion, sliced
1 red bell pepper, seeded and chopped
2 dill pickles, finely chopped

1. Heat avocado oil in a pan over medium heat and put the in pork with ginger paste, salt, and pepper. Cook for 10 to 15 minutes over medium heat while breaking any lumps until the pork is no longer pink.
2. Pat the lettuce dry with a paper towel and in each leaf, spoon two to three tablespoons of the pork mixture, top with onion slices, bell pepper, and dill pickles.
3. Serve immediately.

**Per Serving**

calories: 424 | fat: 28g | protein: 31g
carbs: 4g | net carbs: 1g | fiber: 3g

## Pork Patties with Caramelized Onion Rings

**Prep time: 10 minutes | Cook time: 10 minutes | Serves 6**

2 pound (907 g) ground pork
Pink salt and chili pepper to taste
1 tablespoon olive oil
1 tablespoon butter
1 white onion, sliced into rings
1 tablespoon balsamic vinegar
3 drops liquid stevia
6 low carb burger buns, halved
2 firm tomatoes, sliced into rings

1. Combine the pork, salt and chili pepper in a bowl and mold out 6 patties.
2. Heat the olive oil in a skillet over medium heat and fry the patties for 4 to 5 minutes on each side until golden brown on the outside. Remove onto a plate and sit for 3 minutes.
3. Melt butter in a skillet over medium heat, sauté onions for 2 minutes, and stir in the balsamic vinegar and liquid stevia. Cook for 30 seconds stirring once or twice until caramelized. In each bun, place a patty, top with some onion rings and 2 tomato rings.
4. Serve the burgers with cheddar cheese dip.

**Per Serving**

calories: 490 | fat: 35g | protein: 35g
carbs: 7g | net carbs: 7g | fiber: 0g

## Lemony Pork Chops and Brussels Sprouts

**Prep time: 10 minutes | Cook time: 15 minutes | Serves 6**

1 tablespoon lemon juice
3 cloves garlic, pureed
1 tablespoon olive oil
6 pork loin chops
1 tablespoon butter
1 pound (454 g)
brussels sprouts, trimmed and halved
1 tablespoon white wine
Salt and black pepper, to taste

1. Preheat broiler to 400ºF (205ºC) and mix the lemon juice, garlic, salt, black pepper, and oil in a bowl.
2. Brush the pork with the mixture, place in a baking sheet, and cook for 6 minutes on each side until browned. Share into 6 plates and make the side dish.
3. Melt butter in a small wok or pan and cook in brussels sprouts for 5 minutes until tender. Drizzle with white wine, sprinkle with salt and black pepper and cook for another 5 minutes. Ladle brussels sprouts to the side of the chops and serve with a hot sauce.

**Per Serving**

calories: 400 | fat: 25g | protein: 40g
carbs: 6g | net carbs: 3g | fiber: 3g

## Golden Pork Burgers

**Prep time: 10 minutes | Cook time: 10 minutes | Serves 4**

1 tablespoon olive oil
1 pound (454 g) ground pork
Salt and black pepper to taste
½ teaspoon chili pepper
1 tablespoon parsley
1 white onion, sliced
into rings
½ tablespoon balsamic vinegar
1 drop liquid stevia
1 tomato, sliced into rings
1 tablespoon mayonnaise

1. Warm half of the oil in a skillet over medium heat, sauté onions for 2 minutes, and stir in the balsamic vinegar and liquid stevia. Cook for 30 seconds stirring once or twice until caramelized; remove to a plate. Combine the pork, salt, black pepper and chili pepper in a bowl, and mold out 2 patties.
2. Heat the remaining olive oil in a skillet over medium heat and fry the patties for 4 to 5 minutes on each side until golden brown on the outside. Remove to a plate and sit for 3 minutes.
3. In each tomato slice, place half of the mayonnaise and a patty, and top with some onion rings. Cover with another tomato slice and serve.

**Per Serving**

calories: 380 | fat: 27g | protein: 29g
carbs: 2g | net carbs: 2g | fiber: 0g

## Pork Chops with Blackberry Gravy

**Prep time: 10 minutes | Cook time: 10 minutes | Serves 4**

| | |
|---|---|
| 1 tablespoon olive oil | ½ tablespoon rosemary leaves, chopped |
| 1 pound (454 g) pork chops | 1 tablespoon balsamic vinegar |
| Salt and black pepper to taste | 1 teaspoon Worcestershire sauce |
| 1 cup blackberries | |
| 1 tablespoon chicken broth | |

1. Place the blackberries in a bowl and mash them with a fork until jam-like. Pour into a saucepan, add the chicken broth and rosemary. Bring to boil on low heat for 4 minutes. Stir in balsamic vinegar and Worcestershire sauce. Simmer for 1 minute.
2. Heat oil in a skillet over medium heat, season the pork with salt and black pepper, and cook for 5 minutes on each side. Put on serving plates and spoon sauce over the pork chops.

**Per Serving**

calories: 302 | fat: 18g | protein: 28g
carbs: 4g | net carbs: 2g | fiber: 2g

## Pork Meatballs in Pasta Sauce

**Prep time: 15 minutes | Cook time: 35 minutes | Serves 6**

| | |
|---|---|
| 2 pound (907 g) ground pork | Salt and black pepper to taste |
| 1 tablespoon olive oil | ¼ cup chopped parsley |
| 1 cup pork rinds, crushed | 2 jars sugar-free marinara sauce |
| 3 cloves garlic, minced | ½ teaspoon Italian seasoning |
| ½ cup coconut milk | 1 cup Italian blend kinds of cheeses |
| 2 eggs, beaten | Chopped basil to garnish |
| ½ cup grated Parmesan cheese | |
| ½ cup grated asiago cheese | |

1. Preheat the oven to 400ºF (205ºC), line a cast iron pan with foil and oil it with cooking spray. Set aside.
2. Combine the coconut milk and pork rinds in a bowl. Mix in the ground pork, garlic, Asiago cheese, Parmesan cheese, eggs, salt, and pepper, just until combined. Form balls of the mixture and place them in the prepared pan. Bake in the oven for 20 minutes at a reduced temperature of 370ºF (188ºC).
3. Transfer the meatballs to a plate. Pour half of the marinara sauce in the baking pan. Place the meatballs back in the pan and pour the remaining marinara sauce all over them. Sprinkle with the Italian blend cheeses, drizzle with the olive oil, and then sprinkle with Italian seasoning.
4. Cover the pan with foil and put it back in the oven to bake for 10 minutes. After, remove the foil, and cook for 5 minutes. Once ready, take out the pan and garnish with basil. Serve on a bed of squash spaghetti.

**Per Serving**

calories: 716 | fat: 50g | protein: 50g
carbs: 5g | net carbs: 4g | fiber: 1g

## Garlicky Pork and Bell Peppers

**Prep time: 10 minutes | Cook time: 25 minutes | Serves 4**

| | |
|---|---|
| 1 tablespoon butter | 1 tablespoon olive oil |
| 4 pork steaks, bone-in | 6 garlic cloves, minced |
| 1 cup chicken stock | 1 tablespoon fresh parsley, chopped |
| Salt and black pepper, to taste | 4 bell peppers, sliced |
| A pinch of lemon pepper | 1 lemon, sliced |

1. Heat a pan with 2 tablespoons oil and 2 tablespoons butter over medium heat. Add in the pork steaks, season with black pepper and salt, and cook until browned; remove to a plate. In the same pan, warm the rest of the oil and butter, add garlic and bell peppers and cook for 4 minutes.
2. Pour the chicken stock, lemon slices, salt, lemon pepper, and black pepper, and cook everything for 5 minutes. Return the pork steaks to the pan and cook for 10 minutes. Split the sauce and steaks among plates and sprinkle with parsley to serve.

**Per Serving**

calories: 580 | fat: 39g | protein: 48g
carbs: 7g | net carbs: 6g | fiber: 1g

# Chapter 11 Fish and Seafood

## Blackened Tilapia Tacos

**Prep time: 10 minutes | Cook time: 5 minutes | Serves 4**

1 tablespoon olive oil
1 teaspoon chili powder
**Slaw:**
½ cup red cabbage, shredded
1 tablespoon lemon juice
1 teaspoon apple cider

2 tilapia fillets
1 teaspoon paprika
4 low carb tortillas

vinegar
1 tablespoon olive oil
Salt and black pepper to taste

1. Season the tilapia with chili powder and paprika. Heat the olive oil in a skillet over medium heat.
2. Add tilapia and cook until blackened, about 3 minutes per side. Cut into strips. Divide the tilapia between the tortillas. Combine all slaw ingredients in a bowl and top the fish to serve.

**Per Serving**
calories: 269 | fat: 20.1g | protein: 13.7g
carbs: 5.3g | net carbs: 3.4g | fiber: 1.9g

## Sriracha Shrimp Sushi Rolls

**Prep time: 10 minutes | Cook time: 0 minutes | Serves 5**

2 cups cooked and chopped shrimp
1 tablespoon sriracha sauce

¼ cucumber, julienned
5 hand roll nori sheets
¼ cup mayonnaise

1. Combine shrimp, mayonnaise, cucumber and sriracha sauce in a bowl. Lay out a single nori sheet on a flat surface and spread about $1/5$ of the shrimp mixture. Roll the nori sheet as desired. Repeat with the other ingredients. Serve with sugar-free soy sauce.

**Per Serving**
calories: 220 | fat: 10.2g | protein: 18.6g
carbs: 2.0g | net carbs: 0.9g | fiber: 1.1g

## Tilapia and Red Cabbage Taco Bowl

**Prep time: 10 minutes | Cook time: 15 minutes | Serves 4**

2 cups cauli rice
2 teaspoons butter
4 tilapia fillets, cut into cubes
¼ teaspoon taco seasoning

Salt and chili pepper to taste
¼ head red cabbage, shredded
1 ripe avocado, pitted and chopped

1. Sprinkle cauli rice in a bowl with a little water and microwave for 3 minutes. Fluff after with a fork and set aside. Melt butter in a skillet over medium heat, rub the tilapia with the taco seasoning, salt, and chili pepper, and fry until brown on all sides, for about 8 minutes in total.
2. Transfer to a plate and set aside. In 4 serving bowls, share the cauli rice, cabbage, fish, and avocado. Serve with chipotle lime sour cream dressing.

**Per Serving**
calories: 270 | fat: 23.5g | protein: 16.6g
carbs: 9.1g | net carbs: 3.9g | fiber: 5.2g

## Sicilian Zoodle and Sardine Spaghetti

**Prep time: 5 minutes | Cook time: 10 minutes | Serves 2**

4 cups zoodles (spiralled zucchini)
2 ounces (57 g) cubed bacon
4 ounces (113 g) canned sardines, chopped

½ cup canned chopped tomatoes
1 tablespoon capers
1 tablespoon parsley
1 teaspoon minced garlic

1. Pour some of the sardine oil in a pan. Add garlic and cook for 1 minute. Add the bacon and cook for 2 more minutes. Stir in the tomatoes and let simmer for 5 minutes. Add zoodles and sardines and cook for 3 minutes.

**Per Serving**
calories: 356 | fat: 31.2g | protein: 20.1g
carbs: 8.8g | net carbs: 5.9g | fiber: 2.9g

## Sour Cream Salmon Steaks

**Prep time: 10 minutes | Cook time: 20 minutes | Serves 4**

1 cup sour cream
½ tablespoon minced dill
½ lemon, zested and juiced
Pink salt and black pepper to season
4 salmon steaks
½ cup grated Parmesan cheese

1. Preheat oven to 400ºF (205ºC) and line a baking sheet with parchment paper; set aside. In a bowl, mix the sour cream, dill, lemon zest, juice, salt and black pepper, and set aside.
2. Season the fish with salt and black pepper, drizzle lemon juice on both sides of the fish and arrange them in the baking sheet. Spread the sour cream mixture on each fish and sprinkle with Parmesan.
3. Bake the fish for 15 minutes and after broil the top for 2 minutes with a close watch for a nice a brown color. Plate the fish and serve with buttery green beans.

**Per Serving**

calories: 289 | fat: 23.5g | protein: 16.1g
carbs: 1.5g | net carbs: 1.3g | fiber: 0.2g

## Crab Patties

**Prep time: 10 minutes | Cook time: 5 minutes | Serves 8**

2 tablespoons coconut oil
1 tablespoon lemon juice
1 cup lump crab meat
2 teaspoons Dijon mustard
1 egg, beaten
1½ tablespoons coconut flour

1. In a bowl to the crabmeat, add all the ingredients, except for the oil; mix well to combine. Make patties out of the mixture. Melt the coconut oil in a skillet over medium heat. Add the crab patties and cook for about 2-3 minutes per side.

**Per Serving**

calories: 216 | fat: 11.6g | protein: 15.2g
carbs: 3.6g | net carbs: 3.5g | fiber: 0.1g

## Sriracha Shrimp Stuffed Avocados

**Prep time: 5 minutes | Cook time: 0 minutes | Serves 4**

1 pound (454 g) large shrimp, peeled, deveined, and cooked (tails removed)
⅓ cup sugar-free mayonnaise
2 tablespoons Sriracha sauce
1 teaspoon chopped fresh cilantro, plus more for garnish if desired
1 teaspoon lime juice
2 large ripe Hass avocados

1. Chop the shrimp into bite-sized pieces and place in a medium-sized bowl.
2. Add the mayonnaise, Sriracha, cilantro, and lime juice. Mix until well combined. Place in the refrigerator to chill for 10 minutes.
3. Just before serving, cut the avocados in half and remove the pits. Spoon ½ cup of the spicy shrimp mixture into each avocado half. Serve immediately, garnished with extra cilantro, if desired. If not consuming it right away, store the spicy shrimp mixture in the refrigerator for up to 5 days.

**Per Serving**

calories: 335 | fat: 29.1g | protein: 14.9g
carbs: 7.9g | net carbs: 2.8g | fiber: 5.1g

## Tomato and Olive Tilapia Flillets

**Prep time: 10 minutes | Cook time: 25 minutes | Serves 4**

4 tilapia fillets
2 garlic cloves, minced
2 teaspoons oregano
14 ounces (397 g) diced tomatoes
1 tablespoon olive oil
½ red onion, chopped
2 tablespoons parsley
¼ cup kalamata olives

1. Heat olive oil in a skillet over medium heat and cook the onion for 3 minutes. Add garlic and oregano and cook for 30 seconds. Stir in tomatoes and bring the mixture to a boil. Reduce the heat and simmer for 5 minutes. Add olives and tilapia, and cook for about 8 minutes. Serve the tilapia with tomato sauce.

**Per Serving**

calories: 283 | fat: 15.1g | protein: 22.9g
carbs: 7.9g | net carbs: 5.9g | fiber: 2.0g

## Seared Scallops with Chorizo

**Prep time: 10 minutes | Cook time: 10 minutes | Serves 4**

2 tablespoons butter
16 fresh scallops
8 ounces (227 g) chorizo, chopped
1 red bell pepper, seeds removed, sliced
1 cup red onions, finely chopped
1 cup Asiago cheese, grated
Salt and black pepper to taste

1. Melt half of the butter in a skillet over medium heat, and cook the onion and bell pepper for 5 minutes until tender. Add the chorizo and stir-fry for another 3 minutes. Remove and set aside.
2. Pat dry the scallops with paper towels, and season with salt and pepper. Add the remaining butter to the skillet and sear the scallops for 2 minutes on each side to have a golden brown color. Add the chorizo mixture back and warm through. Transfer to serving platter and top with Asiago cheese.

**Per Serving**

calories: 490 | fat: 32.1g | protein: 35.8g
carbs: 6.0g | net carbs: 4.9g | fiber: 1.1g

## Creamy Herbed Salmon

**Prep time: 10 minutes | Cook time: 10 minutes | Serves 2**

2 salmon fillets
¾ teaspoon dried tarragon
2 tablespoons olive oil
¾ teaspoon dried dill

**Sauce:**

2 tablespoons butter
½ teaspoon dill
½ teaspoon tarragon
¼ cup heavy cream
Salt and black pepper to taste

1. Season the salmon with dill and tarragon. Warm the olive oil in a pan over medium heat. Add salmon and cook for about 4 minutes on both sides. Set aside.
2. To make the sauce: melt the butter and add the dill and tarragon. Cook for 30 seconds to infuse the flavors. Whisk in the heavy cream, season with salt and black pepper, and cook for 2-3 minutes. Serve the salmon topped with the sauce.

**Per Serving**

calories: 467 | fat: 40.1g | protein: 22.1g
carbs: 1.9g | net carbs: 1.6g | fiber: 0.3g

## Chimichurri Grilled Shrimp

**Prep time: 10 minutes | Cook time: 35 minutes | Serves 4**

1 pound (454 g) shrimp, peeled and deveined
2 tablespoons olive oil
Juice of 1 lime

**Chimichurri:**

½ teaspoon salt
¼ cup olive oil
2 garlic cloves
¼ cup red onions, chopped
¼ cup red wine
vinegar
½ teaspoon pepper
2 cups parsley
¼ teaspoon red pepper flakes

1. Process the chimichurri ingredients in a blender until smooth; set aside. Combine shrimp, olive oil, and lime juice, in a bowl, and let marinate in the fridge for 30 minutes. Preheat your grill to medium. Add shrimp and cook about 2 minutes per side. Serve shrimp drizzled with the chimichurri sauce.

**Per Serving**

calories: 284 | fat: 20.4g | protein: 15.8g
carbs: 4.8g | net carbs: 3.6g | fiber: 1.2g

## Pistachio Salmon with Shallot Sauce

**Prep time: 15 minutes | Cook time: 20 minutes | Serves 4**

4 salmon fillets
½ teaspoon pepper
1 teaspoon salt
¼ cup mayonnaise
½ cup chopped pistachios

**Sauce:**

1 chopped shallot
2 teaspoons lemon zest
1 tablespoon olive oil
A pinch of black pepper
1 cup heavy cream

1. Preheat the oven to 370ºF (188ºC).
2. Brush the salmon with mayonnaise and season with salt and pepper. Coat with pistachios, place in a lined baking dish and bake for 15 minutes.
3. Heat olive oil in a saucepan and sauté the shallot for 3 minutes. Stir in the rest of the sauce ingredients. Bring the mixture to a boil and cook until thickened. Serve the fish with the sauce.

**Per Serving**

calories: 562 | fat: 46.8g | protein: 34.1g
carbs: 8.1g | net carbs: 5.9g | fiber: 2.2g

## Macadamia Tilapia

**Prep time: 5 minutes | Cook time: 15 minutes | Serves 2**

| | |
|---|---|
| 2 (4-ounce / 113-g) tilapia fillets | lemon juice |
| ½ cup unsalted macadamia nuts | 2 teaspoons coconut oil |
| 1 tablespoon chopped fresh parsley | ¼ teaspoon garlic powder |
| 1 tablespoon fresh | Lemon wedges, for serving |

1. Preheat the oven to 400°F (205°C). Line a rimmed baking sheet with parchment paper.
2. Rinse the tilapia with cold water, pat dry with a paper towel, and place on the lined baking sheet.
3. Place the macadamia nuts, parsley, and lemon juice in a food processor and pulse/chop until the mixture is slightly chunkier than breadcrumb consistency. Be sure not to overblend, or you will end up with nut butter.
4. Top each fillet with 1 teaspoon of the coconut oil and then macadamia nut mixture, pressing it into the fish. Bake for 10 to 15 minutes, until the top is crisp and slightly golden brown. Serve with lemon wedges on the side.

**Per Serving**

calories: 382 | fat: 32.6g | protein: 22.6g
carbs: 5.4g | net carbs: 2.6g | fiber: 2.8g

## Parmesan Shrimp with Curry Sauce

**Prep time: 10 minutes | Cook time: 5 minutes | Serves 2**

| | |
|---|---|
| ½ ounce (14 g) grated Parmesan cheese | 2 teaspoons almond flour |
| 1 egg, beaten | 12 shrimp, shelled |
| ¼ teaspoon curry powder | 3 tablespoons coconut oil |

**Sauce:**

| | |
|---|---|
| 2 tablespoons curry leaves | ½ cup heavy cream |
| 2 tablespoons butter | ½ ounce (14 g) Cheddar cheese, shredded |
| ½ onion, diced | |

1. Combine all dry ingredients for the batter. Melt the coconut oil in a skillet over medium heat. Dip the shrimp in the egg first, and then coat with the dry mixture. Fry until golden and crispy.

2. In another skillet, melt butter. Add onion and cook for 3 minutes. Add curry leaves and cook for 30 seconds. Stir in heavy cream and Cheddar and cook until thickened. Add shrimp and coat well. Serve.

**Per Serving**

calories: 561 | fat: 40.9g | protein: 24.3g
carbs: 5.0g | net carbs: 4.2g | fiber: 0.8g

## Shrimp and Daikon Noodle Panang

**Prep time: 8 minutes | Cook time: 15 minutes | Serves 4**

| | |
|---|---|
| 1 tablespoon coconut oil | shrimp, peeled and deveined |
| 3 tablespoons red curry paste | 3 cups spiral-sliced daikon noodles (about 10 ounces / 283 g) |
| 2 tablespoons natural peanut butter (no sugar added) | ½ cup sliced red bell peppers |
| 1 (14-ounce / 397-g) can full-fat unsweetened coconut milk | 1 teaspoon sliced Thai red chili peppers (optional) |
| 2 tablespoons fish sauce (no sugar added) | 1 tablespoon lime juice |
| 2 tablespoons granulated erythritol | ¼ cup whole or chopped fresh cilantro leaves, for garnish (optional) |
| 1 pound (454 g) large | |

1. Heat the coconut oil in a large sauté pan over medium heat. Add the curry paste and peanut butter and cook for 2 minutes, stirring constantly. Add the coconut milk, fish sauce, and sweetener and cook for 10 more minutes, or until the sauce has thickened and coats the back of a spoon.
2. Add the shrimp, daikon noodles, bell peppers, and Thai chili peppers, if using, and cook for 3 minutes, or until the shrimp have just turned pink; don't overcook the shrimp or they will be tough and dry.
3. Remove from the heat and stir in the lime juice. Serve hot, garnished with cilantro, if desired.

**Per Serving**

calories: 356 | fat: 27.0g | protein: 24.9g
carbs: 8.9g | net carbs:6.9 g | fiber: 2.0g

## White Tuna Patties

**Prep time: 5 minutes | Cook time: 20 minutes | Serves 3**

2 large eggs
1 tablespoon fresh lemon juice
¼ cup grated Parmesan cheese
¼ cup golden flaxseed meal
2 tablespoons chopped fresh parsley
2 teaspoons Old Bay seasoning

1 (12-ounce / 340-g) can white tuna, in water
¼ cup finely chopped onions
¼ teaspoon salt
¼ cup avocado oil, for frying
Lemon wedges, for serving (optional)

1. In a bowl, beat the eggs with the lemon juice.
2. Stir in the Parmesan cheese, flaxseed meal, parsley, and Old Bay seasoning.
3. Drain the tuna well, removing as much of the water as possible. Add the drained tuna and onions to the Parmesan mixture and mix well. Season with salt and pepper to taste.
4. Shape the tuna mixture into 6 patties.
5. Heat the oil in a large skillet over medium heat. When hot, add half of the patties and fry until golden brown, 3 to 5 minutes per side, then set on a paper towel–lined dish to soak up any excess oil. Repeat with the remaining patties.
6. Serve with lemon wedges, if desired.

**Per Serving**

calories: 306 | fat: 18.1g | protein: 30.9g
carbs: 5.0g | net carbs: 2.0g | fiber: 3.0g

## Alaska Cod with Butter Garlic Sauce

**Prep time: 10 minutes | Cook time: 15 minutes | Serves 6**

2 teaspoons olive oil
6 Alaska cod fillets
Salt and black pepper to taste
4 tablespoons salted butter

4 cloves garlic, minced
⅓ cup lemon juice
3 tablespoons white wine
2 tablespoons chopped chives

1. Heat the oil in a skillet over medium heat and season the cod with salt and black pepper. Fry the fillets in the oil for 4 minutes on one side, flip and cook for 1 minute. Take out, plate, and set aside.

2. In another skillet over low heat, melt the butter and sauté the garlic for 3 minutes. Add the lemon juice, wine, and chives. Season with salt, black pepper, and cook for 3 minutes until the wine slightly reduces. Put the fish in the skillet, spoon sauce over, cook for 30 seconds and turn the heat off.
3. Divide fish into 6 plates, top with sauce, and serve with buttered green beans.

**Per Serving**

calories: 265 | fat: 17.1g | protein: 19.9g
carbs: 2.5g | net carbs: 2.4g | fiber: 0.1g

## Cod Fillet with Summer Salad

**Prep time: 10 minutes | Cook time: 10 minutes | Serves 5**

4 tablespoons extra-virgin olive oil
5 cod fillets
¼ cup balsamic vinegar
1 tablespoon stone-ground mustard
Sea salt and ground black pepper, to season

½ pound (227 g) green cabbage, shredded
2 cups lettuce, cut into small pieces
1 red onion, sliced
1 garlic clove, minced
1 teaspoon red pepper flakes

1. Heat 1 tablespoon of the olive oil in a large frying pan over medium-high heat.
2. Once hot, fry the fish fillets for 5 minutes until golden brown; flip them and cook on the other side for 4 to 5 minutes more; work in batches to avoid overcrowding the pan.
3. Flake the cod fillets with two forks and reserve.
4. To make the dressing, whisk the remaining tablespoon of olive oil with the balsamic vinegar, mustard, salt, and black pepper.
5. Combine the green cabbage, lettuce, onion, and garlic in a salad bowl. Dress the salad and top with the reserved fish.
6. Garnish with red pepper flakes and serve. Enjoy!

**Per Serving**

calories: 276 | fat: 7g | protein: 43g
carbs: 6g | net carbs: 4g | fiber: 2g

## Tuna Cakes with Seeds

**Prep time: 10 minutes | Cook time: 10 minutes | Serves 4**

3 tablespoons sugar-free mayonnaise
1 tablespoon Sriracha sauce
1 teaspoon wheat-free soy sauce
1 teaspoon coconut flour
1 pound (454 g) fresh tuna, cut into ½-inch cubes
2 tablespoons white sesame seeds
1 tablespoon black sesame seeds
2 tablespoons avocado oil or other light-tasting oil, for the pan

1. In a mixing bowl, whisk together the mayonnaise, Sriracha, soy sauce, and flour until smooth. Add the tuna and stir to combine.
2. Combine the white and black sesame seeds and spread on a small plate.
3. Using your hands, form the tuna mixture into 12 small cakes about 2 inches in diameter. Gently dip both sides of the cakes in the sesame seeds to lightly coat them.
4. Heat the oil in a medium-sized nonstick sauté pan over medium heat. Cook the cakes in batches, 1 to 2 minutes per side, until golden brown. Serve warm.

**Per Serving**

calories: 300 | fat: 18.9g | protein: 26.9g
carbs: 2.0g | net carbs: 1.0g | fiber: 1.0g

## Salmon Fillet

**Prep time: 10 minutes | Cook time: 19 minutes | Serves 6**

2 tablespoons peanut oil
2 bell peppers, deseeded and sliced
½ cup scallions, chopped
2 cloves garlic, minced
4 tablespoons Marsala wine
2 ripe tomatoes, pureed
2½ pounds salmon fillets
Sea salt and ground black pepper, to taste
¼ teaspoon ground bay leaf
1 teaspoon paprika

1. Heat the peanut oil in a large frying pan over a moderate flame. Now, sauté the bell peppers and scallions for 3 minutes.
2. Add in the garlic and continue to sauté for 30 seconds more or until aromatic but not until it's browned.
3. Add a splash of wine to deglaze the pan. Stir in the remaining ingredients and turn the heat to simmer.
4. Let it cook, partially covered, for 15 minutes or until the salmon is cooked through. Bon appétit!

**Per Serving**

calories: 347 | fat: 19g | protein: 40g
carbs: 4g | net carbs: 3g | fiber: 1g

## Cheesy Tilapia Omelet

**Prep time: 10 minutes | Cook time: 12 minutes | Serves 4**

2 tablespoons olive oil
½ cup leeks, sliced
1 pound (454 g) tilapia fillets
1 red chili pepper, deseeded and sliced
Sea salt and ground black pepper, to taste
½ teaspoon garlic powder
½ teaspoon fennel seeds
1 cup milk
4 ounces (113 g) cream cheese
8 medium-sized eggs
1 cup goat cheese, crumbled

1. Heat 1 tablespoon of the olive oil in a cast-iron skillet over moderate heat. Once hot, sweat the leeks for 4 to 5 minutes, stirring periodically.
2. Then, add in the tilapia fish and cook for 5 minutes more until flesh flakes apart easily; flake the fish using a fork and reserve.
3. Add in the chili pepper, salt, black pepper, garlic powder, and fennel seeds; stir to combine.
4. In a mixing bowl, whisk the milk, cream cheese and eggs until frothy and well combined. Heat the remaining tablespoon of olive oil. Pour the egg mixture into the skillet.
5. When the eggs are set, spoon the fish mixture over one side, add the goat cheese and fold your omelet over the filling. Heat off.
6. Cover and let stand for 2 minutes in the residual heat until the cheese has melted. Bon appétit!

**Per Serving**

calories: 558 | fat: 38g | protein: 46g
carbs: 7g | net carbs: 7g | fiber: 0g

## Parmesan Baked Salmon with Broccoli

**Prep time: 10 minutes | Cook time: 30 minutes | Serves 4**

2 salmon fillets, cubed
3 white fish, cubed
1 head broccoli, cut into florets
1 tablespoon butter, melted
Salt and black pepper
to taste
1 cup crème fraiche
¼ cup grated Parmesan cheese
Grated Parmesan cheese for topping

1. Preheat oven to 400ºF (205ºC) and grease an 8 x 8 inches casserole dish with cooking spray. Toss the fish cubes and broccoli in butter and season with salt and pepper to taste. Spread in the greased dish.
2. Mix the crème fraiche with Parmesan cheese, pour and smear the cream on the fish, and sprinkle with some more Parmesan cheese. Bake for 25 to 30 minutes until golden brown on top, take the dish out, sit for 5 minutes and spoon into plates. Serve with lemon-mustard asparagus.

**Per Serving**

calories: 355 | fat: 17.2g | protein: 28.1g
carbs: 4.9g | net carbs: 3.9g | fiber: 1.0g

## Crab Cakes with Mixed Greens

**Prep time: 15 minutes | Cook time: 10 minutes | Serves 4**

1 large egg
¼ cup mayonnaise
1 green onion, chopped, plus extra for garnish (optional)
1 teaspoon Old Bay seasoning
1 tablespoon Dijon mustard
1 tablespoon chopped fresh parsley
1½ teaspoons fresh
lemon juice
1 pound (454 g) fresh lump crabmeat
¼ cup golden flaxseed meal
2 to 3 tablespoons avocado oil, for frying
Spring mix greens or arugula, for serving (optional)
Lemon wedges, for serving (optional)

1. In a large mixing bowl, combine the egg and mayonnaise and whisk until smooth. Add the green onion, Old Bay seasoning, mustard, parsley, and lemon juice and mix well.
2. Sort through the crabmeat to ensure that no shells remain in the meat.

3. Then add the crabmeat to the bowl with the egg mixture and gently mix with a spoon until well blended. Be sure to mix gently so that you don't break up the crabmeat too much.
4. Gently fold in the flaxseed meal.
5. Refrigerate the mixture for 20 to 30 minutes, then use your hands to form it into four 4-ounce (113-g) patties.
6. Heat the avocado oil in a large skillet over medium-high heat. When hot, add the crab cakes and pan-fry for 4 to 5 minutes on each side, until golden brown and warm throughout.
7. Serve immediately. If desired, serve each crab cake over a bed of spring mix or arugula with lemon wedges on the side and garnished with extra green onions.

**Per Serving**

calories: 333 | fat: 22.1g | protein: 27.9g
carbs: 3.7g | net carbs: 1.8g | fiber: 1.9g

## Lemony Paprika Shrimp

**Prep time: 10 minutes | Cook time: 20 minutes | Serves 6**

½ cup butter, divided
2 pounds (907 g) shrimp, peeled and deveined
Salt and black pepper to taste
¼ teaspoon sweet paprika
1 tablespoon minced garlic
3 tablespoons water
1 lemon, zested and juiced
2 tablespoons chopped parsley

1. Melt half of the butter in a large skillet over medium heat, season the shrimp with salt, black pepper, paprika, and add to the butter. Stir in the garlic and cook the shrimp for 4 minutes on both sides until pink. Remove to a bowl and set aside.
2. Put the remaining butter in the skillet; include the lemon zest, juice, and water. Add the shrimp, parsley, and adjust the taste with salt and pepper. Cook for 2 minutes. Serve shrimp and sauce with squash pasta.

**Per Serving**

calories: 256 | fat: 22.1g | protein: 12.9g
carbs: 2.0g | net carbs: 1.9g | fiber: 0.1g

## Cheddar Monkfish Fillet

**Prep time: 10 minutes | Cook time: 17 minutes | Serves 6**

2 tablespoons olive oil
6 monkfish fillets
Sea salt and ground black pepper, to taste
2 green onions, sliced
2 green garlic stalks, sliced
½ cup sour cream
1 teaspoon oregano
1 teaspoon basil
1 teaspoon rosemary
½ cup cheddar cheese, shredded
2 tablespoons fresh chives, chopped

1. Heat the olive oil in a frying pan over a medium-high flame. Once hot, sear the monkfish fillets for 3 minutes until golden brown; flip them and cook on the other side for 3 to 4 minutes more.
2. Season with salt and black pepper. Transfer the monkfish fillets to a lightly greased casserole dish. Add the green onions and green garlic.
3. In a mixing dish, thoroughly combine the sour cream with the oregano, basil, rosemary, and cheddar cheese.
4. Spoon the mixture into your casserole dish and bake at 360ºF (182ºC) for about 11 minutes or until golden brown on top.
5. Garnish with fresh chives and serve. Bon appétit!

**Per Serving**

calories: 229 | fat: 13g | protein: 26g
carbs: 2g | net carbs: 2g | fiber: 0g

## Curry Tilapia

**Prep time: 10 minutes | Cook time: 15 minutes | Serves 4**

1 tablespoon peanut oil
3 green cardamoms
1 teaspoon cumin seeds
1 shallot, chopped
1 red chili pepper, chopped
1 red bell pepper, chopped
1 teaspoon ginger-
garlic paste
1 cup tomato puree 1 cup chicken broth
1 tablespoon curry paste
1½ pounds (680 g) tilapia
1 cinnamon stick
Sea salt and ground black pepper, to taste

1. Heat the peanut oil in a saucepan over medium-heat. Now, toast the cardamoms and cumin for 2 minutes until aromatic.
2. Add in the shallot, red chili, bell pepper and continue to sauté for 2 minutes more or until just tender and translucent.
3. Add in the ginger-garlic paste and continue to sauté an additional 30 seconds. Pour the tomato puree and chicken broth into the saucepan. Bring to a boil.
4. Turn the heat to medium-low and stir in the curry paste, tilapia, cinnamon, salt, and black pepper. Let it simmer, partially covered, for 10 minutes more.
5. Flake the fish and serve in individual bowls. Enjoy!

**Per Serving**

calories: 209 | fat: 7g | protein: 35g
carbs: 3g | net carbs: 2g | fiber: 1g

## Tilapia and Shrimp Soup

**Prep time: 10 minutes | Cook time: 21 minutes | Serves 5**

1 tablespoon butter
4 scallions, chopped
1 cup celery, chopped
1 Italian pepper, deseeded and chopped
1 poblano pepper, deseeded and chopped
2 cups cauliflower, grated
2 Roma tomatoes, pureed
4 cups chicken broth
1 pound (454 g) tilapia, skinless and chopped into small chunks
½ pound (227 g) medium shrimp, deveined
2 tablespoons balsamic vinegar

1. Melt the butter in a heavy-bottomed pot over a moderate flame. Once hot, cook your veggies until crisp-tender or about 4 minutes, stirring periodically to ensure even cooking.
2. Add in the pureed tomatoes and chicken broth. When the soup reaches boiling, turn the heat to a simmer.
3. Add in the tilapia and let it cook, partially covered, for 12 minutes. Stir in the shrimp, partially cover, and continue to cook for 5 minutes more.
4. Afterwards, stir in the balsamic vinegar. Ladle into individual bowls and serve warm.

**Per Serving**

calories: 194 | fat: 6g | protein: 26g
carbs: 6g | net carbs: 4g | fiber: 2g

## Mussels and Coconut Milk Curry

**Prep time: 10 minutes | Cook time: 20 minutes | Serves 6**

3 pounds (1.4 kg) mussels, cleaned, de-bearded
1 cup minced shallots
3 tablespoons minced garlic
1½ cups coconut milk
2 cups dry white wine

2 teaspoons red curry powder
⅓ cup coconut oil
⅓ cup chopped green onions
⅓ cup chopped parsley

1. Pour the wine into a large saucepan and cook the shallots and garlic over low heat. Stir in the coconut milk and red curry powder and cook for 3 minutes.
2. Add the mussels and steam for 7 minutes or until their shells are opened. Then, use a slotted spoon to remove to a bowl leaving the sauce in the pan. Discard any closed mussels at this point.
3. Stir the coconut oil into the sauce, turn the heat off, and stir in the parsley and green onions. Serve the sauce immediately with a butternut squash mash.

**Per Serving**

calories: 355 | fat: 20.5g | protein: 21.0g
carbs: 2.5g | net carbs: 0.2g | fiber: 2.3g

## Salmon and Asparagus Bake

**Prep time: 15 minutes | Cook time: 15 minutes | Serves 4**

1½ to 2 pounds (680 to 907 g) asparagus (6 to 8 spears Per Serving)
3 tablespoons coconut oil, melted but not hot
1 teaspoon garlic powder
⅓ cup grated Parmesan cheese
¼ cup plus 2 tablespoons

mayonnaise
1 clove garlic, pressed
4 salmon fillets (about 6 ounces / 170 g each), rinsed and patted dry
Finely chopped fresh dill or dill sprigs, for garnish (optional)
1 lemon, sliced, for serving (optional)

1. Preheat the oven to 350ºF (180ºC).
2. Rinse the asparagus and trim or snap off the tough end of each spear.
3. Place the asparagus, coconut oil, and garlic powder in a zip-top plastic bag, seal, and shake lightly to coat the asparagus.

4. In a bowl, mix the Parmesan cheese, mayonnaise, and pressed garlic.
5. Lay out 4 rectangular pieces of parchment paper, large enough to fit the asparagus and fish with plenty of paper remaining on the sides and ends to fold into packets and seal. Divide the seasoned asparagus evenly among the sheets of parchment.
6. Place the fillets on top of the asparagus, skin side down. Top the salmon with the mayonnaise mixture.
7. Fold the parchment paper over the fish and seal on all sides. The packet should look like a calzone.
8. Place the packets on a rimmed baking sheet and bake for 12 to 15
9. minutes, until the internal temperature of the salmon reaches 145ºF (63ºC).
10. Garnish with fresh dill and lemon slices, if desired.

**Per Serving**

calories: 478 | fat: 33.1g | protein: 38.6g
carbs: 7.3g | net carbs: 3.9g | fiber: 3.4g

## Tilapia Fillet

**Prep time: 5 minutes | Cook time: 10 minutes | Serves 6**

6 tilapia fillets, patted dry
Sea salt and ground black pepper, to taste
1 teaspoon cayenne pepper
6 tablespoons butter

1 teaspoon garlic, minced
1 tablespoon parsley, chopped
1 teaspoon fresh lime juice

1. Brush a nonstick skillet with cooking oil. Heat the skillet over medium-high heat.
2. Once the oil is heated, pan-fry the tilapia until both sides turn golden brown; gently flip them with a tong.
3. Season with salt, black pepper, and cayenne pepper.
4. Prepare the garlic butter sauce by whisking the remaining ingredients. Serve the tilapia with a dollop of garlic butter if desired. Bon appétit!

**Per Serving**

calories: 215 | fat: 14g | protein: 24g
carbs: 1g | net carbs: 1g | fiber: 0g

## Grilled Salmon with Greek Green Salad

**Prep time: 15 minutes | Cook time: 8 minutes | Serves 4**

### Salad:

2 medium heads romaine lettuce, chopped

½ medium cucumber, chopped

¾ cup cherry tomatoes, halved

¾ cup crumbled Feta cheese

½ cup pitted Kalamata olives

½ cup thinly sliced red onions

1 teaspoon dried ground oregano

Pinch of salt

Pinch of ground black pepper

### Dressing:

¼ cup extra-virgin olive oil

¼ cup red wine vinegar

1 large clove garlic, minced

2 teaspoons onion powder

2 teaspoons dried ground oregano

Salt and pepper

### Salmon:

4 (6-ounce / 170-g) skin-on salmon fillets

1 tablespoon extra-virgin olive oil

Salt and pepper

1 tablespoon avocado oil or other cooking oil of choice, for the grill grates Fresh dill, for garnish (optional)

1. In a large bowl, combine all the salad ingredients and toss. Divide the salad among 4 bowls and set aside.
2. Make the dressing: Place the olive oil, vinegar, garlic, oregano, and onion powder in a bowl and whisk to combine. Season with salt and pepper to taste and set aside.
3. Rinse the salmon and pat dry. Brush the salmon with the olive oil and season with salt and pepper.
4. Preheat a grill to medium-high heat, then brush the hot grill grates with the avocado oil.
5. Place the salmon skin side up on the grill, close the grill lid, and cook for 2 minutes. Flip the salmon and cook skin side down for 5 to 6 minutes, until the internal temperature reaches 145ºF (63ºC).
6. Allow the salmon to rest for a few minutes, then place a fillet on top of each salad. Whisk the salad dressing again and drizzle it over the salads.
7. Garnish with fresh dill, if desired, and enjoy!

**Per Serving**

calories: 589 | fat: 41.8g | protein: 42.0g
carbs: 10.2g | net carbs: 7.6g | fiber: 2.6g

## Seared Tuna with Niçoise Salad

**Prep time: 10 minutes | Cook time: 8 minutes | Serves 4**

1 tablespoon sugar-free mayonnaise

1 teaspoon Dijon mustard

½ teaspoon kosher salt

¼ teaspoon ground black pepper

1 pound (454 g) ahi tuna steaks

1 tablespoon avocado oil or other light-tasting oil, for the pan

2 medium heads red or green leaf lettuce, leaves washed and dried

8 hard-boiled eggs, peeled and quartered

2 cups cooked cauliflower florets

2 cups blanched green beans

2 large tomatoes, cut into wedges

### Dijon vinaigrette:

¼ cup extra-virgin olive oil

¼ cup red wine vinegar

¼ cup sugar-free mayonnaise

1 tablespoon Dijon mustard

¼ teaspoon kosher salt

⅛ teaspoon ground black pepper

1. Combine the mayonnaise, mustard, salt, and pepper in a small bowl. Coat the tuna steaks on all sides with the mixture.
2. Heat the oil in a medium-sized nonstick pan over medium-high heat. Add the tuna steaks and sear for about 2 minutes per side for rare or 4 minutes per side to cook them through. Remove from the pan and set aside.
3. Place the lettuce leaves on a serving platter or divide them among 4 individual serving plates. Arrange the eggs, cauliflower, green beans, and tomato wedges around the outer edges on top of the lettuce.
4. Place the tuna steaks, whole or cut into pieces, in the center of the platter or plates.
5. In a medium-sized bowl, whisk together the vinaigrette ingredients. Drizzle over the salad just before serving.

**Per Serving**

calories: 547 | fat: 36.9g | protein: 15.8g
carbs: 12.0g | net carbs: 6.0g | fiber: 6.0g

## Chepala Vepudu

**Prep time: 10 minutes | Cook time: 10 minutes | Serves 3**

3 carp fillets
1 teaspoon chili powder
1 teaspoon cumin powder
1 teaspoon turmeric powder
1 coriander powder
½ teaspoon garam masala

½ teaspoon flaky salt
¼ teaspoon cayenne pepper
3 tablespoons full-fat coconut milk
1 egg
2 tablespoons olive oil
6 curry leaves, for garnish

1. Pat the fish fillets with kitchen towels and add to a large resealable bag. Add the spices to the bag and shake to coat on all sides.
2. In a shallow dish, whisk the coconut milk and egg until frothy and well combined. Dip the fillets into the egg mixture.
3. Then, heat the oil in a large frying pan. Fry the fish fillets on both sides until they are cooked through and the coating becomes crispy.
4. Serve with curry leaves and enjoy!

**Per Serving**

calories: 443 | fat: 28g | protein: 43g
carbs: 3g | net carbs: 2g | fiber: 1g

## Sole Fish Jambalaya

**Prep time: 15 minutes | Cook time: 8 minutes | Serves 2**

1 teaspoon extra virgin olive oil
1 jalapeno pepper, minced
1 small-sized leek, chopped
½ teaspoon ginger garlic paste
¼ teaspoon ground cumin
¼ teaspoon ground allspice
½ teaspoon oregano
¼ teaspoon thyme

¼ teaspoon marjoram
1 pound (454 g) sole fish fillets, cut into bite-sized strips
1 large-sized ripe tomato, pureed
½ cup water
½ cup clam juice
Kosher salt, to season
1 bay laurel
5-6 black peppercorns
1 cup spinach, torn into pieces

1. Heat the oil in a Dutch oven over a moderate flame. Then, sauté the pepper and leek until they have softened.

2. Now, stir in the ginger-garlic paste, cumin, allspice, oregano, thyme, and marjoram; continue stirring for 30 to 40 seconds more or until aromatic.
3. Add in the fish, tomatoes, water, clam juice, salt, bay laurel, and black peppercorns. Cover and decrease the temperature to medium-low.
4. Let it simmer for 4 to 6 minutes or until the liquid has reduced slightly. Stir in the spinach and let it simmer, covered, for about 2 minutes more or until it wilts.
5. Ladle into serving bowls and serve warm. Bon appétit!

**Per Serving**

calories: 232 | fat: 4g | protein: 38g
carbs: 6g | net carbs: 4g | fiber: 2g

## Old Bay Prawns

**Prep time: 10 minutes | Cook time: 10 minutes | Serves 2**

¾ pound (340 g) prawns, peeled and deveined
1 teaspoon Old Bay seasoning mix
½ teaspoon paprika
Coarse sea salt and ground black pepper, to taste
1 habanero pepper, deveined and minced

1 bell pepper, deveined and minced
1 cup pound broccoli florets
2 teaspoons olive oil
1 tablespoon fresh chives, chopped2 slices lemon, for garnish
2 dollops of sour cream, for garnish

1. Toss the prawns with the Old Bay seasoning mix, paprika, salt, and black pepper.
2. Arrange them on a parchment-lined roasting pan. Add the bell pepper and broccoli. Drizzle olive oil over everything and transfer the pan to a preheated oven.
3. Roast at 390ºF (199ºC) for 8 to 11 minutes, turning the pan halfway through the cooking time. Bake until the prawns are pink and cooked through.
4. Serve with fresh chives, lemon, and sour cream. Bon appétit!

**Per Serving**

calories: 269 | fat: 10g | protein: 38g
carbs: 7g | net carbs: 4g | fiber: 3g

## Monkfish Mayonnaise Salad

**Prep time: 10 minutes | Cook time: 9 minutes | Serves 5**

| | |
|---|---|
| 2 pounds (57 g) monkfish | 1 tablespoon balsamic vinegar |
| 1 bell pepper, sliced | ½ cup mayonnaise |
| ½ cup radishes, sliced | 1 teaspoon stone-ground mustard |
| 1 red onion, chopped | Flaky salt, to season |
| 1 garlic clove, minced | |

1. Pat the fish dry with paper towels and brush on both sides with nonstick cooking oil. Grill over medium-high heat, flipping halfway through for about 9 minutes or until opaque.
2. Flake the fish with a fork and toss with the remaining ingredients; gently toss to combine well.
3. Serve at room temperature or well-chilled. Bon appétit!

**Per Serving**

calories: 306 | fat: 19g | protein: 27g
carbs: 4g | net carbs: 3g | fiber: 1g

## Baked Halibut Steaks

**Prep time: 10 minutes | Cook time: 13 minutes | Serves 2**

| | |
|---|---|
| 2 tablespoons olive oil | ½ teaspoon hot paprika |
| 2 halibut steaks | Sea salt cracked black pepper, to your liking |
| 1 red bell pepper, sliced | 1 dried thyme sprig, leaves crushed |
| 1 yellow onion, sliced | |
| 1 teaspoon garlic, smashed | |

1. Start by preheating your oven to 390ºF (199ºC).
2. Then, drizzle olive oil over the halibut steaks. Place the halibut in a baking dish that is previously greased with a nonstick spray.
3. Top with the bell pepper, onion, and garlic. Sprinkle hot paprika, salt, black pepper, and dried thyme over everything.
4. Bake in the preheated oven for 13 to 15 minutes and serve immediately. Enjoy!

**Per Serving**

calories: 502 | fat: 19g | protein: 72g
carbs: 6g | net carbs: 5g | fiber: 1g

## Cod Fillet with Lemony Sesame Sauce

**Prep time: 10 minutes | Cook time: 7 minutes | Serves 6**

| | |
|---|---|
| 6 cod fillets, skin-on | ginger, minced |
| 3 tablespoons olive oil | 1 garlic clove, minced |
| Sea salt and ground black pepper, to season | 1 red chili pepper, minced |
| 1 lemon, freshly squeezed | 3 tablespoons toasted sesame seeds |
| ½ teaspoon fresh | 3 tablespoons toasted sesame oil |

1. Prepare a grill for medium-high heat. Rub the cod fillets with olive oil; season both sides with salt and black pepper.
2. Next, place the cod fillets on the grill skin side down. Grill approximately 7 minutes until the skin is lightly charred.
3. To make the sauce, whisk the remaining ingredients until well combined; season with lots of black pepper.
4. Divide the cod fillets among serving plates. Spoon the sauce over them and enjoy!

**Per Serving**

calories: 341 | fat: 17g | protein: 42g
carbs: 3g | net carbs: 2g | fiber: 1g

## Mahi Mahi Ceviche

**Prep time: 10 minutes | Cook time: 10 minutes | Serves 4**

| | |
|---|---|
| 1½ pounds mahi-mahi fish, cut into bite-sized cubes | 4 scallions, chopped |
| Sea salt and ground black pepper, to taste | 2 Roma tomatoes, sliced |
| 1 teaspoon hot paprika | 1 bell pepper, sliced |
| 2 garlic cloves, minced | 4 tablespoons olive oil |
| | 2 tablespoons fresh lemon juice |

1. Season the haddock fillets with salt, black pepper, and paprika. Brush them on all sides with nonstick cooking oil.
2. Grill over medium heat for 9 to 11 minutes until golden with brown edges. Use a metal spatula to gently lift the haddock fillets.
3. Toss your fish with the remaining ingredients in a large bowl. Taste and adjust seasonings. Divide between four serving bowls and serve.

**Per Serving**

calories: 424 | fat: 30g | protein: 33g
carbs: 6g | net carbs: 4g | fiber: 2g

## Stir-Fried Scallops with Cauliflower

**Prep time: 10 minutes | Cook time: 6 minutes | Serves 5**

1 tablespoon butter
2 medium Italian peppers, deveined and sliced
2 cups cauliflower florets
½ teaspoon fresh ginger, minced
1 teaspoon garlic, minced
2 pounds (907 g) sea

scallops
½ cup dry white wine
½ teaspoon cayenne pepper
½ teaspoon oregano
½ teaspoon marjoram
½ teaspoon rosemary
Sea salt and ground black pepper, to taste
½ cup chicken broth

1. Melt the butter in a large frying pan over medium-high heat.
2. Stir in the Italian peppers, cauliflower, ginger, and garlic. Cook for about 3 minutes or until the vegetables have softened.
3. Stir in the sea scallops and continue to cook for 3 minutes. Stir to coat with the vegetable mixture.
4. Add in the remaining ingredients and let it simmer, partially covered, for a few minutes longer. Bon appétit!

**Per Serving**

calories: 217 | fat: 4g | protein: 24g
carbs: 5g | net carbs: 4g | fiber: 1g


## Sea Bass Fillet with Dill Sauce

**Prep time: 10 minutes | Cook time: 20 minutes | Serves 2**

1 tablespoon olive oil
1 cup red onions, sliced
2 bell peppers, deveined and sliced
**Dill Sauce:**

Se salt and cayenne pepper, to taste
1 teaspoon paprika
1 pound sea bass fillets

1 tablespoon mayonnaise
¼ cup Greek yogurt
1 tablespoon fresh dill,

chopped
½ teaspoon garlic powder
½ fresh lemon, juiced

1. Toss the onions, peppers, and sea bass fillets with the olive oil, salt, cayenne pepper, and paprika.
2. Line a baking pan with a piece of parchment paper. Preheat your oven to 400°F (205°C).

3. Arrange your fish and vegetables on the prepared baking pan. Bake for 10 minutes; turn them over and bake for a further 10 to 12 minutes.
4. Meanwhile, make the sauce by mixing all ingredients until well combined.
5. Serve the fish and vegetables with the dill sauce on the side. Bon appétit!

**Per Serving**

calories: 374 | fat: 17g | protein: 43g
carbs: 6g | net carbs: 4g | fiber: 2g


## New Orleans Halibut and Crabmeat

**Prep time: 15 minutes | Cook time: 22 minutes | Serves 6**

3 teaspoons butter, at room temperature
1 pound (454 g) andouille sausage, sliced
1 red onion, chopped
2 cloves garlic, minced
1 celery stalk, chopped
1 red chili pepper, chopped
2 pounds (907 g) halibut, cut into bite-sized chunks

2 tomatoes, pureed
4 cups water
3 cubes beef bouillon
½ teaspoon Cajun seasoning blend
Flaky salt and ground black pepper, to taste
1 pound (454 g) lump crabmeat
1 teaspoon cayenne pepper
1 tablespoon fresh cilantro

1. Melt 1 teaspoon of the butter in a heavy-bottomed pot over a moderate flame. Now, brown the sausage for 2 to 3 minutes; reserve.
2. Melt the remaining 2 teaspoons of butter and add in the red onion, garlic, celery, and chili pepper; let it cook for 1½ minutes more.
3. Now, stir in the halibut, tomatoes, water, cubes of beef bouillon and bring to a boil. Immediately reduce the heat and let it simmer, partially covered, for 13 minutes.
4. Then, stir in the Cajun seasoning blend, salt, ground black pepper, crabmeat, and cayenne pepper; return the sausage to the pot.
5. Stir to combine well and let it cook for 5 to 6 minutes more. Ladle into individual bowls and serve garnished with fresh cilantro. Enjoy!

**Per Serving**

calories: 441 | fat: 28g | protein: 40g
carbs: 6g | net carbs: 5g | fiber: 1g

## Halászlé with Paprikash

**Prep time: 15 minutes | Cook time: 10 minutes | Serves 2**

1 tablespoon extra virgin olive oil
2 bell peppers, chopped
1 Hungarian wax pepper, chopped
1 garlic clove, minced
1 red onion, chopped
½ pound (227 g) tilapia, cut into bite-sized pieces
1½ cups fish broth
2 vine-ripe tomatoes, pureed
1 teaspoon sweet

paprika
½ teaspoon mixed peppercorns, crushed
1 bay laurel
½ teaspoon sumac
½ teaspoon dried thyme
¼ teaspoon dried rosemary
Kosher salt, to season
½ teaspoon garlic, minced
2 tablespoons sour cream

1. Heat the extra virgin olive oil in a Dutch oven over medium-high heat. Now, sauté the peppers, garlic, and onion until tender and aromatic.
2. Now, stir in the tilapia, broth, tomatoes, and spices. Reduce the heat to medium-low. Let it simmer, covered, for 9 to 13 minutes.
3. Meanwhile, mix ½ teaspoon of minced garlic with the sour cream. Serve with the warm paprikash and enjoy!

**Per Serving**

calories: 252 | fat: 13g | protein: 28g
carbs: 5g | net carbs: 3g | fiber: 2g

## Cod Fillet and Mustard Greens

**Prep time: 10 minutes | Cook time: 13 minutes | Serves 2**

1 tablespoon olive oil
1 bell pepper, seeded and sliced
1 jalapeno pepper, seeded and sliced
2 stalks green onions, sliced
1 stalk green garlic, sliced

½ cup fish broth
2 cod fish fillets
½ teaspoon paprika
Sea salt and ground black pepper, to season
1 cup mustard greens, torn into bite-sized pieces

1. Heat the olive oil in a Dutch pot over a moderate flame. Now, sauté the peppers, green onions, and garlic until just tender and aromatic.

2. Add in the broth, fish fillets, paprika, salt, black pepper, and mustard greens. Reduce the temperature to medium-low, cover, and let it cook for 11 to 13 minutes or until heated through.
3. Serve immediately garnished with lemon slices if desired. Bon appétit!

**Per Serving**

calories: 171 | fat: 8g | protein: 20g
carbs: 5g | net carbs: 3g | fiber: 2g

## Goat Cheese Stuffed Squid

**Prep time: 15 minutes | Cook time: 30 minutes | Serves 4**

8 ounces (227 g) frozen spinach, thawed and drained (about 1½ cup)
4 ounces (113 g) crumbled goat cheese
½ cup chopped pitted olives (I like Kalamata in this recipe)
½ cup extra-virgin olive oil, divided

¼ cup chopped sun-dried tomatoes
¼ cup chopped fresh flat-leaf Italian parsley
2 garlic cloves, finely minced
¼ teaspoon freshly ground black pepper
2 pounds (907 g) baby squid, cleaned and tentacles removed

1. Preheat the oven to 350ºF (180ºC).
2. In a medium bowl, combine the spinach, goat cheese, olives, ¼ cup olive oil, sun-dried tomatoes, parsley, garlic, and pepper.
3. Pour 2 tablespoons olive oil in the bottom of an 8-inch square baking dish and spread to coat the bottom.
4. Stuff each cleaned squid with 2 to 3 tablespoons of the cheese mixture, depending on the size of squid, and place in the prepared baking dish.
5. Drizzle the tops with the remaining 2 tablespoons olive oil and bake until the squid are cooked through, 25 to 30 minutes. Remove from the oven and allow to cool 5 to 10 minutes before serving.

**Per Serving**

calories: 469 | fat: 37g | protein: 24g
carbs: 10g | net carbs: 7g | fiber: 3g

## Shrimp and Sea Scallop

**Prep time: 10 minutes | Cook time: 5 minutes | Serves 2**

1 tablespoon olive oil
½ cup scallions, chopped
1 garlic clove, minced
½ pound (227 g) shrimp, deveined
½ pound (227 g) sea scallops

2 tablespoons rum
½ cup fish broth
¼ teaspoon Cajun seasoning mix
Sea salt and ground black pepper, to taste
1 tablespoon fresh parsley, chopped

1. In a sauté pan, heat the olive oil until sizzling. Now, sauté your scallions and garlic until they are just tender and fragrant.
2. Now, sear the shrimp and sea scallops for 2 to 3 minutes or until they are firm. Add a splash of rum to deglaze the pan. Now, pour in the fish broth.
3. Add in the Cajun seasoning mix, salt, and black pepper; stir and remove from heat.
4. Serve warm garnished with fresh parsley. Enjoy!

**Per Serving**

calories: 305 | fat: 9g | protein: 47g
carbs: 3g | net carbs: 2g | fiber: 1g

## Asian Salmon and Veggies Salad

**Prep time: 20 minutes | Cook time: 5 minutes | Serves 2**

**Salad:**

¼ cup water
¼ cup Sauvignon Blanc
½ pound salmon fillets
1 cup Chinese cabbage, sliced

1 tomato, sliced
2 radishes, sliced
1 bell pepper, sliced
1 medium-sized white onion, sliced Salad

**Dressing:**

½ teaspoon fresh garlic, minced
1 fresh chili pepper, seeded and minced
½ teaspoon fresh ginger, peeled and grated
2 tablespoons fresh lime juice
1 tablespoon sesame

oil
1 tablespoon tamari sauce
1 teaspoon xylitol
1 tablespoon fresh mint, roughly chopped
Sea salt and freshly ground black pepper, to taste

1. Place the water and Sauvignon Blanc in a sauté pan; bring to a simmer over moderate heat.
2. Place the salmon fillets, skin-side down in the pan and cover with the lid. Cook for 5 to 8 minutes or to your desired doneness; do not overcook the salmon; reserve.
3. Place the Chinese cabbage, tomato, radishes, bell pepper, and onion in a serving bowl.
4. Prepare the salad dressing by whisking all ingredients. Dress your salad, top with the salmon fillets and serve immediately!

**Per Serving**

calories: 277 | fat: 15g | protein: 24g
carbs: 5g | net carbs: 4g | fiber: 1g

## Dijon Sea Bass Fillet

**Prep time: 10 minutes | Cook time: 10 minutes | Serves 3**

2 tablespoons olive oil
3 sea bass fillets
¼ teaspoon red pepper flakes, crushed
Sea salt, to taste
⅓ teaspoon mixed peppercorns, crushed

3 tablespoons butter
1 tablespoon Dijon mustard
2 cloves garlic, minced
1 tablespoon fresh lime juice

1. Heat the olive oil in a skillet over medium-high heat.
2. Pat dry the sea bass fillets with paper towels. Now pan-fry the fish fillets for about 4 minutes on each side until flesh flakes easily and it is nearly opaque.
3. Season your fish with red pepper, salt, and mixed peppercorns.
4. To make the sauce, melt the 3 tablespoons of butter in a saucepan over low heat; stir in the Dijon mustard, garlic, and lime juice. Let it simmer for 2 minutes.
5. To serve, spoon the Dijon butter sauce over the fish fillets. Bon appétit!

**Per Serving**

calories: 314 | fat: 23g | protein: 24g
carbs: 1g | net carbs: 1g | fiber: 0g

## Haddock and Turkey Smoked Sausage

**Prep time: 15 minutes | Cook time: 17 minutes | Serves 4**

2 tablespoons butter, at room temperature
1 onion, chopped
2 cloves garlic, sliced
1 bell pepper, sliced
1 celery stalk, chopped
1 cup broccoli florets
4 ounces (113 g) turkey smoked sausage, sliced
Sea salt and ground black pepper, to taste
2 tomatoes, pureed
2 cups fish broth
1 teaspoon chili powder
¼ teaspoon ground allspice
16 ounces (454 g) haddock steak, cut into bite-sized chunks
2 tablespoons fresh coriander, minced
1 teaspoon Creole seasoning blend

1. Melt the butter in a heavy-bottomed pot over moderate heat. Now, sauté the onion, garlic, and pepper, for 2 minutes until just tender and aromatic.
2. Add in the celery, broccoli, turkey smoked sausage, salt, black pepper, pureed tomatoes, and broth. Bring to a rolling boil and immediately reduce the heat to simmer.
3. Add in the remaining ingredients, partially cover, and continue simmering for 15 minutes.
4. Ladle into soup bowls and serve immediately.

**Per Serving**

calories: 236 | fat: 9g | protein: 27g
carbs: 6g | net carbs: 4g | fiber: 2g

## Romano Cheese Cod Fillet

**Prep time: 10 minutes | Cook time: 5 minutes | Serves 3**

3 cod fillets
½ cup almond meal
1 teaspoon cayenne pepper
Sea salt and ground black pepper, to season
1 teaspoon garlic powder
1 teaspoon porcini powder
½ teaspoon shallot powder
1 teaspoon dried rosemary, crushed
1 cup Romano cheese, preferably freshly grated
2 tablespoons butter

1. Pat the cod fillets dry with paper towels.
2. Add the fish, almond meal, and spices to the bag and shake to coat on all sides. Coat them with grated Romano cheese.
3. Melt the butter in a frying pan over medium-high heat.
4. Now pan-fry the fish fillets until flesh flakes easily and it is nearly opaque, about 4 to 5 minutes per side. Serve on warm plates. Bon appétit!

**Per Serving**

calories: 406 | fat: 30g | protein: 32g
carbs: 4g | net carbs: 2g | fiber: 2g

## Mackerel Fillet and Clam

**Prep time: 10 minutes | Cook time: 12 minutes | Serves 3**

2 teaspoons olive oil
2 mackerel fillets, patted dry
1 shallot, finely chopped
2 cloves garlic, minced
½ cup dry white wine
9 littleneck clams, scrubbed
Flaky salt and ground black pepper, to taste
½ teaspoon cayenne pepper
½ teaspoon fennel seeds
½ teaspoon mustard seeds
1 teaspoon celery seeds
1 teaspoon coriander, minced

1. In a large skillet, heat 1 teaspoon of the olive oil until sizzling; now, cook the mackerel fillets for about 6 minutes until cooked all the way through. Make sure to shake the skillet occasionally to prevent sticking; reserve, keeping warm.
2. Heat the remaining teaspoon of olive oil and sauté the shallot and garlic for 1 to 2 minutes or until fragrant.
3. Add in the wine and remaining seasonings; cook until almost evaporated. Fold in the clams and cook for 5 to 6 minutes until they open.
4. Return the fish to the skillet and serve warm. Bon appétit!

**Per Serving**

calories: 379 | fat: 9g | protein: 60g
carbs: 4g | net carbs: 4g | fiber: 0g

## Paprika Tiger Prawns

**Prep time: 10 minutes | Cook time: 10 minutes | Serves 6**

2 tablespoons olive oil
1 teaspoon butter
2 scallions, chopped
2 cloves garlic, pressed
2 bell peppers, chopped
2½ pounds (1.1 kg) tiger prawns, deveined
¼ teaspoon ground

black pepper
1 teaspoon paprika
1 teaspoon red chili flakes
½ teaspoon mustard seeds
½ teaspoon fennel seeds
Sea salt, to taste
½ cup Marsala wine

1. Heat the olive oil and butter in a frying pan over a medium-high flame. Now, sweat the scallions, garlic, and peppers until they are crisp-tender about 2 minutes.
2. Add in the tiger prawns and cook for 1½ minutes on each side until they are opaque.
3. Stir in the remaining ingredients and continue to cook for 5 minutes more over low heat. Taste and adjust seasonings. Bon appétit!

**Per Serving**

calories: 219 | fat: 7g | protein: 39g
carbs: 3g | net carbs: 2g | fiber: 1g

## Salmon Tacos with Guajillo Sauce

**Prep time: 10 minutes | Cook time: 10 minutes | Serves 5**

2 pounds (907 g) salmon
Flaky salt and ground black pepper, to taste
10 lettuce leaves
2 bell peppers, chopped
1 cucumber, chopped
1 avocado, pitted and peeled

1 tomato, halved
2 tablespoons extra-virgin olive oil
1 tablespoon lemon juice
4 tablespoons green onions
1 teaspoon garlic
1 guajillo chili pepper

1. Season your salmon with salt and black pepper. Brush the salmon on all sides with nonstick cooking oil.
2. Grill over medium heat for 13 minutes until golden and opaque in the middle. Flake the fish with two forks.
3. Divide the fish among the lettuce leaves; add the bell peppers and cucumber.

4. Pulse the remaining ingredients in your blender 8 to 10 times or until smooth with several small chunks of tomatoes and scallions.
5. Top each lettuce taco with the guajillo sauce and serve.

**Per Serving**

calories: 342 | fat: 17g | protein: 40g
carbs: 7g | net carbs: 3g | fiber: 4g

## Swordfish with Greek Yogurt Sauce

**Prep time: 10 minutes | Cook time: 25 minutes | Serves 6**

2 tablespoons butter
4 swordfish steaks
1 teaspoon paprika
½ teaspoon ground bay leaf
½ teaspoon mustard seeds
Sea salt and ground black pepper, to season
1 yellow onion, sliced

1 teaspoon garlic, minced
1 cup Greek yogurt
4 tablespoons mayonnaise
2 tablespoons fresh basil, chopped
2 tablespoons fresh dill, chopped
1 teaspoon urfa biber chile

1. Butter the bottom and sides of your casserole dish. Toss the swordfish steaks with the seasonings. Arrange the swordfish steaks in the prepared casserole dish.
2. Scatter the onion and garlic around the swordfish steaks. Bake in the preheated oven at 390ºF (199ºC) for about 25 minutes.
3. Meanwhile, whisk the Greek yogurt with the remaining ingredients to make the sauce. Serve the warm fish steaks with the sauce on the side. Bon appétit!

**Per Serving**

calories: 346 | fat: 23g | protein: 32g
carbs: 3g | net carbs: 3g | fiber: 0g

# Chapter 12 Desserts

## Cream Cheese Chocolate Mousse

**Prep time:10 minutes | Cook time: 0 minutes | Serves 2**

3 ounces (85 g) cream cheese, softened
½ cup heavy cream
1 teaspoon vanilla extract

¼ cup Swerve
2 tablespoons cocoa powder
1 pinch salt

1. Beat the cream cheese in a large mixing bowl with an electric beater until it makes fluffy mixture.
2. Switch the beater to low speed, and add the vanilla extract, heavy cream, salt, Swerve, and cocoa powder to beat for 2 minutes until it is completely smooth.
3. Chill in the refrigerator until ready to serve.

**Per Serving**

calories: 270 | fat: 26.4g | total carbs: 6.0g fiber: 2.0g | protein: 4.2g

## Keto Vanilla Ice Cream

**Prep time:10 minutes | Cook time:0 minutes | Serves 3**

1 cup heavy whipping cream
2 tablespoons Swerve confectioners' style sweetener
1 tablespoon vodka

1 teaspoon vanilla extract
¼ teaspoon xanthan gum
1 pinch salt

1. Add the cream, vodka, xanthan gum, Swerve, vanilla extract, and salt in a large jar.
2. Beat the cream mixture with a hand blender until the cream has thickened, and it makes soft peaks, after 60 to 75 seconds.
3. Cover this cream jar and place in your freezer for 3 to 4 hours, stirring occasionally.
4. Serve the vanilla ice cream in scoops and enjoy.

**Per Serving**

calories: 143 | fat: 14.8g | total carbs: 1.6g fiber: 0g | protein: 0.8g

## Simple Butter Cookies

**Prep time: 10 minutes | Cook time: 20 minutes | Makes 24**

1 cup granulated erythritol–monk fruit blend
8 tablespoons (1 stick) unsalted butter, at room temperature
1 teaspoon vanilla extract
2 large eggs, at room temperature
½ cup full-fat sour cream

2½ cups finely milled almond flour, sifted
1½ teaspoons baking powder
¼ teaspoon sea salt
1¼ cups confectioners' erythritol–monk fruit blend
½ cup full-fat sour cream
½ teaspoon vanilla extract

1. Preheat the oven to 350ºF (180ºC). Line the baking sheet with parchment paper and set aside.
2. In the medium bowl, using an electric mixer on high, combine the granulated erythritol–monk fruit blend, butter, and vanilla for 1 to 2 minutes, until light and fluffy, stopping and scraping the bowl once or twice, as needed.
3. Add the eggs, one at a time, to the medium bowl, then add the sour cream. Mix until well incorporated. Next add the almond flour, baking powder, and salt and mix until just combined. Put the dough in the refrigerator and chill for 30 minutes.
4. Drop the dough in tablespoons on the prepared baking sheet evenly spaced about 1 inch apart. Bake the cookies for 15 to 20 minutes, until lightly browned around the edges. Transfer the cookies to a cooling rack to fully cool, 15 to 20 minutes.
5. In the small bowl, combine the confectioners' erythritol–monk fruit blend, sour cream, and vanilla.
6. Once the cookies are fully cooled, using a spoon or pastry bag, drizzle the icing on top to serve.
7. Store leftovers in the refrigerator for up to 5 days or freeze for up to 3 weeks.

**Per Serving (2 Cookies)**

calories: 235 | fat: 21.9g | protein: 6.0g carbs: 6.0g | net carbs: 4.0g | fiber: 2.0g

## Mocha Mousse

**Prep time: 10 minutes | Cook time: 0 minutes | Serves 6**

1 (13.5-ounce / 383-g) can coconut cream, chilled overnight
3 tablespoons granulated erythritol–monk fruit blend; less sweet: 2 tablespoons

2 tablespoons unsweetened cocoa powder, plus more for dusting
1 teaspoon instant espresso powder
¼ teaspoon salt

1. Put the large metal bowl in the freezer to chill for at least 1 hour.
2. In the chilled large bowl, using an electric mixer on high, combine the coconut cream (adding it by the spoonful and reserving the water that has separated), erythritol–monk fruit blend, the cocoa powder, espresso powder, and salt and beat for 3 to 5 minutes, until stiff peaks form, stopping and scraping the bowl once or twice, as needed. If the consistency is too thick, add the reserved water from the coconut cream 1 tablespoon at a time to thin.
3. Serve immediately in a cold glass, dusted with cocoa powder.
4. Store leftovers in an airtight container for up to 5 days in the refrigerator.

**Per Serving (½ Cup)**

calories: 126 | fat: 11.9g | protein: 0g
carbs: 3.1g | net carbs: 2.0g | fiber: 1.1g

## Cinnamon Cream Cheese Mousse

**Prep time: 15 minutes | Cook time: 0 minutes | Serves 8**

2 ounces (57 g) full-fat cream cheese, at room temperature
1½ cups heavy whipping cream, divided
¼ cup granulated erythritol–monk fruit blend; less sweet: 2 tablespoons
½ teaspoon vanilla extract
½ teaspoon salt

½ cup finely milled almond flour
¼ cup coconut flour
¼ cup granulated erythritol–monk fruit blend
½ teaspoon ground cinnamon
⅛ teaspoon sea salt
4 tablespoons (½ stick) cold unsalted butter, thinly sliced

1. Put the large metal bowl in the freezer to chill for at least 5 minutes.

2. In the large chilled bowl, using an electric mixer on medium high, mix the cream cheese and ¼ cup of heavy cream until well combined. Add the erythritol–monk fruit blend, vanilla, and salt and mix until just combined. Add the remaining 1¼ cups of heavy cream and beat on high for about 3 minutes, until stiff peaks form, stopping and scraping the bowl once or twice, as needed. Refrigerate for at least 1 hour and up to overnight before serving.
3. In the small bowl, combine the almond flour, coconut flour, erythritol–monk fruit blend, cinnamon, and salt. Add the sliced butter and combine using a fork until the mixture resembles coarse crumbs. Set aside until ready to serve.
4. Serve the mousse in short glasses or small mason jars topped with the crumble. Store leftovers in an airtight container for up to 5 days in the refrigerator.

**Per Serving (½ Cup)**

calories: 274 | fat: 28.9g | protein: 3.1g
carbs: 3.1g | net carbs: 1.9g | fiber: 1.2g

## Rum Brownies

**Prep time: 15 minutes | Cook time: 22 minutes | Serves 8**

⅔ cup almond flour
½ cup coconut flour
1 teaspoon baking powder
1 cup xylitol
½ cup cocoa powder, unsweetened
2 eggs
6 ounces (170 g) butter, melted

3 ounces (85 g) baking chocolate, unsweetened and melted
2 tablespoons rum
A pinch of salt
A pinch of freshly grated nutmeg
¼ teaspoon ground cinnamon

1. In a mixing bowl, thoroughly combine dry ingredients. In a separate bowl, mix all the wet ingredients until well combined.
2. Stir dry mixture into wet ingredients. Evenly spread the batter into a parchment-lined baking dish.
3. Bake in the preheated oven at 360ºF (182ºC) for 20 to 22 minutes, until your brownies are set. Cut into squares and serve.

**Per Serving**

calories: 321 | fat: 30.1g | protein: 5.7g
carbs: 6.2g | net carbs: 2.6g | fiber: 3.6g

## Classic Almond Golden Cake

**Prep time: 15 minutes | Cook time: 3 hours | Serves 8**

½ cup coconut oil, divided
1½ cups almond flour
½ cup coconut flour
½ cup granulated erythritol
2 teaspoons baking powder
3 eggs
½ cup coconut milk
2 teaspoons pure vanilla extract
½ teaspoon almond extract

1. Line the insert of a 4-quart slow cooker with aluminum foil and grease the aluminum foil with 1 tablespoon of the coconut oil.
2. In a medium bowl, mix the almond flour, coconut flour, erythritol, and baking powder.
3. In a large bowl, whisk together the remaining coconut oil, eggs, coconut milk, vanilla, and almond extract.
4. Add the dry ingredients to the wet ingredients and stir until well blended.
5. Transfer the batter to the insert and use a spatula to even the top.
6. Cover and cook on low for 3 hours, or until a toothpick inserted in the center comes out clean.
7. Remove the cake from the insert and cool completely before serving.

**Per Serving**

calories: 234 | fat: 22g | protein: 6g
carbs: 3g | net carbs: 2g | fiber: 1g

## Tender Almond Pound Cake

**Prep time: 10 minutes | Cook time: 5 to 6 hours | Serves 8**

1 tablespoon coconut oil
2 cups almond flour
1 cup granulated erythritol
½ teaspoon cream of tartar
Pinch salt
1 cup butter, melted
5 eggs
2 teaspoons pure vanilla extract

1. Lightly grease an 8-by-4-inch loaf pan with the coconut oil.
2. In a large bowl, stir together the almond flour, erythritol, cream of tartar, and salt, until well mixed.
3. In a small bowl, whisk together the butter, eggs, and vanilla.
4. Add the wet ingredients to the dry ingredients and stir to combine.
5. Transfer the batter to the loaf pan.
6. Place the loaf pan in the insert of the slow cooker.
7. Cover and cook until a toothpick inserted in the center comes out clean, about 5 to 6 hours on low.
8. Serve warm.

**Per Serving**

calories: 281 | fat: 29g | protein: 5g
carbs: 1g | net carbs: 1g | fiber: 0g

## Old-fashioned Gingerbread Cake

**Prep time: 10 minutes | Cook time: 3 hours | Serves 8**

1 tablespoon coconut oil
2 cups almond flour
¾ cup granulated erythritol
2 tablespoons coconut flour
2 tablespoons ground ginger
2 teaspoons baking powder
2 teaspoons ground cinnamon
½ teaspoon ground nutmeg
¼ teaspoon ground cloves
Pinch salt
¾ cup heavy (whipping) cream
½ cup butter, melted
4 eggs
1 teaspoon pure vanilla extract

1. Lightly grease the insert of the slow cooker with coconut oil.
2. In a large bowl, stir together the almond flour, erythritol, coconut flour, ginger, baking powder, cinnamon, nutmeg, cloves, and salt.
3. In a medium bowl, whisk together the heavy cream, butter, eggs, and vanilla.
4. Add the wet ingredients to the dry ingredients and stir to combine.
5. Spoon the batter into the insert.
6. Cover and cook on low for 3 hours, or until a toothpick inserted in the center comes out clean.
7. Serve warm.

**Per Serving**

calories: 259 | fat: 23g | protein: 7g
carbs: 6g | net carbs: 3g | fiber: 3g

## Cinnamon Gingerbread Cookies

**Prep time: 15 minutes | Cook time: 15 minutes | Makes 24**

2 cups brown or golden erythritol–monk fruit blend; less sweet: 1¼ cups
3 large eggs
4 tablespoons (½ stick) unsalted butter, at room temperature
1 tablespoon molasses or 1 teaspoon molasses extract (optional)
1 teaspoon vanilla extract
4 tablespoons ground cinnamon
3 tablespoons ground ginger
½ teaspoon ground nutmeg
¼ teaspoon ground cloves
3 cups finely milled almond flour
1 tablespoon psyllium husk powder
1½ teaspoons baking powder
¼ teaspoon salt
¼ cup confectioners' erythritol–monk fruit blend
1 tablespoon heavy whipping cream

1. Preheat the oven to 325ºF (163ºC). Line the baking sheet with parchment paper and set aside.
2. In the large bowl, using an electric mixer on high, beat the brown erythritol–monk fruit blend, eggs, butter, molasses (if using), and vanilla until fully incorporated, stopping and scraping the bowl once or twice, as needed. Add the cinnamon, ginger, nutmeg, and cloves to the mixture and stir to combine.
3. Add the almond flour, psyllium powder, baking powder, and salt and beat on medium high until well incorporated.
4. Place the dough between two sheets of parchment paper and flatten with a rolling pin. Chill the dough in the refrigerator for 30 minutes.
5. Using a small cookie cutter or small-mouthed glass jar, cut the dough into cookies and place them about 1 inch apart, evenly spaced, on the prepared baking sheet. Bake for 12 to 15 minutes, until golden brown. Allow them to cool completely on the cooling rack, 15 to 20 minutes.
6. In the small bowl, combine the confectioners' erythritol–monk fruit blend with the heavy cream 1 teaspoon at a time to make the icing. The icing should have a runny consistency. Decorate the cooled cookies using either a pastry bag for fine detail or drizzle the icing on using a fork for a quick, fuss-free decorated cookie.
7. Store leftovers in an airtight container in the refrigerator for up to 5 days or freeze for up to 3 weeks.

**Per Serving (1 Cookie)**
calories: 107 | fat: 9.0g | protein: 3.0g
carbs: 5.0g | net carbs: 3.0g | fiber: 2.0g

## Pecan Cookies with Chocolate Chips

**Prep time: 10 minutes | Cook time: 15 minutes | Makes 16**

12 tablespoons (1½ sticks) unsalted butter, at room temperature
½ cup golden or brown erythritol–monk fruit blend
½ cup granulated erythritol–monk fruit blend
1 tablespoon sugar-free maple syrup
2 large eggs
1 tablespoon unflavored gelatin
2 cups finely milled almond flour, sifted
¼ cup coconut flour
2 teaspoons baking powder
¼ teaspoon salt
4 ounces (113 g) sugar-free chocolate chips
1 cup chopped pecans

1. Preheat the oven to 350ºF (180ºC). Line the baking sheet with parchment paper and set aside.
2. In the large bowl, beat the butter, golden erythritol–monk fruit blend, granulated erythritol–monk fruit blend, and sugar-free maple syrup until light and fluffy. Add the eggs, one at a time, mixing well after each addition. Sprinkle in the gelatin and combine well.
3. Mix in the almond flour, coconut flour, baking powder, and salt. Fold in the sugar-free chocolate chips and pecans.
4. Drop the dough by heaping tablespoons onto the prepared baking sheet, spacing them evenly about 2 inches apart. Flatten the cookies slightly.
5. Bake for 12 to 15 minutes, until golden. Cool on the rack for 15 to 20 minutes before serving.
6. Store leftovers in an airtight container in the refrigerator for up to 5 days or freeze for up to 3 weeks.

**Per Serving (1 Cookie)**
calories: 254 | fat: 24.0g | protein: 4.8g
carbs: 5.9g | net carbs: 2.1g | fiber: 3.8g

## Super Coconut Cupcakes

**Prep time: 15 minutes | Cook time: 15 minutes | Serves 9**

6 eggs, beaten
½ cup coconut oil, melted
3 tablespoons granulated Swerve
2 tablespoons flaxseed meal
¹/₃ cup coconut flour

1 teaspoon baking powder
A pinch of salt
A pinch of freshly grated nutmeg
1 teaspoon lemon zest
1 teaspoon coconut extract

1. Start by preheating your oven to 360ºF (182ºC). Coat a muffin pan with cupcake liners.
2. Beat the eggs with the coconut oil and granulated Swerve until frothy. In another mixing bowl, thoroughly combine the remaining ingredients.
3. Stir this dry mixture into the wet mixture; mix again to combine. Spoon the batter into the prepared muffin pan.
4. Bake for 13 to 15 minutes, or until a tester comes out dry and clean. To serve, sprinkle with some extra granulated Swerve if desired. Bon appétit!

**Per Serving**

calories: 164 | fat: 16.8g | protein: 2.2g
carbs: 1.6g | net carbs: 0.7g | fiber: 0.9g

## Cream Cheese Chocolate Cake

**Prep time: 15 minutes | Cook time: 20 minutes | Serves 10**

1 stick butter, room temperature
¹/₃ cup full-fat milk
2 eggs
½ cup walnut meal
¹/₃ cup flaxseed meal
¹/₃ cup coconut flour
1 teaspoon baking powder
2 teaspoons liquid stevia
¼ teaspoon ground star anise
¼ teaspoon cinnamon
¼ teaspoon ground cloves

A pinch of flaky salt
2 tablespoons cocoa powder
1 teaspoon rum extract
Cream Cheese Frosting:
¹/₃ cup butter, room temperature
6 ounces (170 g) cream cheese, softened
½ cup Xylitol
½ teaspoon pure caramel extract

1. Cream the butter and milk with an electric mixer; slowly, fold in the eggs and beat again to combine well.
2. In another bowl, mix all types of flours with the baking powder, stevia, spices, cocoa powder, and rum extract.
3. Now, stir this dry mixture into the wet mixture; mix again until everything is well incorporated.
4. Press the batter into a parchment-lined baking pan. Bake in the preheated oven at 400ºF (205ºC) for 18 minutes.
5. Meanwhile, whip the butter and cream cheese with an electric mixer.
6. Add in the Xylitol and caramel extract; continue to beat until the sweetener is well dissolved and the frosting is creamy.
7. Frost your cake and serve well-chilled. Bon appétit!

**Per Serving**

calories: 293 | fat: 29.2g | protein: 5.2g
carbs: 5.4g | net carbs: 3.1g | fiber: 2.3g

## Anise Cookies

**Prep time: 5 minutes | Cook time: 20 minutes | Serves 8**

2 tablespoons coconut oil
1 tablespoon coconut milk
1 egg, whisked
1 cup coconut flour
1 cup almond flour
1 teaspoon baking powder

¼ cup monk fruit powder
1 teaspoon pure anise extract
¼ teaspoon ground cloves
½ teaspoon ground cinnamon
A pinch of salt

1. In a mixing bowl, beat the coconut oil, coconut milk, and egg. In a separate bowl, mix the flour, baking powder, monk fruit, anise extract, ground cloves, cinnamon, and salt.
2. Add the dry mixture to the wet mixture; mix to combine well. Shape the mixture into small balls and arrange them on a parchment-lined baking pan.
3. Bake at 360ºF (182ºC) for 13 minutes. Transfer to cooling racks for 10 minutes. Bon appétit!

**Per Serving**

calories: 143 | fat: 12.9g | protein: 3.6g
carbs: 5.1g | net carbs: 2.7g | fiber: 2.4g

## Peanut and Chocolate Balls

**Prep time: 15 minutes | Cook time: 0 minutes | Serves 6**

| | |
|---|---|
| ½ cup coconut oil | unsweetened |
| ½ cup peanut butter, no sugar added | ¼ cup Xylitol |
| ¼ cup cocoa powder, | 4 tablespoons roasted peanuts, ground |

1. Microwave the coconut oil until melted; add in the peanut butter and stir until well combined.
2. Add the cocoa powder and Xylitol to the batter. Transfer to your freezer for about 1 hour.
3. Shape the batter into bite-sized balls and roll them over the ground peanuts. Bon appétit!

### Per Serving

calories: 330 | fat: 32.5g | protein: 6.8g
carbs: 7.5g | net carbs: 4.9g | fiber: 2.6g

## Coconut Lemon Truffles with Pecans

**Prep time: 30 minutes | Cook time: 0 minutes | Makes 16 truffles**

| | |
|---|---|
| 3 cups shredded unsweetened coconut, divided | Zest and juice of 1 lemon |
| ½ cup pecans | ½ cup monk fruit sweetener, granulated form |
| 2 tablespoons coconut oil | Pinch sea salt |

1. Make the truffle base. Put 2 cups of the coconut and the pecans in a food processor and pulse until the mixture looks like a paste, about 5 minutes.
2. Add the remaining ingredients. Add the coconut oil, lemon zest, lemon juice, sweetener, and salt to the processor and pulse until the mixture forms a big ball, about 2 minutes.
3. Form the truffles. Scoop the mixture out with a tablespoon and roll it into 16 balls. Roll the truffles in the remaining 1 cup of coconut.
4. Store. Store the truffles in a sealed container in the refrigerator for up to one week or in the freezer for up to one month.

### Per Serving (1 truffle)

calories: 160 | fat:16 g | protein: 2g
carbs: 5g | net carbs: 2g | fiber: 3g

## Penuche Bars

**Prep time: 15 minutes | Cook time: 0 minutes | Serves 10**

| | |
|---|---|
| ½ stick butter | sugar-free |
| 2 tablespoons tahini (sesame paste) | A pinch of salt |
| ½ cup almond butter | A pinch of grated nutmeg |
| 1 teaspoon Stevia | ½ teaspoon cinnamon powder |
| 2 ounces (57 g) baker's chocolate, | |

1. Microwave the butter for 30 to 35 seconds. Fold in the tahini, almond butter, Stevia, and chocolate.
2. Sprinkle with salt, nutmeg, and cinnamon; whisk to combine well. Scrape the mixture into a parchment-lined baking tray.
3. Transfer to the freezer for 40 minutes. Cut into bars and enjoy!

### Per Serving

calories: 180 | fat: 18.4g | protein: 1.7g
carbs: 3.1g | net carbs: 2.0g | fiber: 1.1g

## Hazelnut Pudding

**Prep time: 15 minutes | Cook time: 0 minutes | Serves 4**

| | |
|---|---|
| 1 cup double cream | ½ teaspoon vanilla extract |
| ½ teaspoon Swerve | 4 ounces (113 g) hazelnuts, ground |
| 4 tablespoons cream cheese | |

1. Place a mixing bowl in your freezer for 5 to 10 minutes to chill.
2. In the mixing bowl, beat the cream at high speed until the cream starts to thicken. Slowly add in the Swerve and continue beating until stiff peaks form.
3. Add in the cream cheese and vanilla extract; continue to mix an additional minute or so. Fold in the hazelnuts and carefully stir to combine.
4. Serve well chilled and enjoy!

### Per Serving

calories: 342 | fat: 33.1g | protein: 6.5g
carbs: 7.4g | net carbs: 4.4g | fiber: 3.0g

## Almond Fudge Bars

**Prep time: 10 minutes | Cook time: 0 minutes | Serves 7**

1 cup almonds
4 tablespoons coconut flakes
4 tablespoons cacao powder, no sugar
added
3 tablespoons coconut oil
¼ cup monk fruit powder

1. Process all ingredients in your blender until everything is well combined, scraping down the sides as needed.
2. Press firmly into a parchment lined rectangular pan.
3. Cut into squares and serve your bars well chilled. Bon appétit!

**Per Serving**

calories: 80 | fat: 6.9g | protein: 0.6g
carbs: 4.6g | net carbs: 3.5g | fiber: 1.1g

## Chocolate Brownie Cake

**Prep time: 10 minutes | Cook time: 3 hours | Serves 12**

½ cup plus 1 tablespoon unsalted butter, melted, divided
1½ cups almond flour
¾ cup cocoa powder
¾ cup granulated erythritol
1 teaspoon baking
powder
¼ teaspoon fine salt
1 cup heavy (whipping) cream
3 eggs, beaten
2 teaspoons pure vanilla extract
1 cup whipped cream

1. Generously grease the insert of the slow cooker with 1 tablespoon of the melted butter.
2. In a large bowl, stir together the almond flour, cocoa powder, erythritol, baking powder, and salt.
3. In a medium bowl, whisk together the remaining ½ cup of the melted butter, heavy cream, eggs, and vanilla until well blended.
4. Whisk the wet ingredients into the dry ingredients and spoon the batter into the insert.
5. Cover and cook on low for 3 hours, and then remove the insert from the slow cooker and let the cake sit for 1 hour.
6. Serve warm with the whipped cream.

**Per Serving**

calories: 185 | fat: 16g | protein: 5g
carbs: 7g | net carbs: 6g | fiber: 1g

## Cream Mousse

**Prep time: 10 minutes | Cook time: 0 minutes | Serves 4**

2 cups double cream
4 egg yolks
½ teaspoon instant coffee
1 teaspoon pure coconut extract
6 tablespoons Xylitol

1. Heat the cream in a pan over low heat; let it cool slightly.
2. Then, whisk the egg yolks with the instant coffee, coconut extract, and Xylitol until well combined.
3. Add the egg mixture to the lukewarm cream. Warm the mixture over low heat until it has reduced and thickened.
4. Refrigerate for 3 hours before serving. Enjoy!

**Per Serving**

calories: 290 | fat: 27.7g | protein: 6.0g
carbs: 5.0g | net carbs: 5.0g | fiber: 0g

## Almond Chocolate Squares

**Prep time: 10 minutes | Cook time: 0 minutes | Serves 10**

½ cup coconut flour ½ cup almond meal
1 cup almond butter
¼ cup erythritol
2 tablespoons coconut
oil
½ cup sugar-free bakers' chocolate, chopped into small chunks

1. Mix the coconut flour, almond meal, butter, and erythritol until smooth.
2. Press the mixture into a parchment-lined square pan. Place in your freezer for 30 minutes.
3. Meanwhile, microwave the coconut oil and bakers' chocolate for 40 seconds. Pour the glaze over the cake and transfer to your freezer until the chocolate is set or about 20 minutes.
4. Cut into squares and enjoy!

**Per Serving**

calories: 235 | fat: 25.2g | protein: 1.6g
carbs: 3.5g | net carbs: 2.2g | fiber: 1.3g

## Blueberry and Strawberry Trifle

**Prep time: 10 minutes | Cook time: 40 minutes | Serves 10**

4 tablespoons unsalted butter, at room temperature, plus more for greasing
1¼ cups finely milled almond flour, sifted
1 teaspoon baking powder
¼ teaspoon salt
¾ cup granulated erythritol–monk fruit blend; less sweet: ½ cup
4 ounces (113 g) full-fat cream cheese, at room temperature
1 teaspoon vanilla extract
4 large eggs, at room temperature
1 cup fresh or frozen blueberries
8 ounces (227 g) fresh or frozen strawberries, thinly sliced
2 tablespoons granulated erythritol–monk fruit blend; less sweet: 1 tablespoon
½ tablespoon freshly squeezed lemon juice
2 cups heavy whipping cream
8 ounces (227 g) full-fat cream cheese, at room temperature
¼ cup granulated erythritol–monk fruit blend; less sweet: 2 tablespoons
1 teaspoon vanilla extract

1. Preheat the oven to 350ºF (180ºC). Grease the loaf pan with butter, line with parchment paper, and set aside.
2. In a medium bowl, combine the almond flour, baking powder, and salt. Set aside.
3. In a large bowl, using an electric mixer on high, cream the butter with the erythritol–monk fruit blend for 2 to 3 minutes, stopping and scraping the bowl once or twice, as needed, until the mixture is light and fluffy and well incorporated.
4. Add the cream cheese and vanilla and mix well. Add the eggs, one at a time, making sure to mix well after each addition. Add the dry ingredients to the wet ingredients and mix well until the batter is fully combined. Scrape the batter into the prepared loaf pan.
5. Bake for 30 to 40 minutes, until golden brown on top and a toothpick inserted into the center comes out clean. Remove from the oven and set aside to cool before slicing.
6. While the cake is baking, in another large bowl, combine the blueberries, strawberries, erythritol–monk fruit blend, and lemon juice. Toss until fully coated and set aside.
7. In a third large bowl, using an electric mixer on high, whip the heavy cream for 3 to 5 minutes, until stiff peaks form, stopping and scraping the bowl once or twice, as needed.
8. In another medium bowl, using an electric mixer on medium high, beat the cream cheese and erythritol–monk fruit blend for 1 to 2 minutes, until smooth and creamy, then stir in the vanilla. Gently fold the whipped cream into the cream cheese mixture until well combined.
9. Assemble the trifle by breaking the slices of the cake into pieces that fit into the bottom of the trifle dish. Add one-third of the berry mixture, followed by one-third of the whipped cream. Alternate the layers two more times, ending with the whipped cream on top.
10. Store leftovers covered in an airtight container for up to 3 days in the refrigerator.

### Per Serving
calories: 440 | fat: 41.9g | protein: 8.0g
carbs: 8.9g | net carbs: 7.0g | fiber: 1.9g

## Strawberries in Chocolate

**Prep time: 5 minutes | Cook time: 1 minute | Serves 2**

¼ cup sugar-free dark chocolate chips
1½ teaspoons coconut oil
10 medium-sized fresh strawberries, rinsed and drained

1. Melt the chocolate chips by placing it in a small microwave-safe bowl and microwaving it for 1 minute or until it's completely melted.
2. Remove the bowl from the microwave, add chocolate chips into the bowl and mix until it completely dissolves.
3. Add the oil to the melted chocolate and mix thoroughly.
4. Line the parchment paper on a baking sheet. Dip ⅔ of each strawberry inside the melted chocolate and set it on the parchment paper.
5. Place the baking sheet inside a refrigerator for 15 minutes to allow the chocolate to set.
6. Remove them from the refrigerator and serve chill.

### Per Serving
calories: 133 | fat 12.6g | total carbs 5.6g
fiber: 1.2g | protein 0.4g

## Chocolate Popsicles

**Prep time: 5 minutes | Cook time: 0 minutes | Serves 8**

1¾ cups plain yogurt
4 tablespoons full-fat milk
5tablespoons cocoa
powder
½ teaspoon pure vanilla essence
¾ cup Swerve

1. Place all ingredients in a bowl of your food processor.
2. Pour into popsicle molds and freeze. Bon appétit!

### Per Serving

calories: 60 | fat: 2.5g | protein: 3.0g
carbs: 5.4g | net carbs: 4.1g | fiber: 1.3g

## Cheesecake

**Prep time: 15 minutes | Cook time: 25 minutes | Serves 8**

3 tablespoons coconut oil
$1/_3$ cup coconut flour
$2/_3$ cup almond flour
½ teaspoon cardamom
A pinch of salt 3 tablespoons xylitol
Filling:
8 ounces (227 g) cream cheese, at
room temperature
6 tablespoons xylitol
1 teaspoon vanilla extract
$1/_3$ cup sour cream
2 egg
½ teaspoon cinnamon powder
1 teaspoon ground anise

1. Mix all of the crust ingredients until everything is well incorporated. Press the crust mixture into a lightly greased springform pan.
2. Bake in the preheated oven at 320ºF (160ºC) for 8 minutes.
3. In a mixing bowl, mix the cheese and xylitol until well combined. Add in the remaining ingredients and mix until smooth using a mixer set at low-medium speed.
4. Spread the filling over the prepared crust. Cover with strips of aluminum foil. Bake at 300ºF (150ºC) approximately 16 minutes or until the edges are set. Bon appétit!

### Per Serving

calories: 260 | fat: 24.2g | protein: 6.1g
carbs: 5.0g | net carbs: 3.5g | fiber: 1.5g

## Coconut Brownies

**Prep time: 10 minutes | Cook time: 20 minutes | Serves 10**

½ cup butter, melted
1¼ cups coconut flour
1 teaspoon baking powder
$1/_3$ cup cocoa powder, unsweetened
1 cup Xylitol

1. Mix all ingredients in the order listed above.
2. Scrape the batter into a parchment-lined baking pan.
3. Bake in the preheated oven at 360ºF (182ºC) approximately 20 minutes or until a tester comes out clean.
4. Transfer to a cooling rack for 1 hour before slicing and serving. Bon appétit!

### Per Serving

calories: 124 | fat: 12.8g | protein: 0.8g
carbs: 3.2g | net carbs: 1.4g | fiber: 1.8g

## Easy Dark Chocolate Fudge

**Prep time: 15 minutes | Cook time: 0 minutes | Makes 30 pieces**

1 cup coconut oil, melted
1 cup cocoa powder
1 teaspoon vanilla extract
½ cup monk fruit sweetener, granulated form
Pinch sea salt

1. Prepare a baking dish. Line a 9-by-9-inch glass baking dish with plastic wrap and set it aside.
2. Make the fudge. Place the coconut oil, cocoa powder, vanilla, sweetener, and salt in a blender and process until the mixture is smooth and blended. Pour the mixture into the baking dish and place more plastic wrap over it.
3. Refrigerate. Place the fudge in the refrigerator for at least 4 hours, until it is set up and firm.
4. Cut and store. Remove the fudge from the baking dish, cut it into roughly 1½-inch squares and store in the freezer in a sealed container for up to one month.

### Per Serving (2 pieces)

calories: 139 | fat: 15g | protein: 1g
carbs: 3g | net carbs: 1g | fiber: 2g

## Citrus Raspberry Custard Cake

**Prep time: 15 minutes | Cook time: 3 hours | Serves 8**

| | |
|---|---|
| 1 teaspoon coconut oil | ½ cup coconut flour |
| 6 eggs, separated | ¼ teaspoon salt |
| 2 cups heavy (whipping) cream | Juice and zest of 2 limes |
| ¾ cup granulated erythritol | ½ cup raspberries |

1. Lightly grease a 7-inch springform pan with the coconut oil.
2. In a large bowl, using a handheld mixer, beat the egg whites until stiff peaks form, about 5 minutes.
3. In a large bowl, whisk together the yolks, heavy cream, erythritol, coconut flour, salt, and lime juice and zest.
4. Fold the egg whites into the mixture.
5. Transfer the batter to the springform pan and sprinkle the raspberries over the top.
6. Place a wire rack in the insert of the slow cooker and place the springform pan on the wire rack.
7. Cover and cook on low for 3 hours, or until a toothpick inserted in the center comes out clean.
8. Remove the cover and allow the cake to cool to room temperature.
9. Place the springform pan in the refrigerator for at least 2 hours, until the cake is firm.
10. Carefully remove the sides of the springform pan. Slice and serve.

**Per Serving**

calories: 165 | fat: 15g | protein: 6g
carbs: 4g | net carbs: 3g | fiber: 1g

## Chocolate Lava Cake

**Prep time: 15 minutes | Cook time: 10 minutes | Serves 4**

| | |
|---|---|
| 2 tablespoons coconut flour | heavy cream |
| 4 tablespoons cocoa powder, unsweetened | A pinch of Himalayan salt |
| ½ teaspoon baking powder | ¼ teaspoon cardamom |
| 3 eggs | ½ teaspoon cinnamon |
| 1½ ounces (43 g) butter, melted | ½ teaspoon rum extract |
| 1½ ounces (43 g) | ½ teaspoon vanilla extract |
| | 6 tablespoons xylitol |

1. Thoroughly combine the flour, cocoa powder, and baking powder.
2. In another mixing bowl, whisk the eggs with the butter and heavy cream; fold this wet mixture into the dry mixture.
3. Add in the remaining ingredients; mix until everything is well blended. Spritz 4 ceramic mugs with nonstick cooking spray; pour the batter into the prepared mugs.
4. Bake in the preheated oven at 350ºF (180ºC) for 10 minutes or until the edges have set but the middle is still soft.
5. Lift each lava cake onto a serving plate with a spatula. Bon appétit!

**Per Serving**

calories: 169 | fat: 15.7g | protein: 4.4g
carbs: 6.0g | net carbs: 3.4g | fiber: 2.6g

## Blueberry-Vanilla Pudding

**Prep time: 10 minutes | Cook time: 10 minutes | Serves 6**

| | |
|---|---|
| 3 cups coconut milk | 1 tablespoon coconut oil |
| ⅓ cup monk fruit sweetener, granulated form | 1 tablespoon pure vanilla extract |
| ¼ cup arrowroot flour | 1 cup fresh blueberries |
| 1 egg | |

1. Cook the base. In a large saucepan, whisk together the coconut milk, sweetener, and arrowroot. Bring the mixture to a boil then reduce the heat to low, whisking constantly, until the pudding is thick, about 5 minutes. Whisk the egg into the pudding and cook, while still whisking, for about 30 seconds.
2. Add the remaining ingredients. Whisk the coconut oil and vanilla into the pudding until it's smooth.
3. Cool. Transfer the pudding to a medium bowl and cover it with plastic wrap, pressing the wrap down to the surface of the pudding, then place it in the refrigerator to cool completely, about 2 hours.
4. Serve. Spoon the pudding into bowls and top with the blueberries.

**Per Serving**

calories: 286 | fat: 27g | protein: 3g
carbs: 9g | net carbs: 7g | fiber: 2g

## Almond Chocolate Cookies

**Prep time: 15 minutes | Cook time: 10 minutes | Makes 20 cookies**

1 cup grass-fed butter, at room temperature
¾ cup monk fruit sweetener, granulated form
2 eggs
1 tablespoon vanilla extract
3½ cups almond flour
1 teaspoon baking soda
½ teaspoon sea salt
1½ cups dark chocolate chips

1.  Preheat the oven. Set the oven temperature to 350°F (180°C). Line a baking sheet with parchment paper and set it aside.
2.  Mix the wet ingredients. In a large bowl, cream the butter and sweetener until the mixture is very fluffy, either by hand or with a hand mixer. Add the eggs and vanilla and beat until everything is well blended.
3.  Mix the dry ingredients. In a medium bowl, stir together the almond flour, baking soda, and salt until they're well mixed together.
4.  Add the dry to the wet ingredients. Stir the dry ingredients into the wet ingredients and mix until everything is well combined. Stir in the chocolate chips.
5.  Bake. Drop the batter by tablespoons onto the baking sheet about 2 inches apart and flatten them down slightly. Bake the cookies for 10 minutes, or until they're golden. Repeat with any remaining dough. Transfer the cookies to a wire rack and let them cool.
6.  Store. Store the cookies in a sealed container in the refrigerator for up to five days, or in the freezer for up to one month.

**Per Serving (2 cookies)**
calories: 226 | fat: 27g | protein: 3g
carbs: 1g | net carbs: 0g | fiber: 1g

## Pumpkin-Almond Fat Bombs

**Prep time: 10 minutes | Cook time: 0 minutes | Makes 16 fat bombs**

½ cup butter, at room temperature
½ cup cream cheese, at room temperature
1/3 cup pure pumpkin purée
3 tablespoons chopped
almonds
4 drops liquid stevia
½ teaspoon ground cinnamon
¼ teaspoon ground nutmeg

1.  Line an 8-by-8-inch pan with parchment paper and set aside.
2.  In a small bowl, whisk together the butter and cream cheese until very smooth.
3.  Add the pumpkin purée and whisk until blended.
4.  Stir in the almonds, stevia, cinnamon, and nutmeg.
5.  Spoon the pumpkin mixture into the pan. Use a spatula or the back of a spoon to spread it evenly in the pan, then place it in the freezer for about 1 hour.
6.  Cut into 16 pieces and store the fat bombs in a tightly sealed container in the freezer until ready to serve.

**Per Serving (1 fat bomb)**
calories: 87 | fat: 9g | protein: 1g
carbs: 1g | net carbs: 1g | fiber: 0g

## Peanut Butter Cupcake

**Prep time: 15 minutes | Cook time: 3 to 4 hours | Serves 8**

2 tablespoons coconut oil, divided
1 cup almond flour
1 cup granulated erythritol, divided
1 teaspoon baking powder
¼ teaspoon salt
¾ cup natural peanut butter
½ cup heavy (whipping) cream
1 teaspoon pure vanilla extract
1 cup boiling water
¼ cup cocoa powder

1.  Lightly grease the insert of a 4-quart slow cooker with 1 tablespoon of the coconut oil.
2.  In a large bowl, stir together the almond flour, ½ cup of the erythritol, baking powder, and salt.
3.  In a medium bowl, whisk together the peanut butter, heavy cream, and vanilla until smooth.
4.  Add the peanut butter mixture to the dry ingredients and stir to combine.
5.  Transfer the batter to the insert and spread it out evenly.
6.  In a small bowl, stir together the remaining ½ cup of the erythritol, boiling water, and cocoa powder.
7.  Pour the chocolate mixture over the batter.
8.  Cover and cook on low for 3 to 4 hours.
9.  Let the cake stand for 30 minutes and serve warm.

**Per Serving**
calories: 244 | fat: 20g | protein: 11g
carbs: 6g | net carbs: 3g | fiber: 3g

## Banana Fat Bombs

**Prep time: 10 minutes | Cook time: 0 minutes | Makes 12 fat bombs**

| | |
|---|---|
| 1¼ cups cream cheese, at room temperature | (whipping) cream |
| | 1 tablespoon pure banana extract |
| ¾ cup heavy | 6 drops liquid stevia |

1. Line a baking sheet with parchment paper and set aside.
2. In a medium bowl, beat together the cream cheese, heavy cream, banana extract, and stevia until smooth and very thick, about 5 minutes.
3. Gently spoon the mixture onto the baking sheet in mounds, leaving some space between each mound, and place the baking sheet in the refrigerator until firm, about 1 hour.
4. Store the fat bombs in an airtight container in the refrigerator for up to 1 week.

**Per Serving (1 fat bomb)**

calories: 134 | fat: 12g | protein: 3g
carbs: 1g | net carbs: 1g | fiber: 0g

## Simple Blueberry Fat Bombs

**Prep time: 10 minutes | Cook time: 0 minutes | Makes 12 fat bombs**

| | |
|---|---|
| ½ cup coconut oil, at room temperature | ½ cup blueberries, mashed with a fork |
| ½ cup cream cheese, at room temperature | 6 drops liquid stevia |
| | Pinch ground nutmeg |

1. Line a mini muffin tin with paper liners and set aside.
2. In a medium bowl, stir together the coconut oil and cream cheese until well blended.
3. Stir in the blueberries, stevia, and nutmeg until combined.
4. Divide the blueberry mixture into the muffin cups and place the tray in the freezer until set, about 3 hours.
5. Place the fat bombs in an airtight container and store in the freezer until you wish to eat them.

**Per Serving (1 fat bomb)**

calories: 115 | fat: 12g | protein: 1g
carbs: 1g | net carbs: 1g | fiber: 0g

## Coconut-Chocolate Treats

**Prep time: 10 minutes | Cook time: 3 minutes | Makes 16 treats**

| | |
|---|---|
| ⅓ cup coconut oil | Pinch sea salt |
| ¼ cup unsweetened cocoa powder | ¼ cup shredded unsweetened coconut |
| 4 drops liquid stevia | |

1. Line a 6-by-6-inch baking dish with parchment paper and set aside.
2. In a small saucepan over low heat, stir together the coconut oil, cocoa, stevia, and salt for about 3 minutes.
3. Stir in the coconut and press the mixture into the baking dish.
4. Place the baking dish in the refrigerator until the mixture is hard, about 30 minutes.
5. Cut into 16 pieces and store the treats in an airtight container in a cool place.

**Per Serving (1 treat)**

calories: 43 | fat: 5g | protein: 1g
carbs: 1g | net carbs: 1g | fiber: 0g

## Keto Almond Butter Fudge

**Prep time: 10 minutes | Cook time: 0 minutes | Makes 36 pieces**

| | |
|---|---|
| 1 cup coconut oil, at room temperature | (whipping) cream |
| 1 cup almond butter | 10 drops liquid stevia |
| ¼ cup heavy | Pinch sea salt |

1. Line a 6-by-6-inch baking dish with parchment paper and set aside.
2. In a medium bowl, whisk together the coconut oil, almond butter, heavy cream, stevia, and salt until very smooth.
3. Spoon the mixture into the baking dish and smooth the top with a spatula.
4. Place the dish in the refrigerator until the fudge is firm, about 2 hours.
5. Cut into 36 pieces and store the fudge in an airtight container in the freezer for up to 2 weeks.

**Per Serving (2 pieces)**

calories: 204 | fat: 22g | protein: 3g
carbs: 3g | net carbs: 2g | fiber: 1g

## Hazelnut Shortbread Cookies

**Prep time: 10 minutes | Cook time: 10 minutes | Makes 18 cookies**

½ cup butter, at room temperature, plus more for greasing
½ cup granulated sweetener
1 teaspoon alcohol-free pure vanilla extract
1½ cups almond flour
½ cup ground hazelnuts
Pinch sea salt

1. In a medium bowl, cream together the butter, sweetener, and vanilla until well blended.
2. Stir in the almond four, ground hazelnuts, and salt until a firm dough is formed.
3. Roll the dough into a 2-inch cylinder and wrap it in plastic wrap. Place the dough in the refrigerator for at least 30 minutes until firm.
4. Preheat the oven to 350ºF (180ºC). Line a baking sheet with parchment paper and lightly grease the paper with butter; set aside.
5. Unwrap the chilled cylinder, slice the dough into 18 cookies, and place the cookies on the baking sheet.
6. Bake the cookies until firm and lightly browned, about 10 minutes.
7. Allow the cookies to cool on the baking sheet for 5 minutes and then transfer them to a wire rack to cool completely.

**Per Serving (1 cookie)**

calories: 105 | fat: 10g | protein: 3g
carbs: 2g | net carbs: 1g | fiber: 1g

## Coconut-Vanilla Ice Pops

**Prep time: 10 minutes | Cook time: 5 minutes | Makes 8 ice pops**

2 cups almond milk
1 cup heavy (whipping) cream
1 vanilla bean, halved lengthwise
1 cup shredded unsweetened coconut

1. Place a medium saucepan over medium heat and add the almond milk, heavy cream, and vanilla bean.
2. Bring the liquid to a simmer and reduce the heat to low. Continue to simmer for 5 minutes.
3. Remove the saucepan from the heat and let the liquid cool.
4. Take the vanilla bean out of the liquid and use a knife to scrape the seeds out of the bean into the liquid.
5. Stir in the coconut and divide the liquid between the ice pop molds.
6. Freeze until solid, about 4 hours, and enjoy.

**Per Serving (1 ice pop)**

calories: 166 | fat: 15g | protein: 3g
carbs: 4g | net carbs: 2g | fiber: 2g

## Vanilla-Raspberry Cheesecake

**Prep time: 10 minutes | Cook time: 25 to 30 minutes | Serves 12**

⅔ cup coconut oil, melted
½ cup cream cheese, at room temperature
6 eggs
3 tablespoons granulated sweetener
1 teaspoon alcohol-free pure vanilla extract
½ teaspoon baking powder
¾ cup raspberries

1. Preheat the oven to 350ºF (180ºC). Line an 8-by-8-inch baking dish with parchment paper and set aside.
2. In a large bowl, beat together the coconut oil and cream cheese until smooth.
3. Beat in the eggs, scraping down the sides of the bowl at least once.
4. Beat in the sweetener, vanilla, and baking powder until smooth.
5. Spoon the batter into the baking dish and use a spatula to smooth out the top. Scatter the raspberries on top.
6. Bake until the center is firm, about 25 to 30 minutes.
7. Allow the cheesecake to cool completely before cutting into 12 squares.

**Per Serving (1 square)**

calories: 176 | fat: 18g | protein: 6g
carbs: 3g | net carbs: 2g | fiber: 1g

## Spicy Almond Fat Bombs

**Prep time: 10 minutes | Cook time: 4 minutes | Serves 12**

¾ cup coconut oil
¼ cup almond butter
¼ cup cocoa powder
3 drops liquid stevia
⅛ teaspoon chili powder

**SPECIAL EQUIPMENT:**
A 12-cup muffin pan

1. Line a muffin pan with 12 paper liners. Keep aside.
2. Heat the oil in a small saucepan over low heat, then add the almond butter, cocoa powder, stevia, and chili powder. Stir to combine well.
3. Divide the mixture evenly among the muffin cups and keep the muffin pan in the refrigerator for 15 minutes, or until the bombs are set and firm.
4. Serve immediately or refrigerate to chill until ready to serve.

**Per Serving**
calories: 160 | fat: 16.8g | total carbs: 2.0g fiber: 1.2g | protein: 1.5g

## Healthy Blueberry Fat Bombs

**Prep time: 10 minutes | Cook time: 0 minutes | Serves 12**

½ cup cream cheese, at room temperature
½ cup coconut oil, at room temperature
½ cup blueberries, mashed with a fork
Pinch ground nutmeg
6 drops liquid stevia

1. Use the silicone mold or line a mini-sized muffin tin with paper liners. Keep it aside.
2. Combine the cream cheese with coconut oil in a medium mixing bowl and stir to blend well.
3. Fold in the blueberries, nutmeg, and stevia, and mix well.
4. Spoon the mixture into the muffin cups evenly and keep the muffin tin or mold in the refrigerator for 3 hours or until firm.

**Per Serving**
calories: 119 | fat: 12.5g | total carbs: 1.3g fiber: 0.2g | protein: 0.6g

## Chia Pudding with Blueberries

**Prep time: 10 minutes | Cook time: 0 minutes | Serves 2**

1 cup unsweetened vanilla almond milk
1½ tablespoons stevia
¼ cup chia seeds
4 to 6 fresh blueberries

1. Put the milk and stevia in a blender and process for 1 minute to combine well.
2. Pour the chia seeds in a glass and add the mixture.
3. Make the pudding: Stir the mixture well and then cover the glass with plastic wrap and refrigerate for 6 to 8 hours.
4. Transfer the pudding into a glass and add the blueberries on top before serving

**Per Serving**
calories: 125 | fat: 10.2g | total carbs: 12.9g | fiber: 9.8g | protein: 5.2g

## Macadamia Nut and Chocolate Fat Bombs

**Prep time: 5 minutes | Cook time: 1 minute | Makes 8 fat bombs**

¼ cup sugar-free dark chocolate chips
Sea salt, to taste
1 tablespoon coconut
oil
24 raw macadamia nut halves

**SPECIAL EQUIPMENT:**
8 baking cups or truffle molds

1. Melt the chocolate chips in a microwave for 50 seconds and mix it with sea salt and oil. Stir it until well mixed.
2. Arrange 3 macadamia nut halves inside each small baking cup and completely cover the nuts in chocolate by spooning the melted chocolate over each nut. Sprinkle a pinch of sea salt over the chocolate.
3. Place the cups inside the freezer for 30 to 40 minutes or until solid.

**Per Serving**
calories: 161 | fat: 14.8g | total carbs: 7.5g fiber: 2.2g | protein: 1.7g

# Appendix 1 Measurement Conversion Chart

## VOLUME EQUIVALENTS(DRY)

| US STANDARD | METRIC (APPROXIMATE) |
|---|---|
| 1/8 teaspoon | 0.5 mL |
| 1/4 teaspoon | 1 mL |
| 1/2 teaspoon | 2 mL |
| 3/4 teaspoon | 4 mL |
| 1 teaspoon | 5 mL |
| 1 tablespoon | 15 mL |
| 1/4 cup | 59 mL |
| 1/2 cup | 118 mL |
| 3/4 cup | 177 mL |
| 1 cup | 235 mL |
| 2 cups | 475 mL |
| 3 cups | 700 mL |
| 4 cups | 1 L |

## VOLUME EQUIVALENTS(LIQUID)

| US STANDARD | US STANDARD (OUNCES) | METRIC (APPROXIMATE) |
|---|---|---|
| 2 tablespoons | 1 fl.oz. | 30 mL |
| 1/4 cup | 2 fl.oz. | 60 mL |
| 1/2 cup | 4 fl.oz. | 120 mL |
| 1 cup | 8 fl.oz. | 240 mL |
| 1 1/2 cup | 12 fl.oz. | 355 mL |
| 2 cups or 1 pint | 16 fl.oz. | 475 mL |
| 4 cups or 1 quart | 32 fl.oz. | 1 L |
| 1 gallon | 128 fl.oz. | 4 L |

## TEMPERATURES EQUIVALENTS

| FAHRENHEIT(F) | CELSIUS(C) (APPROXIMATE) |
|---|---|
| 225 °F | 107 °C |
| 250 °F | 120 °C |
| 275 °F | 135 °C |
| 300 °F | 150 °C |
| 325 °F | 160 °C |
| 350 °F | 180 °C |
| 375 °F | 190 °C |
| 400 °F | 205 °C |
| 425 °F | 220 °C |
| 450 °F | 235 °C |
| 475 °F | 245 °C |
| 500 °F | 260 °C |

## WEIGHT EQUIVALENTS

| US STANDARD | METRIC (APPROXIMATE) |
|---|---|
| 1 ounce | 28 g |
| 2 ounces | 57 g |
| 5 ounces | 142 g |
| 10 ounces | 284 g |
| 15 ounces | 425 g |
| 16 ounces (1 pound) | 455 g |
| 1.5 pounds | 680 g |
| 2 pounds | 907 g |

# Appendix 2 Recipe Index